MW00648806

a little book about believing

The Transformative Healing Power of Faith, Love, and Surrender

Cash Peters

PENNER

Published and distributed by Penner Inc., Beverly Hills, California 90210.

Book and cover design by Sonia Fiore

E-book ISBN: 978-1-4507-7654-7

Paperback ISBN: 978-1-4507-7655-4

1st Edition: May 2011

Printed in the United States of America.

‘Believe it can be done.
When you believe something can be done, really believe,
Your mind will find ways to do it.
Believing there’s a solution paves the way to a solution.’

David Schwartz

Contents

Foreword

This is an important book because of the issues it raises. What is the nature of spiritual and physical healings? How do they occur? What is the relationship of the body to the mind? What is the role of belief in relationship to the physical body and to illness or health? Or placebo? Or invisible or spiritual forces?

We live in a time that is experiencing the benefits of considerable material and technological progress. One could say that the gift of western culture to the rest of the world has been its elucidation of the physical laws of the universe. Because of that great work, we have warm homes, computers, medicines and smartphones; and unparalleled material wealth.

One could also argue, however, that in some ways we remain as impoverished as before, at least from a spiritual perspective. People are still lonely and broken, and although the illnesses from which we suffer may be somewhat different in character, evidence suggests that in some ways we have not made as much progress as one would wish, given the amount of energy and research that has been invested. In some ways we are sicker than ever before, with more and more doctor visits, involving more medicines and technologies, yet with diminishing returns in regard to the major causes of morbidity and mortality: depression, heart disease, cancer, and chronic illnesses in general.

Perhaps we're missing something.

One possibility is that we need to take the next step. If it's true that we are both physical and spiritual beings, then perhaps we need a paradigm of health and healing that understands what this means. We are a culture that believes in the reality of the physical world - in what we can see and touch. If we are also spiritual beings, then perhaps we need to understand what this really means.

Now that the physical laws of the universe have been defined, maybe we need to take the next step and begin to define the *spiritual* laws of the universe. Perhaps what have been called 'miracles' for thousands of years are really events that have participated at some level in something congruent with those spiritual laws. Even the physical world seemed to behave in strange ways until we began to better understand its laws.

Cash Peters and I may quibble or have fascinating discussions about small issues - e.g., from my perspective as a physician, it seems clear that some of what goes on at the Casa can be explained as sleight of hand - but I am fascinated and gripped by how well he addresses the larger, more important issues about whether and how spiritual events can genuinely heal physical illness.

I myself traveled to the Casa de Dom Inaçio, but as a skeptic, and, though there's much I don't understand, I am convinced that places and people such as those described in this book raise questions and issues that we must explore further. The research is complicated, but we are fortunate to live in a time when spiritual events can be more easily examined without the overlay and interpretation of any particular religion. Because of this, the events can be more easily examined for what they are in themselves, with their similarities and differences being seen across a variety of religions. Early evidence suggests that there are powers of mind and heart that we have not adequately understood, and that they are a more primary and real force than the world that we can see and touch with our senses.

There is much that we need to understand. For example, from the spiritual perspective, the point is not always to get rid of the illness. Sometimes the illness is meant to serve a higher function in our lives. Sometimes the point is not the alleviation of illness, but finding the grace to allow the furnace of suffering to separate out the gold from the dross so that we become more aware of who we are.

Cash raises large questions in this book. As a psychiatrist, every day I see people who have great difficulty understanding how their false beliefs about themselves, and about the world, can lie at the root of their suffering. It's easier to see this in others than in ourselves. How does one help a fish understand what 'wet' is? If a patient believes that she is a faulty or defective person, then this is the lens through which she views the world. It's difficult for her to see that this is simply the lens that she has adopted, and that it is not true. But who would have guessed? Most of us aren't even aware of what our deep, unconscious beliefs are. Just look at all the people who say they believe in God, and God's love, but actually live lives characterized more by fear or control, and a lack of faith in something larger than themselves. Most of us don't even know our true beliefs, much less how to go about changing them at a deep level.

Cash is zeroing in on something that appears to be critical and life-changing: contrary to the belief of many religious and popular teachings - that there is something fundamentally wrong or defective in the very structure of human life, whether that be inherent badness, childhood deficits or neurochemical defects – in the end what heals people seems to be something connected with an experience of their inherent dignity and unrepeatable uniqueness and goodness. There is a deep perfection lying within all of us - what we know in our better moments as the Image of God - and the point of our lives is to get to the point where we can experience and know ourselves in this way. As Cash says so well: 'Healing happens at the point where expanded expectation meets raised consciousness.'

I highly recommend this book and further efforts to examine these issues. They are critical to our time, and to the challenges we must rise to meet.

JEFFREY D. REDIGER M.D., M.DIV.
MEDICAL DIRECTOR OF THE MCLEAN HOSPITAL SOUTH EAST,
HARVARD MEDICAL SCHOOL.

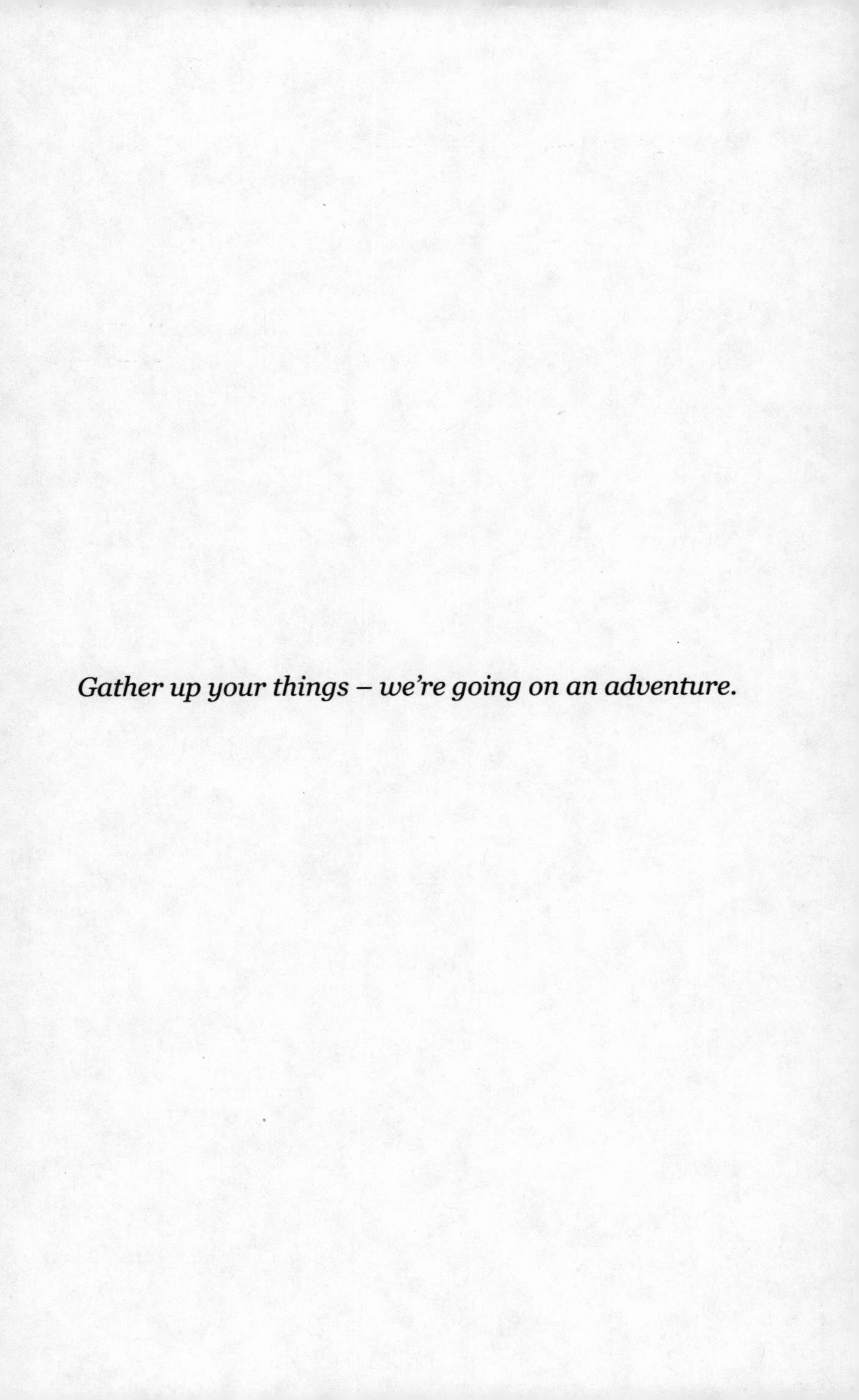

Gather up your things – we're going on an adventure.

1

What If There's Another Way?

Your first morning at the Casa is the trickiest. Everyone tells you that. 'Get the first morning out of the way,' they say, 'and the process starts to make sense.'

I do hope so, because right now I have no idea at all what's going on.

And I'm not alone; nobody else in the Great Hall seems to know either. People sit, people stand. Some people stand, then sit, then, sure suddenly that they must be doing the wrong thing, stand up again. As they do, they're picked off one by one by the uniformed attendants and wrangled into single file, ready for healing.

Below the corrugated rafters, chrome fans barely trouble the stagnant morning air, while scabby wild dogs, the flesh between their ribs rippled like fingerprints in warm plasticine, flop exhausted under chairs, with their tails tucked under to avoid getting stepped on by people standing in line. A line that weaves toward a blue door at the far end. *The* Blue Door.

Not fully understanding what happens to us on the other side of that door has everyone jittery. But a good jittery. The kind that kids feel at Christmas when their parents drive them into town to meet Santa. All we've been told ahead of time is that it leads to a room of mysteries and miracles. Once you cross the threshold, you give your life over to someone else. Or, more accurately, to some *thing* else. It's this part of the story that's making us jittery.

'Excuse me...'

The accent is British, but faint. I look up to find a skeleton lowering itself with difficulty onto the bench beside me. Assorted human odds and ends sheathed in grayish translucent flesh and topped by a neat bob of brown hair, her one concession to aesthetics.

'...where are we supposed to be, d'you know?' Wincing, the girl drops the last ten inches or so to the seat, landing with an ooof! 'I was wondering if I should be in line, or just hang around.'

'Did they give you a ticket when you came in?'

She's not sure. Anorexic fingers dip into the pocket of her skirt and fish out a voucher with the words '2a Vez' on it. *Segunda vez.* 'This?'

'Ah, I think you're in the second-time group over there. If I were you, I'd get in line now. It's almost half-past. They'll be going in any minute.'

'Okay. Thank you.'

Using my shoulder as a crutch, she unfolds to the vertical with the stiff jerks of a rusty angle-poise, before shuffling off across the Great Hall to join the back of a lengthening queue. I watch her go, transfixed. Such a weak light she has; so frail. And she's by no means the exception. Dozens, if not hundreds more, either inside the hall or streaming toward us across the grounds, are in the same boat. Answer-seekers like myself. The lost, the blighted, the broken, arriving on sticks, canes, in wheelchairs, or supported by stronger arms. Not to be overdramatic, but death is in the air today. You can taste it. Circling the compound like ravenous jackals, it stakes out its prey, sifting the weak from the strong, debating which ones to take down first.

Even though I know it's not looking for me, I'm still on edge. My whole body's tingling. With anxiety mostly. I put this down to Susan – one of our tour guides – and a little pep talk she gave us in the battered minivan late last night as we drove into town. Since then I've not been able to settle.

'Welcome to Abadiânia everyone,' she shouted over the rattle of the suspension. 'Tonight you are at a major turning point in your lives. Incredible things are about to happen. The fact that you're with us means you were invited. You're meant to be here, and I promise you, you'll look back on the next two weeks as one of the defining events of your lifetime.'

The old woman in the seat next to me let loose a loud 'Oooooh', then turned and asked, wide-eyed, 'Is this your first time?', to which I nodded a firm yes. 'Wow,' she said, grinning. 'It's gonna blow your mind.'

With a grind of gears, the bus began to slow.

As we bounced through a final series of potholes up to the hotel door, Susan told us, 'You are about to have an incredible experience that will change the way you look at the world forever', concluding with a cryptic: 'There's life before Brazil and life after Brazil. Things will never be the same again.'

And we all cheered, little realizing in most cases, I'm sure, how truly prophetic this was.

The starting point for this intriguing excursion to Brazil was a wedding reception in Newport Beach. That's where I met Geena.

Though not particularly tall or imposing, the instant this vivacious blonde entered the room she had waiters thirty years her junior running after her with wine-bottles.

For some reason – and I no longer believe in chance, so it had to be providential - we ended up sitting at the same table. Naturally, we got chatting. About me a little bit, but mostly about her. And thank goodness we did. For, on that warm Californian night, over several glasses of Merlot and five gourmet courses, including two desserts, Geena turned out to be the bearer of the most insightful information I had heard in years. It concerned health. Not a subject I was particularly interested in to begin with. Like most people, I find anything to do with my body, illness, and healing, a little bit icky. Something I choose not to think about until I'm actually ill, which my parents taught me was always the best way. But Geena's vibrant manner, her enthusiasm, and her obvious passion for the breakthroughs she'd recently experienced, cast a spell. That's the only way I can put it - an entrancing spell. And by the time we parted a mere three hours later I was hooked.

There aren't too many what I'd call 'tentpole' moments in the average year for me. Meeting Geena, though, I now realize, was one such moment. In the course of recounting her personal story, she exposed me to a revolutionary perspective I'd never considered before. On health, longevity, and what it takes to meet, treat, and beat disease. What's more, by doing so, she altered the entire course of my life.

And it's not often you can say that.

Geena's Story

Originally from Texas, she'd been married three times, she said. Most recently to a German industrialist, a real high-flyer. One of those invincible, up-and-at-'em, force-of-nature mogul types who are constantly stressed out from being 'on' all the time: meeting deadlines, crisscrossing the globe, working nonstop, sleeping four hours a night, yakking on their cellphones, eating at their desk, and juggling a thousand commitments and responsibilities simultaneously.

By every measure we use to evaluate success, the guy was a winner. And his commitment to being number one had paid off in all the ways you'd expect, with millions in the bank, a set of golden handcuffs, a corporate jet, a bottomless expense account, extensive stockholdings, a beautiful wife, and homes on three continents. The American Dream, we call it. Though of course all the success, wealth, power, influence, status, stockholdings, wives, and homes in the world aren't worth a red cent if you're too sick to enjoy them. Which, sadly, is what happened. After working hard for thirty-some years to get where he was, this poor man ended up in hospital, where doctors told him he had cancer in two organs, as well as a brain tumor the size of a baby's fist, and he was dying.

Nothing, they said, could save him. This included the drastic cocktail of medical treatments he was being subjected to, which only served to ravage his already-depleted body still further, threatening to make his remaining days more wretched than they might otherwise have been.

Naturally, seeing him in such a terrible state drove Geena to the brink of despair. 'The doctors are killing him,' she thought. 'There *has* to be another way.'

It was at that moment that some kind of eleventh-hour survival switch flicked on in her head, inspiring her to do more than just sit there and watch her partner disintegrate before her eyes. Instead, she decided to take control of the situation and stage an intervention.

First stop: the Internet.

Out of some pretty intensive research came a slew of health facts that, being a lay person with no medical knowledge at all, she'd been entirely unaware of previously.

About chemotherapy, for instance.

Health fact number one: chemo has a shockingly low success rate in the longer term. According to a 2004 issue of the *Clinical Oncology Journal*, a patient who starts a five-year program of cytotoxic chemotherapy today has only 2.1% chance of surviving to year six. If this is true, and you were to expose one hundred cancer patients to chemo this week, then five years from now ninety-eight of them would be dead.[1] Is it me, or are those *appalling* odds?

Health fact number 2: conservatively, up to 98,000 Americans die in hospital each year from what's called 'iatrogenic illness', that is to say as a direct result of medical errors - incorrect diagnosis, surgical mistakes, wrong prescriptions, and so on. And I'm not the one saying this, by the way; it comes from a report by the Institute of Medicine published in 2000[2]. Bottom line: physicians are far from infallible.

Thankfully, there are many doctors out there who are honest and reliable and consistently good at what they do. We'd be lost without them.

When Arizona Representative Gabrielle Giffords was shot in the head in January 2011 during a planned assassination attempt in Tucson, neurosurgeons put her in a chemically-induced coma right away and, very methodically, over the next few hours and days, went about saving her life. The doctors who performed this medical miracle gave press conferences on TV. They were treated like rock stars, and deservedly so. There can be no doubt at all that, without their dedication and expertise, Gabrielle Giffords would have died.

It's a scenario that's repeated every day all over the world: doctors routinely saving and extending lives.

But statistics show they also end quite a few lives too, and that's where we need to be on our guard.

---

[1] For more on this, read *Knockout* by Suzanne Somers (2009, Random House)

[2] 'Errors in the healthcare industry are at an unacceptably high level,' it said, adding, 'Preventable adverse events are a leading cause of death in the United States....' During 2009's healthcare debate in the House of Representatives, Rep Bruce Braley cited this report and went on to say, 'Every year there are fifteen million incidents of medical harm in this country... [M]edical errors add $17-28 billion of cost, most of it in additional medical care that we end up paying for as consumers in healthcare.'

In 2009, for example, eleven California hospitals were fined $25,000 each for multiple violations, including failing to follow proper surgical procedures. 20% of these cases involved foreign objects left inside patients after they were sewn up. Nowadays, death by medicine is the third leading cause of fatalities in the U.S., after cancer and heart disease. In fact, the National Institute of Nutrition, in its own statistics in 2003, ranked iatrogenic illness *first*, claiming that there were 7.5 million unnecessary medical and surgical procedures undertaken each year, with 783,936 patients dying that didn't need to.[3]

When facts like these started coming to light, Geena was shocked. Which is an understandable reaction, though not one I happen to share. Mainly because I, too, have had unnecessary surgery.

A few years ago, I began experiencing sharp pains in my liver area. Surprisingly, this was put down to my unending appetite for cakes and pastries. To a native of the north of England, cake is considered a staple. Muffins, cookies, and pies too. Problem is, over time, eating junk like this can clog your system with stones, which is what had happened. So, on the advice of my physician, I let a surgeon remove my gallbladder.

'Don't worry. It's a useless organ anyway,' he assured me, 'you don't need it.'

Well, he lied. You do need your gallbladder. When it's not there doing its work of regulating bile flow as you eat, mealtimes become a minefield. This has led to all manner of discomfort since.

How was I to know, as a mere layman, that, for many surgeons, whipping out gallbladders is their bread and butter? It puts their kids through college, buys them a second home in the mountains, and a fast car with which to reach it. No wonder

---

[3] *Death by Medicine*, 2003, National Institute of Nutrition. Compiled by Gary Null PhD, and others.

it's the number one surgery in America today. Half a million gallbladders are removed every year, oftentimes unnecessarily, when really all that may have been required was a change of diet perhaps, or a thinning of the bile, or a simple flush of the system. No mention, however, was ever made to me about viable alternatives. First resort every time seems to be the operating theater.

Undoubtedly, it was this bitter experience that fueled my fascination with what Geena was saying, and everything that came after.

At first, she told me, she was a little overwhelmed by the situation with her husband. But that didn't last long, as she started trawling websites for news of reliable alternatives to standard allopathic treatments for cancer. Some of these she reeled off over dinner. I've forgotten most of them now, though I do recall there was talk of using Asian mushrooms, as well as coffee enemas, hemp oil, and also a certain blend of tea.

Plus one other remedy.

'There's this thing called spiritual surgery.'

'Oh yeah?' And I smirked, which is what everyone does. 'What's that?'

'Faith healing. There are mystical healers in the Philippines, South America, and other places. Healers so powerful that they've been known to rid people of deadly diseases – boom, just like that. Spontaneous remission. I've read testimonials. It's incredible.'

Incredible, and also very, *very* risky, I should think. Who were these guys? I'm all for having faith in people, but why would you trust your life to a complete stranger like that? Someone with zero qualifications.

Geena, however, didn't have the luxury of excessive scrutiny. Time was running out. She needed a quick fix and a new kind of treatment, before doctors set about killing the man she loved the old-fashioned way. Since spiritual surgery, as outlandish as it seemed at first, was fast and could be arranged at short notice, this, wisely or unwisely, was the route she chose.

Alas, things didn't go according to plan. Before she could bundle her husband onto a plane to South America, the disease accelerated its advance and he passed away. 'A few more days and that was it, he was gone.'

'Hang on. Wait a second. *You're telling me he died???'*

'Yes,' she said. 'Six weeks ago.'

Great heavens - but that's terrible.

I admit, I'd been expecting an upbeat movie kind of ending. A gleeful 'And it worked!' perhaps. Or a triumphant 'He survived. It's a miracle.' - as a robust, silver-haired German tycoon waved at us from across the dance floor, clearly at the peak of health thanks to the spiritual surgeon found for him at the last minute by his dear wife.

But that's not how it went.

Tragically, the chemo didn't work, the cancer won out, and Geena lost her third husband.

What's astonishing is that she didn't view this as a defeat. If anything, I'd say it only strengthened her resolve. Despite the setback - or perhaps because of it - she became gripped by an elevated spirit of hope. Not for herself, but for those who, like her husband, might be afflicted with serious diseases - including cancer, of course, but many others too - who've been told a cure doesn't exist and there's nothing anybody can do, when in actual fact hope may not be lost after all.

'There has to be another way,' she assured me. 'What if a natural remedy for these diseases is staring us right in the face? We just have to be persistent. That's what I'm taking away from this.'

And on that tragic note, her face brightened and she changed the subject.

'So, any travel plans for the summer?'

Travel-wise, I'd half-decided to take a trip to Argentina. Show up on spec maybe, do the rounds of Buenos Aires for a few weeks, make friends, maybe learn to tango, then, after gathering enough fascinating experiences to fill a new book, return home to Los Angeles to write it. A little vague; not what you'd call an actual plan, but that's how I like my adventures – structureless and freewheeling.

It's an approach I learned on a Buddhist retreat in England years ago, and it can be summed up as follows:

'Trust yourself. Trust life. Embrace uncertainty. Dive fearlessly in, holding nothing back. Expect a positive outcome *always*, and marvel at how things turn out better than anything you could have designed yourself. Above all, remember: the unknown is where all the fun happens.'

I love that message!

To me, it translates as: 'Don't plan unnecessarily. Give your all to whatever you're doing in every moment. Loosen your grip and go intuitively with the flow.'

Easily said, of course, but much harder in practice.

Most of us don't trust life enough. We say we do. We say we have faith, and we may pay lip service to the idea of a higher force watching over us and guiding our step. Meanwhile, can we relax and let it happen? No. Our ego gets in the way, constantly craving control. If we don't feel like we're in charge every second of every day, our foundations start to rattle and we become anxious and afraid.

There's a prayer:

Father Almighty, I put myself in your hands.
Do with me whatsoever you wish.
Whatever it is, I give you thanks.
I am ready for anything; I accept it all...

Nowadays, I'm trying to be that way. More and more, I live in a state of surrender, especially when I travel. And Geena and I were just discussing this philosophy over our second dessert...

Thump thump thump thump....

...when the band struck up, bringing our conversation to an abrupt close. It's not that she stopped talking, just that I stopped hearing what she was talking *about*.

...thump thump thump thump....

Partly it was the music. But also...

When I mentioned my disastrous gallbladder operation just now, I did so for good reason. You'll find out why it's important a little later. But there's one other thing you need to know as well, and it's this: I'm slowly going deaf.

Not something I admit to very often. As a professional radio broadcaster, I find it embarrassing. And unfortunate.

The causes of deafness are varied. In my case they include years of foolishly wearing headphones with the volume turned up far too high, which is how we tend to do things in radio. Also, my work has not been kind in other ways. I had a travel show on TV once. Our shooting schedule was punishing; fifteen months of sleep deprivation, junk food, and non-stop stress. Eventually, the air pressure from countless take-offs and landings left me with a horrible blockage in one ear that cut off 90% of the hearing on my left side.

As a result, I wound up in hospital again.

Doctors did their best. They poked around, blew air into it, prodded and scratched, ran tests, x-rayed it, but failed to come up with very much. If the condition kept on deteriorating, it was decided, and I didn't find an answer soon, I might end up deaf in both ears, at which point my radio career would be over.

...thump thump thump thump...

'SO,' Geena raised her voice above the din, 'WHERE WILL YOU GO?'

'I'm considering a month in Buenos Aires. Thought I'd learn to tango.'

'Oh *no,* don't do that,' she shouted, shaking her head 'til wild tongues of hair dropped into her eyes. 'You should go to Brazil. BRAZIL, my dear!!!'

'Why?'

'There's a man you must see. A spiritual surgeon. He's *the real deal.* The town he's in, Abadiânia, is a magnet to curious minds. A lot of switched-on people go there – Seekers, they're called - with all kinds of problems and questions, and they find BIG answers.'

'Answers to what?'

'You name it. Life, love, the universe, themselves, who they are, what they're doing here, why they have diseases....it's an incredible place.' With a sly wink, she added, 'Trust me, save the tango for next time. Go to Brazil and...'

...thump thump thump thump...

The rest vanished into the music. Knocking over her chair and staggering onto the dance floor, she scanned the crowd for a pair of vacant arms.

'BUT WHY,' I called after her, 'WOULD I WANT TO SEE A SPIRITUAL SURGEON?'

I was genuinely mystified.

From ten feet away, she jabbed at the side of her head with a finger, playing Charades. Three words. Three syllables.

FOR. YOUR. EARS.

I think it's fair to say that the reaction of my friends to the news that I was heading off to Brazil for two weeks to visit a faith healer on the advice of some woman I'd met at a wedding was less than enthusiastic and, as I recall, accompanied by a lot of eye-rolling.

Nobody but me, it seems, was buying Geena's 'crazy mystical woo-woo nonsense,' as they insisted on calling it. A couple even suggested she was acting as a shill for a South American religious cult and I'd probably get sucked in and disappear forever. Others were alarmed – *shocked,* actually, they said - that an award-winning journalist of twenty-five years' standing would give over a moment of his time to the voodoo mumbo-jumbo of a quack, much less take it halfway seriously by writing a book about healing.

'Why would you do this?' they groaned. 'You can't give medical advice. You have no qualifications.'

To them, and to anyone else who would query my credentials for this mission, what can I say, other than 'You're right'?

But that's okay. As far as the Brazil trip is concerned, and also this book, I want you to think of me, not as a health expert – which I most definitely am not - but as Everyman. Someone who had one of his organs removed when it didn't need to be. Someone who, like Geena - like most of us, actually, who have witnessed friends, colleagues, and loved ones succumb to serious illness and die over the years - is bewildered by the soaring disease statistics in this country and puzzled by modern medicine's seeming inability to do anything to reduce them on our behalf, despite billions of dollars being poured into research, treatment, and the quest for solutions. Just a regular guy who'd had a bunch of questions building up inside of him like a pressure cooker for the longest time, but who'd never been able to find a credible answer to them. Such as:

- Does a cure for major diseases, especially cancer, already exist, but for whatever reason we're simply not being told what it is?
- Are there healthier alternatives to the usual trifecta of solutions offered by conventional doctors: drugs, surgery, and radiation?

- Is there something to faith healing? Does faith have a practical application in helping heal the body? In Scripture we find a wealth of examples where believers were cured at the hands of the Divine. It even says in Matthew 21: 'And all things, whatsoever ye shall ask in prayer, *believing*, ye shall receive.' Can that same power be harnessed today to deal with serious health problems?
- When a doctor hands down a death sentence, is that it? The end of the line? Do we have to abide by that prognosis, or should we treat it merely as the first step in a process, prompting us to acknowledge his or her words for what they are: an informed opinion, before simply taking matters into our own hands?

If my stay in Brazil managed to resolve even a fraction of these issues, including bringing back my hearing, as Geena hinted that it might, then I'd consider it money and time well spent.

One last thing: I realize that alternative health and especially faith healing are controversial areas. By the same token, I never cease to be amazed at how fixed people tend to be in their views on this subject, and how defensive or even angry they become at anyone who has the nerve to suggest that maybe conventional medicine doesn't have all the answers, or that it may, in some cases, by its heavy-handed and often harsh and harmful treatments, actually make things far worse.

I've brought these issues up at dinner parties before now, only to be shot down by friendly fire. Or mocked mercilessly for being so naïve. When you're talking about saving lives and healing bodies, you run into a lot of entrenched thinking. People's trust in modern medicine is strangely absolute.

In this book we are crossing a bridge into the unknown, ready to challenge some of our holiest preconceptions about health and healing. In my view that's a good thing. The mere fact that we're discussing this topic at all will surely bring us to a place of new understanding. A place where hopefully someday we, the ordinary people, may not be such easy prey for serious illness and can instead choose to be its master, or even avoid it altogether.

It's an exciting journey, one that requires a flexible mind, a willing heart, and a readiness to release ingrained attitudes. But, above all, it requires that we believe. Belief, as you'll see, is the key of keys when it comes to being healthy. Without it, true healing seems to be a lot harder to nail down.

Knowing what I now know, I'm finally coming around to the view that there was nothing accidental about that night in Newport Beach with Geena. A firmer hand was on the tiller for sure. This was a woman I feel I was destined to meet. Someone who would not only positively affect *my* life, but the lives of everyone who came into contact with these revolutionary insights into the healing process.

And yes, looking back, I can honestly say I now agree with her: there may well be another way - *Geena was right.*

Now, let's get going. I have a lot to tell you.

2

The Revolution Starts Here

The Great Hall of the Casa de Dom Inaçio is painted a glossy sky blue up to chest-level and white the rest of the way, a design quirk echoed all over the compound.

Three of the walls are decorated with portraits of Jesus and various saints, while the fourth opens up along its full length onto a walkway filled with milling apparitions dressed identically in all-white, their faces blanched by stark sunlight. Outside, coaches are still pulling in. One from Mexico a while ago, now another, this one from Peru, spilling forty people apiece, and with them forty new sets of problems, into the gentle autumnal heat. Quite a scene. An exodus in reverse.

It's 8.20am - ten minutes to go 'til **He** arrives – and the place is really popping, as, out of bedlam, at long last emerges some kind of system.

Knots of strangers gabble in whispers, clutching scraps of notepaper and ballpoints, the way they were told to, their white smocks and cotton shirts billowing in a warm breeze. One couple even showed up in matching judo outfits, which is nothing short of inspired. Conforming without being conformist. I like that. On Wednesdays, Thursdays, and Fridays, the days that **He** is on site, everyone within the Casa compound must wear white, that's the rule, white being a color of high vibration, apparently, which enhances the human aura and encourages the free flow of energy in and around us.

'Pai! Dai ao culpado o arrespendimento...,' On a shallow dais, an elderly woman mumbles words into a microphone in Portuguese. *'...ao Espiritu, a verdade...'*

'What's she saying? Anyone know?'

'It's a prayer, I t'ink,' a light voice behind me guesses. 'For de sick people 'n' all, like.'

Dermot is the first guy I met stepping off the bus. Lovely man. Mid-forties, I'd say. Prematurely graying. His sad, wet Irish eyes, pressed deep into a fleshy face, betray an unusual vulnerability. Though he may carry himself with the robust swagger of an entry-level dockworker, he's actually nothing of the sort. In fact, I discover that he's a businessman, overseeing a family-run chain of dry-cleaning stores in Boston. Or *was*. Until his diagnosis came through. Prostate cancer, stage four. One of the incurables. Unstoppable by drugs, radiation, surgery, basically whatever his doctors threw at it. In the end, with an operation and an unsuccessful bout of chemotherapy behind him, and the cancer still advancing, he gave up on the usual medical approach and became a Seeker.

Life, he figured, is a matter of interpretation. It's not what happens to you that's important, it's what you do with it. Just because something seems bad, or because other people tell you it's bad – or incurable or unstoppable – doesn't mean it is. We can, if we choose, be the architects of our own destiny.

Then one night he was watching TV and caught a documentary about some strange compound in South America, a place where miracles are allegedly generated every day. And something about what he saw triggered in him a sense of new hope. Figuring he wasn't going to let doctors have the last word on this, he decided to stage his own intervention. Next day he went out and booked a flight to Brazil.

'I told my sister, it's wort' a shot, like. You don't know if you don't try, do you?'

Slumped in his shadow, a stiff, forlorn-looking woman offers a faint smile.

'Of course if dis fails,' he chuckles bleakly, 'it's curtains. My Last Chance Saloon, like.' The wet eyes grow dim and he lapses into glum silence. Only for a moment, though. Then, laughing - 'Boy, it's bloody warm in here, don't you t'ink? Makes me wish I'd worn my bat'ing suit, so it does.' - he springs up off the bench, stretches his L white Polo shirt over his XXXL stomach, a legacy from years of good times, by the look of it, tucks it into his shorts, and, with a bounce in his step that gives no clue to how sick he is, rushes off to the toilet, leaving his sister staring after him gloomily.

8.35am.

Angela, our main tour guide, sweeps in with breaking news. '**He's** arrived. **He** is in the building and almost ready to begin.'

Murmurs of anticipation greet the opening of the blue door. On a command from one of the smiling attendants, the '*Segunda Vez*' crowd – those visiting **Him** for the second time - some of whom have been waiting patiently for an hour or more, begin their slow plod inside. This takes a while.

Once the last patient has trudged across the threshold, the door closes.

Only a couple of hundred of us are left now, including Dermot, bustling back from the restroom, much to the relief of his sister.

In many ways, these two are fairly typical of the kind of people you meet at the Casa. Regular folk. Our group of twenty-four is made up mostly of professionals: therapists, a gynecologist, three businessmen, a teacher, two real estate agents, a few retirees, and an engineer. We even have a circuit judge from the State of Maine with us. In other words, not flakes or New Age crazies or fools, but prosperous, educated, well-rounded and grounded individuals.

At the same time, they're aware they don't belong here. That they are refugees from a different world: a sophisticated, progressive world of choice and privilege contrasting sharply with the decrepit landscape they now find themselves in, of unpaved roads, spotty sanitation, fallen-down adobe houses with the occupants still inside – you can peek at them through little holes in the wall; processed food that may or may not be contaminated with *ecoli* – 'You'll just have to try it and see.' - and strange sticky flies that hover in the air close to your face for the longest time, then, when you try to brush them away, glom onto your fingers and won't come off.

I dare say adjusting to the hardships of Abadiânia will take days. For now, though, such minor inconveniences are unimportant. We're on the starting grid of an exciting adventure, something transformative, ready for our lives to be changed for the better. So if there is a mutiny brewing over the sobering state of our humble surroundings, then everyone's keeping it to themselves.

'Assim como nós perdoamos a quem nos tenha ofendido...'

Out of range of my one good ear, the gray-haired matron resumes her muttering at the microphone, forcing those of us who were too lazy to buy a Portuguese phrase book to take comfort in the cadence and tone of her voice alone. There's a general assumption around here, I've noticed, that if you've come all this way, then you'll at least have taken the time to learn a little of the native language before setting off. Enough to get by. Well, let me say this: I admire their optimism, but to my mind that's what tour guides are for.

'...Santificado seja o Vosso nome, venha nõs a Vosso reino...'

On cue, Angela reappears, amused by our baffled faces. 'The rest of you will be going in shortly.' She has a voice that carries. Every word is a scythe hacking through thickets of background chatter. 'Did everyone remember to get their questions translated?'

I wave my scrap of paper eagerly.

On the first day, you're given Three Wishes. They're not called that, *obviously*, but in effect that's what they are. Direct pleas to **Him**, and therefore indirectly to the Universe itself, to God, for much-needed change in your life – insight, direction, enlightenment, physical healing. No restrictions are placed on what you can and can't ask for. It doesn't even have to be health-related. Marty, an architect from Minnesota, tells me he stops by the Casa at least once a year for a healing. And sometimes while he's here he seeks investment advice. Advice that **He,** the Big Man, willingly imparts.

'And is he right?'

Marty nods. 'Always.'

So clearly the field's wide open.

Even so, you're urged to choose wisely. After all, who knows when you'll pass this way again? It might be your one shot at getting what you need. 'So don't go squandering your requests on trivialities,' we were told over breakfast, 'or on something you might regret down the road.'

Understood.

All the same, the process of whittling a myriad possibilities down to three is harder than it looks. You think you know what you'd do in this situation. After all, three wishes - it's what every child dreams of. But then, when it finally arrives and the pressure's on, you get flustered. Or at least I did. I was up 'til gone midnight last night trying to squeeze all my current desires – and believe me, there's a lot of things I don't have that I'd like - into three pithy sentences that covered all the bases without seeming forced, crass, or greedy. That takes skill.

Once you've settled on your list, there's a kiosk outside the main hall where a little man stands waiting to translate it into Portuguese.

Shunting slowly to the head of the line, I was still very busy tweaking and honing, substituting this word for that, crossing out 'enthusiastic' and scribbling in 'passionate', when the man grabbed the paper from my hand, read what I'd written, chuckled at it, glanced up at me as if to say, 'Well, okay, if you're absolutely *sure* this is what you want...', transcribed it into Portuguese, and handed it back, swiftly moving onto the woman behind me.

The process is startlingly slick.

Weirdly, after all the build-up and ballyhoo and the many weeks of waiting, the Casa, this magical compound we've heard so much about, turns out to be rather unremarkable: a single featureless hangar, plus a few basic outbuildings, ringed by modest but well-tended gardens. Not that it matters. Nobody came here expecting sophistication. And anyway, it's not the compound but rather its location that makes it unique, as well as entirely wondrous and awe-inspiring in ways that few other places on the planet even come close to being. Sedona in Arizona has something similar, I believe. And Miami too. But nothing on this scale. Nothing quite as powerful.

At breakfast in our hotel - or *pousada*, as it's called – we received a brief orientation class. Maps were handed out, plus a schedule of our healing sessions for the week, followed by a Q & A. Unfortunately, I caught only a small portion of what was said. I was too busy eavesdropping.

At a neighboring table, a Norwegian couple - old hands who make the pilgrimage to Abadiânia once a year - were priming first-timers about what lay ahead. Their little group was seated over to my left, my bad side, and some way away, so I couldn't hear everything that was said, though what I did pick up gave me chills. There was talk of miracles. Of diseases being banished from people's bodies in inexplicable ways. One of the older guys, speaking with deadly earnestness, told of an incident the previous summer when he'd witnessed glowing objects - orbs, he called them - 'in the field over here behind the *pousad*a.'

The other guy went further still. Claimed to have laid eyes on 'a strange being.' A non-human form had entered his bedroom late one evening apparently, manifesting itself to the sleeping occupant, then – poufff! – vanished.

'The entities are everywhere hereabouts,' the first guy picked up, matter-of-factly. 'You can see them quite often over by...' - this part of the conversation got lost in the general restaurant chitchat – '...though during the healing process they will find you, and you can...' - something, something – '...them.'

What? I can *what* them?

But as usual I couldn't hear, and nobody else seemed willing to explain.

'Nope. I can't tell you,' Marty the architect said when I asked him.

He's a smart guy. Thirty-nine years old, bespectacled, a bit on the small, stocky side, but with the quiet presence of a man twice his height. He's also, I found out, another cancer survivor. Like Dermot, he had grown tired of conventional medicine messing with his precious body, so he took up his bed and walked, so to speak - or rather *flew;* Marty's wealthy enough to have his own plane - to Brazil. So far he's been here five times. If the Norwegians were right and there are indeed orbs and spirits in Abadiânia, you'd imagine that he, of all people, would have stories galore. But for some reason he became evasive.

'Isn't the very idea of a voyage of self-discovery that you discover it for yourself?' he said. From behind thick glasses two fishbowl eyes swam with amusement.

By contrast, Wendy, the excitable elderly woman I met on the bus, turned out to be a lot more forthcoming. She's from Denver, Colorado, where she runs an antique furniture store with her husband. On the side she's an amateur nutritionist, with a slim face contoured by sensible eating, and a demeanor that's gentle, almost grandma-ish in some ways, but infused with quiet passion when it comes to the subject of health and healing.

'Abadiânia is one of the few places on the planet,' she confided breathily, sweeping two gray tails of hair out of her eyes, only to have them fall back down again, 'with an energy vortex, a force field running through it. The membrane between the mortal world and the spiritual world is gossamer-thin here. That's what makes the Casa so special. It means the lines of communication between the two dimensions are open, like a gate, enabling God to speak to us directly.'

This was the first time in my life I'd heard anything even remotely like this.

'So okay, let me get this straight. You're saying there's a gate between Heaven and Earth, and Abadiânia is at the center of it?'

'Not an *actual* gate, but kinda, yes.'

'And when God speaks to you, what does he say?'

'Whatever he figures you need to hear most, I guess.'

'So it's a voice in your head?'

'More like a direct download into your mind. Normally, our lives are so frantic, the messages get lost. We make ourselves so busy all the time and our heads are so full of....of .... ' Darting hands flicked at the air. '...*clamor* and stress; it's hard to still the mind and just, y'know, receive. Well, that's what the Casa is for. You can still your mind here, and, when you do, incredible things happen. You learn all kinds of amazing stuff about life and about yourself.'

'Because of the vortex.'

'Exactly.'

The Abadiânia Energy Vortex

Brazil is the third largest country in the Americas, after Canada and the USA. It's advanced and primitive both – a big, prosperous industrial economy skirted by pockets of sweeping rural poverty and no-holds-barred urban gang violence.

As well as being one of the world's biggest sugar exporters, Brazil is also extremely rich in mineral and ore deposits, especially in the central plateau region where we are right now.

The Casa de Dom Inaçio was built here in the 1960s, by **Him,** the Big Man, above a special rock formation: a sheet of metamorphic crystal that extends across half the country. What geologists call a Precambrian Shield. According to Wendy, the energy generated by this massive crystal bed, combined with the earth's magnetism, produces a vortex – a spiral tunnel of energy so strong that it causes a kink in the laws of physics.

Now, before we go on, let me just say that, whatever you're thinking about all of this as you read it, I'm right there with you. I thought the same thing when I first heard it too. A kink in the law of physics? Caused by crystals? *Are you nuts?*

But if I'm being absolutely honest, I have to admit that there's definitely something here. The energy at the Casa is like nothing else I've ever experienced. Something between an overwhelming infusion of electricity and a subtle warmth that seeps through your body the way wifi does, invisibly. It's hard to explain - how can you put your finger on a sensation? The best I can offer at this early stage is that it's like a homecoming. As if you've been away a long, long while to a distant place, visiting relatives you don't much care for, and now you're back among your own. Relief – that's it. You're *relieved* to be home.

It's not essential that you be a native to succumb to its power either. Even as your tourist jet is touching down in Brazil, your blood starts to pump a little faster and your senses become attuned to a new, higher vibration. Coincidentally – or not - within seconds of landing in Rio de Janeiro, my cellphone went dead and hasn't worked since, a not uncommon side-effect of this freak energy breach that has Abadiânia locked at its epicenter. The resulting vortex, Wendy says, makes it possible for thousands upon thousands of entities - invisible beings, that would otherwise be stuck on the other side of the etheric divide - to swarm through and float among us. And when they do, they are able to achieve miraculous things. They're said to heal visitors at the Casa, for instance.

Josie RavenWing, in *The Book of Miracles*, a series of essays about events in Abadiânia, writes, 'To pass through the gates of the Casa de Dom Inaçio is to pass through a portal into a parallel world. In this world is a spiritual hospital in which the medical personnel are spirits, the chief administrator is God, and daily miracles of healing are the norm.'

Well, quite honestly, I'd never heard anything so preposterous and I wanted to laugh. That's what journalists do, we mock stuff we don't understand. In this case, however, it would be a mistake. There are numerous dependable, sane eyewitnesses – the Norwegians at the next table, for instance - who will tell you categorically that they have not only felt the power of the vortex in Abadiânia and experienced its incredible healing powers, but were actually *visited by entities and other strange beings* while they were here.

But this is where it gets tricky. The spirits can't make the trip alone. They need a channel. Someone local. A human connection on our side of the divide, the earth side, to act as a go-between, directing these energies into ordinary folks like us. Which is where **He** comes in. That's what **He** does. **He's** that guy. The guy that channels spiritual entities between Heaven and Earth, doing so with such incredible precision, it is said, that, by **His** hand, even the most chronic diseases can be vanquished forever. The Big Man treats more patients each week than the average western hospital does in a year, with an overall total that must be close to nine million by now.

'So when you meditate,' Wendy told me, 'make it your sacred intent to trust **Him** and the wonderful things **He** can do for you. Open your mind to the entities, and to receive messages from divine intelligence, and you will.'

'Such as what? What kind of messages?'

'About ways to heal yourself and your life.' Her eyes rolled up into her head while she recalled an example. 'In my case, it was all about taking care of my body. One of the things I was told the first time I came here was: 'Wendy, you have to take better care of your health and your body.'

'Why would God say that to you?'

'Oh, come on, look around. Have you *seen* the state of most people today?' she hissed, indicating the group, especially those with rolls of flab to spare. 'They've abused themselves. They're overloaded with toxins. Now they're here, trying frantically to undo it all – but *after* the fact, when they're already sick. Doctors couldn't do anything, so they came to a place like this hoping for magic and miracles." She shook her head in despair. "Neglect a car, Cash, and eventually it starts rusting and won't drive. Well, how is the human body any different? Neglect it, fail to give it what it needs, and it falls ill and stops working. Period. I mean, I'm not throwing stones. I was as guilty as anyone. Years ago, before I knew this stuff, I was lazy, overweight, toxic, and sick too. And borderline diabetic. Until I came here and learned how to make myself well again.'

'So what are you saying? That serious diseases can be cured?'

'Cured?' She became guarded, lowering her voice. 'Cured is, y'know, a forbidden term these days. But...' Choosing her words carefully. '...effectively treated? Sure, in some cases. And prevented? I wouldn't be surprised.'

I guess it makes sense. For every one of the things we do to ourselves that put our health in jeopardy – smoking, stress, drugs, alcohol, wolfing down junk food, candy, pastries and cake – most likely there are other things we could do to get ourselves out of trouble, if we only knew what they were.

'We were born to be healthy,' Wendy continued very earnestly, sensing she'd found a ready audience. 'Healthy into old age, without arthritis, without cancer, or weak and failing bodies. That's what we have an immune system for. It's like a...' She floundered for a moment, searching for the right metaphor. '... like a built-in shock absorber. It helps ward off disease. But it can only do that if we support it and keep it strong. Disease is a simple lack of ease. A lack of harmony and balance within the body. Often we just need to bring ourselves back into balance, by cleansing, detoxifying, getting adequate rest, eating the right foods, thinking positive, exercising, and so on.'

'And that's enough to prevent cancer, you think?'

'There was no cancer in ancient Egyptian times – did you know that? Scientists have run tests on mummies. No trace. Cancer is a modern plague. A sign of *our* times. It's something we're doing to ourselves. It's environmental, it's a lifestyle thing, it's about what we put in our mouths. We eat sugary, starchy junk food filled with chemicals, that quite honestly have no – zero - nutritional value to them at all. And I mean *at all*. We breathe bad air, we get fat, we shower in chlorinated water, we take drugs, stress out over every little thing, we don't sleep enough, we pollute our minds with anger and resentment, and so on, a whole long list of poisonous acts. Then we're shocked – scared, *freaked out,* when our bodies pack up and we end up in hospital with diabetes, tumors, Parkins...!'

Mid-sentence, she stopped.

She'd just realized – about the same time I realized – that all the time she'd been talking, I was eating cake. The chocolate cake they bake at our *pousada* tastes fabulous, almost gourmet, even though all available evidence points to the fact that it comes out of a packet.

'Want some?' I said, nudging the plate toward her. 'It's delicious.'

She grimaced. 'No way. Did you know that refined sugar ravages the human body? In health terms it's like swallowing glass. When your body can't metabolize all the sugar you're feeding it and is exhausted from trying, it develops diabetes.'

'I do know,' I told her, taking another bite. 'But I can't help it. I just love cake.'

For several seconds, disappointed gray eyes searched my face for something other than crumbs, some glimmer of understanding. Finding none, she fell into a gloomy silence.

'Alright, everyone, let's move it,' Angela cried, rushing in. 'You don't want to be late on your first day. There's a lot to do. This way. Follow me.'

Thanking Wendy for her little lecture, I stuffed the rest of the cake in my mouth, swilled it down with gulps of *Diet Pepsi*, and, suitably fortified, joined the rest of the group, delighted - *thrilled* - to be on my way at last.

This was it, the moment. Our first encounter with **Him**.

The miracle man they call John of God.

3

João

'Okay, guys...' Angela, a dervish of efficiency this morning, steers us across the main assembly hall, her pale face almost completely hidden behind two vertical drapes of dark hair. '...come over here and form an orderly line.'

Since it's only day one, and what's known as the Casa Effect – a soporific trance state that apparently engulfs you after you've been here a while - has yet to kick in, the crowd makes a quick stampede to the blue door.

Watching them leap up and go like that leaves me quite shocked. Shocked that here, of all places, in a retreat tailor-made to induce tranquility and spiritual wholeness, people still feel the need to scramble to be first, the way they do at home. As though this is the DMV, or they're applying for a passport. They'll all get through the door; they'll all be attended to. What's the rush?

Not long ago, someone compiled a global happiness index. Unbelievably, Nigeria, one of the poorest, most struggling economies in the world, topped the list, taking the rest of us by surprise. Turns out, they have more happy people in Nigeria than anywhere else. Meanwhile, out of 50 countries polled, guess where the United States came. *46th!* Why is that? Why would the population of the richest, most powerful nation on earth be so miserable?

The seed of the answer, I suggest, lies in what I saw just now - that grim determination to be first in line.

Although it's a fairly international crowd here today, the majority of people, I know without being told, are American. It's pretty obvious. Americans bring their American-ness with them wherever they go. The bustle. The need for instant gratification. The sense of purpose, of always driving toward something. This is not a criticism, by the way. It's these traits that make them so successful and their lifestyle the envy of the world. They're raised to believe that they can be (indeed, must *strive* to be) number one in their chosen endeavor. The best. Top of the heap, successful, a winner. And if you're not a winner, you're automatically a loser; you can't be trying hard enough. I see it all the time. It's the old Darwinian dog-eat-dog model: survival of the fittest. You are what you do, what you have, what you own, and where you're placed in society's pecking order. Performance is everything.

This philosophy has spread like pollen around the world in recent years, even though, when you get down to it, none of it is true.

And not only is it not true, but the sheer incongruence caused by struggling for success no matter what, of maintaining an image and trying to be something you're not, puts a lot of pressure on the body. Think back to Geena's husband. He was the perfect example of what we would class these days as a winner - always trying to prove himself, to be richer, more powerful - yet look what happened to him.

That, however, is not the way things work in Abadiânia. There's no adrenaline at the Casa. No racing pulse. You're not here to win. To succeed. To outwit, outrun, or beat anyone. You're here to submit. To surrender to the process. To give your lowly state of being up to something higher. There's no rivalry, no contest - you versus everyone else. At the end of the day this is a private matter. It's between you and God.

Clearly, for some people, that's quite a climbdown, and very humbling.

One of the best pieces of advice I ever received was given to me during that Buddhist retreat I mentioned before, and it's this: life is not a competition.

Write that up and stick it on your fridge so you won't forget.

Life is not a competition, the monks would say. It's not a race against your neighbor, or your workmates, or your friends. It's not about winning or losing. Nor is it a comparative exercise, a peacock strut of one-upmanship, constantly showing off and trying to prove yourself, seeing whom you can outshine in any given endeavor. If you really must compete, compete with yourself. Work at being better, kinder, more loving, more accepting, more grateful, more mindful, more forgiving, and more generous. Do those things today more than you did yesterday and you will make people around you happier. This happiness then reflects back onto you, making you happier also. And in the end, what matters most in life? That you're happy, of course!

If you're happy just as you are, with exactly what you have, then in spiritual terms you're already a success. You beat the odds. Congratulations, you made it. You won. Nothing more can be asked of you.

The idea that it's more complicated than this is a lie. That you must pretend to be better than you are, or brighter, or more efficient, or work longer hours, cloud your days with stress and worry, go without adequate sleep to get more done, eat badly and sporadically, and burn yourself out, just to stay ahead and keep up with the Joneses, always striving for more – more status, more money, more stuff, more houses, more technology, more cars, more of everything - and feeling like a failure if you don't get it; this nonstop frazzled struggle is toxic to the body. It makes your system acidic, and diseases thrive in an environment that's too acidic.

Anxiety, frustration, tension, anger, and fatigue, the monks said, exact a toll on our biology. Same with unnecessary conflicts, bitterness, greed, protracted disharmony. Same with traumas such as divorce, moving house, exams, unemployment, depression, poverty, the death of a loved one. All highly stressful, enough to have a detrimental effect on our body, slowly weakening the cell structure. Stress has been found to lie at the root of many of our worst diseases: ulcers, depression, cardiovascular disease, even HIV/AIDS[4] and cancer[5].

Of course, Buddhist monks aren't doctors. I couldn't vouch that any of what they were telling us was medically sound. But there's something about the truth that resonates with the soul, I find, and their words stirred something in me. Ultimately, they said, all that's required in order for you to be considered a winner in life is authenticity and inner peace. Somehow this made perfect sense. Not that you 'be the best' every time, but that you '*do* your best with who you are and what you have, and *enjoy* yourself.'

I particularly remember that word coming up over and over: enjoy.

In his classic 1976 book, *The Relaxation Response*, Dr. Howard Benson revealed the results of years of research into stress, and how it leads to higher blood pressure, an increased heart-rate, a faster metabolism, and many other physical

---

[4] Study by Sheldon Cohen of Carnegie Mellon University, published in the *Journal of the American Medical Association.*

[5] In the 1970s, Dr. Hans Selye, a Canadian endocrinologist, conducted some heavy research into stress and its effects. He divided it into two kinds: eustress – physical or mental exercise from challenging and rewarding work or strength training that is beneficial to the body – and distress, the kind of persistent overwrought coping or adaptation response that heightens anxiety or results in withdrawal or depression, and which can over time lead to physical disease.

symptoms. 'The stress response,' he said recently in an interview with ABC News, 'brings patients to doctors in over 60% of visits.'

Struggle and discord make for a sick body, whereas being congruent with your inner truth and being joyful and at peace with your life places far less strain on your cell structure. Your muscles and organs don't clench up. Your digestive and elimination systems work more easily. Blood flow is strong. In fact, everything flows more easily. Reach this point, and the struggle to be first, to win, to be a success will suddenly seem redundant, because you're already there; you're already a winner.

Happiness alone is the litmus for success. Or, as Eckhart Tolle calls it, 'the radiant joy of Being.'

Since that retreat, I've traveled extensively, visiting all corners of America and the world, and it's shocking to me how many millions of people haven't yet figured this out.

The queue files slowly - six inches, stop, six inches, stop - through the blue doorway into a broad L-shaped waiting room, the better part of which disappears out of sight around a corner. It's here that **He,** John of God, sits waiting for us.

Before greeting the Big Man, you must take an energy bath. That's what the first part of the room is for. To our immediate left is a large pool of people, of all ages, all nationalities, all hairstyles, clad in white T-shirts, smocks, and of course judo outfits. These are **His** worker bees. Gatekeepers of the portal. Participants in a well-coordinated ritual of love, each one connected in consciousness to all the rest, subjugating his or her own individual will for the good of the whole. It's quite moving to see. They sit rigid, eyes closed, staring without seeing, bodies tranquilized by deep meditation, like a recently-disinterred terracotta army. Or a silent choir, one that's *thinking* its song, spurred on *sotto voce* by a woman in a nurse's uniform moving between them up and down the rows.

'Let your thoughts be butterflies of hope,' she's saying, pacing back and forth, 'fluttering over a landscape of sickness and despair, bringing life and joy and peace and love to the world, in Jesus's name.'

Two other women stand to one side. These are the volunteer mediums. The Casa has around sixty altogether. It's their job, we're told, to harness the healing current of energy, which apparently is whirling around us unseen at all times, and keep it moving throughout the room, purifying the patients as they – we - shuffle by. Hard to say at this stage if this is actually a real process, meant to draw out sickness and disease, or just a visualized ideal. For now, though, we're asked to take it on trust, which I willingly do.

With *Ave Maria* lilting in the background, the line of restless white cotton moves excruciatingly slowly. Six inches, stop. Six inches, stop. Canes clatter, wheelchairs squeak, people cough, bored children wriggle in their parents' arms. One woman is sobbing into a tissue. Six inches, stop. Six inches, stop.

When my turn comes to peer around the corner, I'm dazzled by a sunny grotto filled with still more worker bees. Dozens of them. A strong current of love, fierce as a riptide and very palpable, flows through here. Love for **Him**, love for the afflicted as they parade by, love for divine intelligence and the miraculous wonders it can weave.

This second part of the room acts like a repair shop, an etheric scaffold erected around the Big Man to support him during the time he's taken over by entities. The technical term for the trance he goes into is 'incorporation.' That's when the human being we know as John of God is reduced to a state of absent presence; a husk through which source energy, if you care to call it that, is then better able to operate.

Despite his formidable reputation, he staunchly refuses to label himself a *curandeiro* (healer) or, worse still, a *milagreiro* (miracle man). '*Quem cura é Deus eu não curo ninguem,*' he insists to reporters and critics when they ask.

In English: 'I do not heal anyone, it is God that heals. I am only an instrument in His divine hands.'

If I'm honest, when I hear something like that, my first thought as a journalist is: he must be saying it for legal reasons. If João did purport to heal someone and the procedure resulted in serious injury or death, he'd be laying himself wide open to multiple lawsuits, I should think, and very possibly criminal action. Whereas the passive approach – 'I do nothing, it's all God's work' - is less risky and gives him a free pass, since it merely echoes Jesus's words: 'I can of mine own self do nothing.' And also: 'The Father that dwelleth in me, he doeth the works.'

Six inches, stop.

The line ahead of me shuffles unevenly along a center divide, drawing ever closer to a slumped figure in a chair. I can see a shoulder and an elbow, but no more; there are too many bobbing heads in the way, all angling for their first glimpse.

Several minutes to go yet before it's my turn.

So, while we're waiting, why don't we quickly take a look at the basic nutshell of João's life story?

John of God

João Teixeira de Faria – John's birth name – was born into a Catholic family in a dirt-poor neighborhood in the backwoods of Brazil. The son of a simple tailor, he was, by all accounts, a difficult and rebellious child. Over many years his despairing parents tried placing him in several schools, with no luck. In the end, because the family needed food on the table and quite clearly the whole education thing wasn't going anywhere, João dropped out to work as a cloth cutter in his father's shop.

One day, desperately poor and hungry, the sixteen-year-old boy went down to the local river to bathe. At the water's edge - or so the story goes – he fell prey to a magnificent vision. A stunning, fair-haired woman called Rita came to him in a pillar of light, saying, 'There's something I want you to do. Go to a temple called The Spiritist Center of Christ the Redeemer, and when you get there....well, you'll see.'

The temple was a long way away. To walk there took an entire day, without food or water. When he arrived, João found the place thronged with people, each one afflicted with a serious disease. But by then the kid was worn out. Before he could ask what was going on, he collapsed from exhaustion.

That's when a miracle took place.

Three hours later, as he surfaced, someone stepped up with a surprise. They told him he'd just cured every last one of the people in the temple.

'You were possessed by the spirit of King Solomon,' the elders said. 'By his mighty power working through you, you healed the sick.'

To say João was shocked is an understatement. Although the evidence of his powers lay all around him, it seemed an outrageous proposition - 'Heal people? *Me?*' – and he refused to take his phenomenal powers seriously. Only months later, after a short stint in the army and a few go-nowhere jobs had failed to capture his imagination, did he begin to realize that he was going in the wrong direction in life, forcing him to reconsider.

From that day on, he quit resisting his destiny and agreed to let himself be used as a channel by spirit, setting off with a bag of medicinal herbs into the Brazilian backwoods to minister to the sick and dying.

Not unexpectedly, his treatments made headlines.

Wherever he went, patients boasted of spontaneous

remissions from disease, or else spectacular recoveries within days of meeting him. It wasn't long before communities far and wide began to hear of this amazing young prodigy and to seek him out – though not always for the right reasons. Often he'd show up in a town, only to be hounded out again by angry doctors and priests, or beaten up and jailed for illicitly practicing medicine without a license. In time, this cemented his image as a major anti-establishment figure.

By 1993, João had decided to capitalize on his growing reputation as a metaphysician by settling in Abadiânia, a small agricultural community 71 miles south of the capital, Brasilia, comprising two dairies, a meat-packing operation, and a brick factory. Here, he set up an early, primitive version of the Casa and waited for patients to come by, which of course they did, in their hundreds at first, then their thousands. On foot and by bicycle, in cars and taxis, and eventually vans, coaches, and planes. Until in the end the descending multitude of pilgrims got to be so absurdly large that João was forced to expand his operation, taking over a few rural acres off main street, which he turned into a full-service faith-healing center, a sort of Latin Lourdes, with a snack bar, an infirmary, a gift shop, a pharmacy, and its own waterfall. He named the center the Casa de Dom Inaçio de Loyola[6], after St. Ignatius de Loyola.

Once you learn of the road João took to get here, as well as the phenomenal extent of his powers he's said to have, and also

---

[6] St. Ignatius de Loyola, known as Dom Inaçio, is one of John of God's heroes. He was a Spanish nobleman in the 16th Century who founded a gentlemen's club called the Society of Jesus, also known as The Jesuits. This he did after being hit in the leg with a cannonball. To take his mind off the surgery, which involved stitching him up without anesthetic, a friend gave him a book to read about Christ's life. And that was pretty much it. Instantly he was converted to the teachings of Jesus. Nowadays, St. Ignatius, you're asked to believe, is the head surgeon at this facility. Though dead, obviously, he oversees its daily workings from a special vantage point in the spirit world. Since you have no evidence that indicates otherwise, you end up subscribing to this idea.

the problems he faced in bringing his healing abilities to South America's Christian community, it makes your first audience with him both daunting and at the same time exhilarating. For me, it's like meeting Mick Jagger or the Pope. Even Oprah's done a show about him and says she wants to pay a visit. The guy is a legend.

I confess, I'm nervous.

Three people to go. Two people to go. This is it.

Angela beckons. 'Okay, Cash. You're up. Come on.'

Beaming to cover my nerves, I step out of the line and launch myself at João Teixeira de Faria.

So, okay, let me say this first: he is not at all what I imagined.

His bio says he's six feet tall, though you'd never think that to look at him. He seems a lot smaller in person. Flopped in a modest wooden armchair flanked by statues of Jesus and Mary, the Big Man comes across as fairly frail. Tired, indifferent, looking older than his sixty-odd years, and depressingly out of condition, with a fleshy face and extra-large earlobes. His only concession to the vibrancy of youth is a striking flop of brown hair that might be dyed, it's hard to tell. At any rate it appears quite out of place today against his old man skin.

Patti Conklin, another of the Abadiânian tour guides, puts João's poor physical state some days down to a relentless dedication to good works. Quoted in *The Book of Miracles*, she says, '[H]is cellular structure is becoming weakened, and that is very, very typical....On a cellular level it's exhausting to keep moving that kind of energy day after day, year after year...it seems to be an occupational hazard of this kind of work.'

But it's more than that. When João is possessed by a spirit, he will often take on the physical characteristics of that spirit. His posture becomes crumpled, his face changes shape and texture. It's a wonder to behold.

Now that I'm here before him, I'm not sure what to do.

Watery blue eyes peer past me from behind sensible spectacle frames. He seems annoyed. Not once during our entire encounter does he pay me any attention.

'How come he keeps looking past people while they're talking to him?' I ask Angela. 'It's so rude.'

'No it's not,' she mumbles discreetly. 'He's watching the spirits. They're floating up and down the line, inspecting people, cleansing them, figuring out what their problems are and what kind of treatment they need. It's really the spirits handling the workload, not him.'

Heather Cumming and Karen Leffler throw light on this in their very detailed book, *John of God: The Brazilian Healer Who's Touched the Lives of Millions:* 'The entities view the body as a hologram; they are able to see our energetic field and have access to our complete karmic history (the cumulative effects of all our actions). As we stand before the entities and ask for healing, we must understand that we are entering into a partnership: we are co-creating healing by using our free will in a proactive way and making a concerted effort to change our lifestyle, habits, and anything else that no longer serves our highest good.'

Since João is a trance medium, his body at such times, we're told, becomes an unpiloted drone, vacated by his own soul and possessed by beings of a higher vibration. It could even be two or three beings in succession,[7] drawn from a pool of thirty-seven 'spirit doctors' - ghosts of reputable theologians,

---

[7] According to various biographies, João's mentors, on his road to becoming John of God, were a mixed bag of hypnotists, psychics, and magicians. He is known to be a devotee of Allan Kardec (1804-1869), a 'spiritist' who was an authority on séances and 'spirit-tapping.' The Spiritism movement embraces the belief that, not only do ethereal beings walk the earth, but these beings reincarnate again and again on their long, homebound journey to enlightenment, and they can be contacted through spirit-tapping. Only, in Kardec's case, it turned out *not* to be ethereal beings doing the tapping, alas, but his friends knocking on the underside of a table with their knuckles. Despite this slight credibility hiccup, spiritism remains important to Brazilians even today.

physicians, surgeons and therapists, each one of whom was, during his lifetime, considered a master in his field. These include St. Francisco Xavier[8], a good friend of St. Ignatius de Loyola. ('Francisco simply loves doing tooth extractions,' I was told enthusiastically by Wendy on the way here.) Then there are a couple of specialists. The first is Dr. José Valdevino, who stops by now and then to fix up quadriplegics. The other's called Dr. Augusto de Almeida, a one-time military doctor who's good with wounds. Or, if you're really lucky, St. Ignatius de Loyola himself may make an appearance. According to Angela, you know when Ignatius takes over because João develops a limp.

On top of these there's said to be an entire brigade, or 'phalange', of invisible entities - hundreds, and possibly thousands of them – circulating around this compound, attending to, examining, diagnosing, and healing the patients. It's the spiritual equivalent of a Swiss army knife, offering something for every occasion.

And these aren't just wild, unsubstantiated claims, by the way. Rigorous testing has been conducted on João over the years by those who would challenge his credibility, with outstanding results that only go to cement his reputation.

One time, a tech guy working on a TV documentary for ABC Television showed Angela a piece of sound equipment, she told me. Just before João entered the current room, the machine went berserk, producing, according to her, a 'graph of black frequencies' that blew right off the scale.

On another occasion dowsing rods were used to monitor João's aura. The results were dazzling enough to scotch most doubts about his unseen power. When the Big Man was not 'in entity', that is to say when he was just being himself, researchers found that the energy field around him extended out roughly

8 A small but very motivated 16th Century Jesuit missionary who traveled the world letting people of all races know that his God was better than theirs, with mixed results.

four feet or so, which is normal. Ours – mine and yours - are about the same. But all this would change dramatically the instant he incorporated. At that point, the dousing rods went haywire. At once, he became a spiritual lighthouse, his beam sweeping seventy feet in all directions. That, for many people, was all the proof they needed that João was certainly not your ordinary everyday guy, but rather a phenomenon blessed with extraordinary God-given abilities.

'Good morning,' I say to him quietly, handing him my three wishes.

In return I receive a nod of somber acknowledgement.

As I said, it was difficult honing them into a workable list. The first wish, like you might expect, went to my left ear (*orelha esquerda)*, my primary reason for coming. 'I wish to have it unblocked and full hearing restored,' I wrote. For a guy who broadcasts on stereo radio to be functioning in mono only is highly unfortunate. Not to say inconvenient. My phone will ring in my pocket and I won't hear it. The TV volume has to be turned way up. And I regularly sleep through the alarm. The whole situation's getting to be a drag.

After that, though, I was stumped. In every other respect I'm perfectly okay. What else could I put on my wish list?

Ultimately, this is the deal: coming to the Casa is a threshold moment, an opportunity to instigate big changes and rid one's life of anything negative that might be getting in the way of harmony, happiness, abundance, or growth.

So I went full out. I made #2: 'Reconciliation with my father' (I'll explain more later), and followed that with #3, a rather sweeping: 'Please unblock my life and career; help me find a way to escape public radio and move on to other work I'm really passionate about.' Too broad, of course, but it's the best I could come up with without seeming brash or greedy.

After a quick glance at my paper, John of God leans over the arm of his chair and grunts something to the attendant in a low voice, which, because of my blocked ear, I miss completely. With that, he straightens up again and, handing back my list, stares past me to the next person in line.

Wait, *that's it?*

Unsure what to do next, I hesitate. As I'm waiting, I suddenly feel a dagger-like stabbing sensation under my right eyebrow. It comes on in a flash, similar to the barometric headaches I get at home occasionally that presage an upcoming turn in the weather. But this is far worse, and – 'Ouch!' – very painful.

With a hand over my eye, I stumble out of the door into the next room.

'What happened there?' I ask Angela, still referring to the awkward few seconds I stood before João. At the very least I was expecting a little chitchat, an interaction, some kind of profound personal contact, but already I'm dismissed.

'He doesn't need long. He knows what he's doing,' she says, consulting her written notes. 'What's wrong with your eye?'

'I don't know. Something weird just happened.'

I give her the bullet points. And this is where things get spooky, because, while she's wondering what the cause of the pain might be, she traces the arc of her own right eyebrow with a finger. 'Hm. This area of the face here is on the liver-gallbladder meridian. So the entities were probably checking you out and they found some kind of problem with your gallbladder. It's that th...'

'But...' And you know what's coming next. '...I don't *have* a gallbladder,' I tell her. 'I had it removed two years ago.'

At this, a smug little smile crosses Angela's face. 'Well, there you go! Obviously, the entities found you had no gallbladder and, as they went through your body, checking you out, you felt pain.'

In some part of my mind, I must admit, I want to put this freakish incident down to coincidence and leave it at that. But quite honestly it's beyond uncanny.

'Anyway...'- back to her notes - '...João said come back for surgery at two.'

'Oh yeah? And what does that mean exactly?'

'It *means* come back for surgery at two o'clock. The entities inspected you and found something they need to work on...'

'They did?'

'...so he wants you to return this afternoon. For an operation.'

Lunch at the Casa is free. On the menu this morning: hearty minestrone soup. On the menu *every* morning, as a matter of fact; they only have one course and one recipe. The soup is made fresh each day in a cramped kitchen at the heart of the compound, then blessed with divine energy by one of João's assistants, before being ladled from steaming vats into bowls and passed, along with a bread roll, through little windows to the long lines gathered outside.

After the reverential hush of the current room, the covered patio alongside the kitchen has the feel of a Stock Exchange trading pit: buzzy, frenzied, everyone chatting and piling in at once. Scanning for familiar faces, I spot our group at a far table comparing notes – what João said, who's scheduled for what and when.

One glance tells me there's someone missing. 'Where's Dermot?'

The group goes quiet.

Uh-oh. 'Something wrong?'

'João wrote an X on his sheet,' Wendy informs me with great solemnity.

'And an X means...?'

Her blank stare tells me everything. Dermot, it seems, arrived at the Casa with barely a minute to spare. Fearing the chunky Irishman might die, or 'disincarnate', as it's called around here, João ordered he be whisked into surgery straight away.

A woman called Mary, a therapist from Wisconsin who talks in short sharp bursts like railway station announcements, proceeds to improvise a small prayer 'to help Dermot fight his cancer.' A beautiful thought.

The very idea, though, seems to annoy Wendy.

'Why must we always talk of *fighting* disease?' she says quietly. 'When we get sick, especially if it's life-threatening, our first instinct is to – ' She adopts a boxer pose, fists up. '... fight it, you know? The terminology of war. Always war. 'The *battle* against cancer.' 'The *struggle* to survive.' '*Combating* a disease.' Everything's about conquering, overcoming, winning and losing. It's such an imperialistic, territorial attitude, and it only stresses the body out even more, making things worse. 'The enemy has invaded; we must expel it and triumph.' When, really, going to war against a disease is as futile as staging a 'war on terror,' and you know how badly that went.'

I notice some people drifting away to another table. Her words are too harsh for their delicate ears. The shutters have come down.

But to a certain extent Wendy is right. We're told constantly in the media that there's a battle against cancer. One and a half million Americans are diagnosed with the disease each year. According to a recent article in the *New York Times,* the National Cancer Institute alone has spent, altogether, $105 billion on researching a cure. And *they're* the National Cancer Institute! They do nothing else all day but turn over rocks looking for some kind of breakthrough. Frankly, if they can't find one, who can? Despite this, and despite the hundreds of millions of dollars that have been donated to cancer charities, all the sponsored bike-rides, all the billions invested in studies and applied research, not to mention all the boatloads of hope and prayers that have been expended – cancer has us licked. It's running neck and neck with heart disease for the title of 'Number one killer in the country', and, given current growth rates, is predicted to be striking down an estimated 21 million of us each year by 2030[9].

Everyone knows someone who fell foul of the Big C and died, or who is currently engaged in a battle for survival.

Cancer even took the life of my mother and her sister.

I remember, years ago, after the loss of my mom, being, first sad – she was only in her sixties; these days that's ridiculously young - but then very angry. I got to thinking, as many people do when they see their friends and loved-ones die, 'What's going on here? How come there's no cure? Why aren't doctors doing something? These guys were supposed to be our champions. We charged them with a mission: to hunt down this dragon and slay it once and for all. And you're telling me that *still* nobody has a handle on it?'

'Why do we think that the best way to eradicate cancer,' Wendy picks up, 'is by making an enemy of it, fighting it, cutting it out, blasting it with radiation? When all that does is make it more hostile. You think you wiped out one group of cells and for a time everything's good, but often all you did was stall them. More spring up elsewhere later on. Before you know it, you're back in hospital having more treatment. That's what makes our western medical system so out of date.'

This earns a few sage nods around the table, though I wonder if people are thinking what I'm thinking: how radical this seems. Almost heretical to the untutored ear. Outside of

---

[9] The International Agency Research on Cancer, an agency of the United Nations, reporting in 2010.

this place, you never hear anyone talk as bluntly as Wendy does about disease. At least, I don't.

'Doctors don't think outside the box, that's the problem,' a small, rather severe woman with a gray crop chips in. 'They're still following the same tired old ways. Still chasing the symptoms and trying to suppress them.'

Wendy beams broadly. She's found an ally. 'When what they should be doing is finding the source, the *cause* of the symptoms, and tackling those...'

'....by cleansing the body,' the second woman, who's called Sheila, completes the thought, 'relaxing it, giving it the nutrition and rest it needs, detoxing it of metals and chemicals. People need to make different lifestyle choices. They need to be asked, 'What are you doing in your life that caused you to get sick?'

'That's right. And they need to be told, 'Don't fight disease - embrace it, own it.' Diseases are there to teach you something. It's just your body's way of trying to get your attention.'

A pause while Wendy scoops up a spoonful of soup allows me to step in and play Devil's advocate. 'So if you die of a disease, you're saying it's basically your fault?'

'Not always.' Sheila replies for her. 'But a lot of the time, sure.'

Since the death of my mother, I've read a couple of books about this, including one by health guru Andreas Moritz.[10] He, too, says we have cancer all wrong. It's not a disease as such, it's a sign that the body is panicking, and '...the result of many crises of toxicity that have as their common origin one or more energy-depleting influences.' He goes on to list stimulants, emotional trauma, repressed emotions, dehydration, an irregular lifestyle, stress reactions, lack of sleep, and an accumulation of chemicals and toxins in the liver, kidneys, colon, and so on, as

[10] Author of *Cancer is Not a Disease, It's a Survival Mechanism* – Ener-chi.com, 2008.

major hindrances to the system's attempt to remove billions of dead cells each day. 'When these accumulate in any part of the body, they naturally lead to a number of progressive responses that include irritation, swelling, hardening, inflammation, ulceration, and abnormal growth of cells.'

'True healing,' Wendy insists, 'comes from the inside out, not the outside in. I know it's a cliché, but your body's like an exquisite temple. It will stand firm and strong for the longest time if you look after it. Neglect it, though, and the roof caves in.'

'But...' For a moment I lapse into my default settings and become a journalist again. '...what about people who die very young? Children, babies? They haven't abused their bodies, have they? Yet their roofs cave in anyway.'

'Some people's roofs cave in early,' she returns with a shrug. 'That's just how it is. There's a bigger plan at work. Each of us has a moment to die, and that's theirs. They're born for a reason, but their life is intended to be shorter than most, then they're called home. It's not for us to question Divine Consciousness. We need to stop putting ourselves through the wringer, trying to figure out the plan, or plea-bargaining with God, asking 'Why me?' Always the ego wants to know why. Well, sometimes there is no 'why'. Or at least no 'why' we're meant to understand. Our current adventure is at an end and a new one is about to begin. That's it. So accept it, let go. That's the best you can do.'

I don't deny there may be some truth to this. All the same, let's hope she doesn't blurt out anything quite so hard-edged to poor Dermot. The guy's not in a fit state right now to take on board Wendy's theories about terrorism and health.

Almost every member of our group, one way or another, it turns out, is listed for some sort of procedure today.

'And how about...?' Mary turns to me.

'Me? Oh, surgery. Today at 2pm.'

Surgery. Good grief, what am I saying? I'd naïvely pictured the process to be less complicated. That João would snap his fingers or pray over me, or maybe do some jiggery-pokery with his nose like Samantha does in *Bewitched*, or whatever, and my hearing would come galloping back clearer than ever. But not so. Whatever's wrong, it's going to take a full-blown operation to correct it. Naturally I'm worried what that might entail.

In need of comfort food, I return to the soup line for a second helping, where I bump into tour-leader Susan, a wafting wisp of a woman, tall and fair, in an ankle-length silk skirt that billows and foams in on itself like the coiling smoke from a snuffed-out candle.

'There are two kinds of surgery: invisible and physical,' she says. 'Invisible means there's no actual incision. Whereas physical surgery – well, it's what it says. The Entity operates on you directly.'

'And does he explain beforehand which kind it'll be? Y'know, before he administers the anesthetic?'

'Erm....' Something happens at this point. I'm not sure what. Susan becomes a little distant for a second, then: 'What anesthetic?'

With no further elaboration, she drifts off toward the Casa shop, leaving me with a full bowl of soup and suddenly no appetite.

The guy operates on you *without anesthetic*? Is that what she just said?

Oh - my – lord.

4

The Hypnotic Power of the Physician's Word

The pocket of real estate acquired by João all those years ago for his spiritual hospital has evolved organically ever since, morphing into the cultivated tropical fantasy that surrounds us today, an oasis of flowerbeds and statuary intermingled with trees of avocado and mango. On the far reaches of the Casa gardens he built a small pagoda-like viewing deck, a pleasant hilltop sanctuary where people sit for hours, meditating, and staring out across a shallow crease of rolling green pastureland uncluttered by more than a few jack fruit trees and a drifting herd of white Brahma cattle, moving with the plodding, aimless stumble of a species that must have had big dreams once, but has since lowered its expectations.

Done with my soup, and feeling thoroughly relaxed - perhaps too much so for a man who's down for surgery in under ninety minutes - I commune for a few moments with the pastoral isolation of the viewing platform, then cut a path back across the trimmed lawn, washed an almost hallucinogenic green by noonday sunlight, through the parking lot and out onto the main street.

Our *pousada* is situated two blocks up from the Casa.

Brazil is very proud of its *pousadas*. The two-story pink hacienda we've been booked into is typical of its kind and quite attractive. Better still, it's only thirty dollars a night. For that, you get a poky little room that offers the basics – a ceiling and door, for instance – but no closet. Well, that is to say, it does have a closet, it just doubles as a bathroom, that's all – sink, toilet, shower, everything kept very simple and functional. Though we were given warnings about the showers in our block. Seems one or two were inadvertently wired up to the mains. 'People have been electrocuted,' Angela told us, 'so take care with that.'

I promised I would.

During check-in last night, I noticed Amy, a delightful and very glamorous businesswoman from Arizona, simpering quietly as she surveyed the walls of Reception in mild horror. 'My god, it's a *minus* three-star motel,' she hissed out of the corner of her mouth. I half-expected her to start sobbing.

On first impressions, I had Amy down as someone who'd consider herself to be slumming if she were downgraded from a stateroom at the *Four Seasons* to a mere suite. But I'm wrong. She's remarkably game for this adventure, even though, with her well-honed elegance, fashionable *Saks* knitted poncho - she refers to herself smilingly as 'the Poncho Diva' - and forearms jangling with a pipeline of bangles, she blends into the downbeat Abadiânian landscape the way, say, Liberace might, or an astronaut.

This morning we walked to the Casa together. En route, she stopped off at one of the roadside jewelry stores to admire a clutch of crystal pendants in the window. 'Oh, I really *love* this,' she cooed. 'I think I'm going to buy it.'

'Oh yeah?' There were three pendants side by side. 'Which one?'

She looked puzzled, then laughed. 'Not the pendant, *the store*.'

That's how she is. It's hysterical.

Aside from the low nightly rate, there's one other major advantage to staying at our *pousada,* or *The One Season* as we now call it: it has its own restaurant. Believe it or not, for that measly thirty bucks, they throw in three hearty cooked meals a day, making it tip-top value. Even Amy's impressed.

As I said before, our group has twenty-four members altogether. That's a lot of new faces to become acquainted with in such a short time. The easiest approach, I've found, is to do it in shifts: move about the dining room, sitting at a different table every meal, and pick out somebody new to talk to each time.

That's how I get to meet Lukas, a spry, fresh-faced Swiss guy whose disposition is bursting with cheery bonhomie. In fact, apart from the slightly worn-down aura that hovers about his shoulders, which goes hand in hand with clinging onto life by your fingernails, you'd never even know he was sick.

Back home in his native land, Lukas, though still relatively young, is a well-respected gynecologist. A card-carrying member of the Western medical establishment with a practice in Zurich for twenty years or more, until he was forced to give it up following a traumatic run-in with cancer that for the very first time in his life put him on the wrong end of a surgeon's knife. The initial outbreak was intestinal, he says. So doctors went in and cut out a sizeable chunk of damaged tissue from the stomach, hoping that might work. Well, it didn't. Later, they found that the cancer had spread to his bladder. So they operated again. Which *also* didn't work.

Wendy may be right on target when she likens Western medicine to the military's clumsy war efforts. At the first sign of a tumor, their first impulse is to go on the offensive. The way Lukas tells it, his surgeons did just that. They thundered in like a surgical S.W.A.T. team, hacking and slicing, chasing the cancer cells around his body as if they were at a funfair playing whack-a-mole. Meanwhile, the possible root cause of the disease, which is the real problem, went unidentified and unaddressed, and lived on to cause him even more problems.

'Later,' he says, 'they found tumors in my anus. So they replaced that.'

'The whole thing?'

'I am the original bionic man!'

Joking, of course. Gallows humor stemming from a place of dark despair.

I don't know him well enough to press further, but I long to ask the obvious question: '*What on earth were you thinking, dude?* How could you let your own profession carve up your body like that, hacking chunks out, irradiating the rest, then showering you in pills? Rationally speaking, did you not think they might be doing more harm than good?'

According to Andreas Moritz, cancer cells are natural to the human body. Up to 95% of tumors appear and disappear of their own accord, he claims, before we realize they're there. He goes on to add, 'In truth, relatively few cancers are 'terminal'. However, once diagnosed, the vast majority of all cancers are never even given a chance to disappear on their own. They are promptly targeted with an arsenal of deadly weapons such as chemotherapy drugs, radiation, and the surgical knife. The problem with cancer patients is that, terrified by the diagnosis, they submit their bodies to all these cut/burn/poison procedures that, more likely than not, lead them to the final day of sentencing...'[11]

---

[11] In his book *Cancer Is Not a Disease,* Moritz quotes leading cancer researcher Dr. Hardin Jones of U.C. Berkeley: 'It is most likely that, in terms of life expectancy, the chance of survival is no better with, than without, treatment, and there is the possibility that treatment may make the survival time of cancer less.' And later: 'My studies have proven conclusively that cancer patients who refuse chemotherapy and radiation actually live up to four times longer than treated cases, including untreated breast cancer cases.'

But I guess that's the thing about doctors – they wield an immense amount of power over us. The white coat says 'authority', the equipment and protocol are mesmerizing. We believe everything they tell us. In fact, this tendency we have for falling under the spell of our physician even has a name. It's called the Shaman Effect. Luckily, our trust is usually justified. Doctors, most times, are professionals doing a tough job, often in very trying circumstances. Such is our admiration for them that we can forget that they're just human beings. This is a dangerous level of power to invest in any one stranger, much less one who requires that you be sick in order for him to make a living, but who otherwise may not have any personal investment in whether you live or die.[12]

'Last year,' Lukas continues, finishing off a salad and dabbing his lips with a napkin, 'they did further tests on me and found that the cancer had gone higher, into the bowel. They told me they wanted to operate and take out even more. Well, that was it.' His thick, gurgly Swiss accent rises from submissive to indignant. 'That's when I said, 'No way, y'know? Enough. I'm done. I'll try something else.'

Now he's here. John of God is the 'something else' he's trying. The last 'something else' on his list, by the sound of it. The man's run out of options; he's pretty close to the end. The jackals almost have him. By shunning allopathic medicine, he feels he may have bought himself some time, but not much. A miracle is needed, and soon.

---

[12] Nothing you'll read here is intended as a blanket dismissal of the medical profession. Far from it. If you break a leg, get yourself to a hospital. If glass flies into your eye, let the guys in the E.R. remove it. Break a hip, need a blood test, treatment for traumatic injuries, childbirth, long-term care, strokes, brain hemorrhages, a transfusion, or a hundred other things? All are the rightful province of the medical profession. Plus, if you develop cancer or some other serious disease, by all means consult a healthcare professional. Wisdom dictates it. Accumulate all the facts – you'd be a fool not to – then make up your own mind about what's right for you.

*

Certain aspects of the Casa operation resemble a country spa. Not intentionally, but they do.

Returning to the compound after lunch, I stop by the gift shop to sign up for a session of 'crystal bed therapy'. Angela describes it as a spiritual workout - 'Very therapeutic; you'll love it' – hawking the benefits with such enthusiasm that I'm left wondering if maybe she gets a cut from every booking. Then again, she's such a believer and so earnest about all of this that it's impossible to distrust her. So I take out my billfold and bag myself a slot for Friday afternoon.

João's known for being a very shrewd entrepreneur, and it shows. His gift shop is a goldmine, raking in around $400,000 a year. This goes a long way toward paying for the upkeep of the Casa, but it's still not enough. Luckily, he owns a couple of ranches, an emerald mine, and various other business interests on the side. It's the profits from these that help keep the place solvent. They also fund his other charity work, including a soup kitchen at the other end of town. In that respect, the guy's a living saint.

Aside from selling crystal bed treatments, the gift shop does a roaring trade in religious knickknacks: rosaries, jewelry, crystal pendants, books, and also mysterious wooden triangles. These come in three sizes and I assume serve a vital purpose, though I have no idea what that might be. Maybe they give off heat, because I see people walking around hugging them to their chest the way two-year-olds clutch teddy bears.

After buying a bottle of water that's been blessed by a Casa official, the same way the soup is, I squeeze through the crowd of white-clad bodies glowing in the hot sun and join the 'Surgery at 2 o'clock' line inside the main hall where sixty or so people are locked in a holding pattern before the blue door.

'Have you decided which one you're going to have?'

I turn to find Susan standing behind me. 'Which what?'

'Kind of surgery - physical or spiritual?'

João only tackles a few physical operations each day, so space is limited. Usually, the big, unwieldy stuff - removing surface tumors, cysts, fixing painful chronic hernias, etc – takes priority. Clearly, compared to something as grave as cancer, my own problem seems positively trivial. I'd feel terrible if a blockage in my left ear took precedence over someone who might otherwise die.

In the end, the kind of surgery I choose depends on one factor only: 'Does the hands-off approach actually work, or is my ear more likely to be healed if João tackles the issue physically?'

'There's really no difference,' Susan assures me. 'Some people have doubts, that's all. They need proof. So João proves it to them by doing physical incisions.'

'Without anesthetic?'

'The entities see to all of that. The patient feels nothing.'

Hm. I've heard about this. 'Spiritual anesthesia', it's called. It induces a kind of numbness bordering on apathy in the body and around the incision, leaving the patient fully conscious and aware, but feeling no pain. It's remarkable, and quite baffling to regular science. Maybe there's some discomfort afterwards, but very little, and even this disappears quickly. How this works is shrouded in mystery and it's puzzled skeptics for fifteen years. João doesn't even seem to sterilize his surgical instruments, which you'd think would be the minimum precaution when human lives are at risk. In any other environment it would be inviting infection. But not here.

'So the anesthesia – is it completely effective?' I ask.

Susan smiles coyly - 'You'll be fine.' – and strides away.

*

The afternoon session begins much the same way the morning one did.

Promptly at 2pm, we file in through the blue doorway, shuffling past the hundreds of worker bees with their eyes closed, busy generating waves of love, and trek slowly by João's empty throne and out the other side into a mysterious, darkened bunker beyond, which they call The Surgery Room, where we're invited to take a seat on long benches.

'Who will be volunteering for physical surgery this afternoon?' an attendant asks once we're settled. 'Please stand up.'

A few brave souls rise from their seats. Eight or nine. Wow, that's a sizeable number. 'Good for you,' I think to myself, watching them leave.

'Anyone else?' The attendant pauses expectantly.

A part of me wants to go with them. Though not a particularly big part, I must say, otherwise I wouldn't still be sitting here with my eyes fixed on the floor.

Problem is, I've seen documentaries. You probably have too. Scathing exposés of so-called 'psychic healers,' in particular those bands of shameless rogues operating out of Australia and the Philippines, where regulations on scamming people are evidently quite relaxed and they can avoid scrutiny. These guys claim to be able to cure major diseases, and will blithely don scrubs and a surgeon's cap to perform elaborate heart and liver operations, amazing everyone with their professional dexterity, when really all they're doing is a bunch of conjuring tricks and sleight of hand. Sometimes there's a spare cow's liver hidden under the table. Or they have the guts of a duck in a bag. This is kept concealed in their pocket until a messy tumor is supposedly being cut out, when, hey presto, the surgeon squeezes it and blood flies everywhere. Or in some cases, there's a secret rubber tube, carefully positioned, that squirts fake blood at the point of incision.

Yet despite the obvious trickery, patients, because they're desperate, still flock to see them, prompting the U.S. Federal Trade Commission in 1975 to get tough with a handful of Californian travel agencies, ordering them to quit sending people to the Philippines for psychic surgery, calling the procedure 'a total hoax.'

A website dedicated to blowing the lid off flimflam and the work of New Age quacks recently went even further in condemning this kind of practice. 'False hope for the seriously ill is the cruelest form of quackery because it lures victims away from effective treatment... [T]hose who buy false hope can get stuck in an attitude of denial. They waste not only financial resources but what little remaining time they have left.'[13]

Which is all well and good. I too am against shysters preying on people's trust. But here's the thing: what if not all spiritual healers are born equal?

In the same way that not all lawyers fit the stereotype of greedy, self-serving, ambulance-chasing opportunists, and not all rock stars are violent, drug-addicted lotharios, is it not possible that, in among all the many charlatans, there are some people out there who do have a spiritual gift, one that can't be explained away rationally by scientific testing? If a gateway does exist between our world and the next, maybe there's also a handful of geniuses out there who hold a key to it. Not me, not you, but *some*one. Dig deep enough among the long list of healers rubbished as quacks, and it's not unthinkable, is it, that you might turn up someone who actually is 'the real deal'?

A fine example, to my mind, is Mata Amritanandamayi Devi. This venerated Hindu mystic is already a global phenomenon, thanks to her passion for selflessly projecting unconditional love at people who come to see her. She does this by the simplest of

---

[13] www.quackwatch.com.

means: a hug.

The effects are stunning. Pilgrims who succumb to her embrace experience a feeling akin to being tied to a radiator in winter. A current of strong, penetrating warmth vibrates through them, affecting their bodies, but also their emotions too, bringing comfort, rejuvenation, and relief. So far, 29 million have received a hug from 'Amma', as she's known. Many weep or break down in her presence; many more claim to have been healed.

Of course, detractors are quick to rubbish her efforts, dismissing her (and her followers) as delusional. But what if focused love energy is similar to electricity? You can't see electricity, and there's no proof it's there. At least, not 'til you plug into it, at which point that same invisible force can power an entire city. Maybe love energy, projected from a guileless heart, works in the same way. What if it is able, by some means we don't yet understand, to penetrate the body of another, affecting the cell structure and bringing about a healing? It's possible.

In light of this, I'm wondering if the terminology we use about John of God is faulty in some way.

Maybe calling what João does 'spiritual/psychic surgery' is misleading. Especially if, by labeling him 'psychic', we're lumping him in with a bunch of crooks, showmen, conjurors, conmen, and nutjobs, because, from what little I've seen, he seems very much on the level. For a start, he doesn't charge for what he does. His services are rendered for free. Anyone who shows up at the Casa looking for a healing will be taken care of no matter what. That, right there, forestalls accusations of exploitation, engendering a lot of trust. Also, there's no underhanded conjuring involved, as far as I can tell. His healing acts are done openly, in full view, and, he claims, totally unconsciously.

In an interview with the *Beliefnet website,* TV journalist John Quinones, a reporter for ABC's *Primetime Live,* tells how he investigated John of God's activities at the Casa, and, no doubt to the supreme annoyance of doubters, came away more than halfway convinced that the Big Man was the real deal. A lot of journalists have arrived at the same conclusion. It's easy to pour scorn from afar, but see this stuff up-close and you soon change your tune.

In his report, Quinones quotes João as saying, 'When I look at a person and somebody is ailing, the spirits come to me and incorporate my body. They're the ones that instruct my hands to do whatever they need to do to cure someone.'

Later, when João was shown footage of his operations, he recoiled in horror, declaring, 'That's not me!' Turns out, he remembered nothing, on account of being possessed at the time. 'It's God using me as an instrument.'

The story, as I say, is very convincing, and never more so than when you're here at the Casa among hundreds of people who trust John of God completely, way more in many cases than they trust their own doctors.

For these reasons, then, my mind is made up. Given that I have to make a choice one way or the other, I decide to opt for the physical operation – if only so that I can later say I overcame my fear and found the courage to do something I normally wouldn't have dared. Sometimes you just have to step out in faith.

I adore the words of Maya Angelou: 'Life loves to be taken by the lapel and told: 'I'm with you, kid. Let's go.'

Too many people nowadays are wallflowers. Afraid to live, they shy away from any new experience that might lead to discomfort or feelings of insecurity, in case they trip, or fail, or make a fool of themselves, when in fact tripping, failing, and making a fool of yourself is what life is all about.

At times like these I fall back on something called *The Risk-Taker's Protocol* – a four-step routine to follow prior to leaping into the unknown. It goes like this:

Show up
Say yes
Take a deep breath
Dive in and get it over with.

After all, the unknown is where the fun happens. We know that now.

So physical surgery it is!

Unfortunately, on this occasion, I'm too late.

By the time my deliberations of the pros and cons are done, the offer has been withdrawn. Not that it matters; physical or non-physical, it all adds up to the same result, according to Susan. Still, as the small group of volunteers is escorted away and the door closes, I couldn't be more disappointed.

Or, between you and me, relieved.

'Maybe next time,' I tell myself, knowing full well there won't be one.

In their wake, a hush settles over the room.

'Please, everyone,' the elderly attendant drops her voice, 'I want you all to close your eyes and keep them closed.'

With my good ear, I catch nervous fidgeting around me. Outside the window, a pair of squabbling songbirds escalates a petty dispute into violence, then flies off, still bickering. In the flower garden behind us, passers-by chat. At one time I could have heard what they said. No longer. Without fanfare, a door over to my right creaks open and several pairs of unidentified feet shuffle in. John of God, I presume, arriving with his entourage of mediums.

Before he can do any surgeries, João must incorporate, a transition that nobody who's about to be operated on is allowed to witness. You're free to watch surgeries being performed on other people, just not on yourself. The way Angela tells it, this meddles with the energy flow, causing the entities to flee back up the vortex. And nobody wants that.

Luckily, I have a vague idea what's going on. Before I left home, I did some research. Found a video of this process on *YouTube*, shot by someone smart enough to keep his eyes closed but leave his camera phone turned on.

So this much I know: first, João braces himself, becoming rigid for a moment, in that peculiarly mannered way that bad actors do in silent movies to suggest exaggerated shock. Often he will grip onto people standing close by. Then he breathes in sharply, emitting a small noise – 'Erk!' This tells you his body is being invaded by a transcendent spirit. Once it has, he adopts a posture entirely different from his normal one, becoming taller or more imposing. Or he may develop a limp. Depends on which etheric being is entering his physical form.

'Erk!'

Jeepers, that was fast.

My radar picks up movement four rows ahead. Feet shifting, a crackling, a rustle. I'm still trying to identify what it might be when – *'Ffffff-pshhhh-ssss!'* –there's a sharp hissing sound. Hard to describe it to someone who's not here with us. But you know the noise a *Pepsi* bottle makes if you shake it hard and rip the cap off? Something like that. It makes me jump anyway.

'Nome de deus todos os filhos foi operado,' a gruff voice says.

Fffffff-psch-sssssssssssssssssssssssss.

The operation's underway.

Should I be feeling something? Twinges? A shift? If there are transcendent spirits in the room, are we supposed to sense their presence? How'm I supposed to know this is working if nothing twitches or aches or throbs?

More movement. More footsteps, more rustling, an incantation in Portuguese, then the same door closes and everything falls silent. When I open my eyes, João and his entourage have vanished. Only the original attendant is left, smiling benignly at the wakening crowd.

Is that it?

Everyone's dazed. People afflicted by greater problems than mine start to rub their legs, their arms, their chest, groping for signs of a change. One woman frowns, clutching her head; the guy beside her is weeping quietly, smearing tears off his cheeks with the ball of his hand. Others seem to be equally impacted, stretching hard, as if awakening from a Sleeping Beauty kind of slumber. Obviously, this was a very profound moment for many.

Less so for me.

I run a quick all-systems check, snapping my fingers next to each ear separately.

Right ear – snap! – clear as a bell, same as always.

Left ear – snap...90% deaf. Exactly as before.

On a covered terrace behind the current room, forty or so people, their senses suspended at a point somewhere between shocked and confused, sit listening while a well-spoken middle-aged American man in a white tunic stands before us issuing strict do's and don'ts for the coming week. These are rules we must stick to no matter what, he says: 'This is important.' Going on to add that the surgery we've just been through is not the healing itself – ah, that explains it, then - but the commencement of healing, a process that starts today and will continue.

'Every one of you has had surgery this afternoon. Often, the entities will perform up to nine operations simultaneously, depending on what you need.'

To the novice, this sounds far-fetched. But according to Josie RavenWing, X-rays have been taken of patients who received invisible healing at the Casa. Shockingly, the images revealed *actual scar tissue from stitches on their organs*, even though there was no sign of any incision.

'For the next forty days, you will need to take good care of yourself,' the man tells us. 'During that time, all your energy must go into healing. That means...'

He proceeds to reel off a list of hard and fast rules, including 'no sex', 'no sitting in direct sunlight' and 'no heavy lifting.' These, and other ordinary, everyday activities, from masturbation to yoga, and even eating pepper apparently, can deplete the body's energy, lowering its vibration. And lowered vibrations nix the healing process.

'At this moment, ladies and gentlemen,' he concludes, 'your channels are wide open. When you leave here today, head directly to your *pousada*. Go to bed. Stay there for the next twenty-four hours. I urge you NOT to leave your room during that time. Make arrangements for meals to be brought to you. Rest, sleep, remain calm, and let the entities do their work. Above all, don't forget your medicinal herbs. As you're taking them, think of the entities. Imagine your link with divine intelligence. Focus on the healing power the entities bring to your body and spirit.' The man then moves among us, handing out sheets of paper. 'Please write down your name and where you'll be sleeping eight days from today. Which *pousada*, which room.'

'What's so special about eight days' time?' I wonder.

Before I can ask this out loud, the guy answers it.

'That night, between twelve midnight and 5am, the entities will come to your room and remove your stitches. So it's important to wear white to bed. This will help the flow of healing energy. During this time, do not open your eyes. No matter what you hear or what you think is going on around you, or how curious you are, *do not open your eyes*.'

More excited than ever now, the group starts to disperse.

Just in time, Angela arrives from the *farmacia,* sheaths of raven hair folding into the wind behind her, arms laden with bags containing plastic pots filled with our medicinal herbs.

Years ago, the herbs were a liquid mixed by mediums in the pharmacy, crowding around vats. Nowadays they're in pill form, which is easier to handle. Each tiny pot sports a colorful portrait on the label, of a bearded, bald St. Ignatius de Loyola staring up to Heaven. Slightly alarming is that all the pots are identical, with identical labels and even, I discover, identical contents: passiflora, or ground-up passionflower.

Passionflower is a mystical plant with soothing properties when taken internally. Its components are tied by mythology to the crucifixion of Jesus. The spiky fringe in particular is said to represent Christ's crown of thorns.

'But if they're all the same,' I ask her, sounding a little too skeptical, I'm sure, 'how can they specifically treat my hearing problem?'

'Your herbs are charged with your own special energy. When you take them, it's like a tracking device that helps the entities find you.'

'Really? Er....but how can that work?'

The mediums in the pharmacy used to ask the same question. How could it work? But it's one of those odd things that you're forced to accept. Apparently no set of herbs is ever the same. They start off the same, but then they become imbued with the energy of each individual patient. Not only that, but each pot smells different, looks different, and has different effects, even though, ostensibly, they're all exactly the same. It's just another unaccountable wonder of the Casa.

'Remember: the herbs are a sacrament, not a supplement,' Angela says. 'A subconscious reminder of what's going on, helping you stay true to the process while you're taking them, and that's important. Now, anyone else...?'

And she quickly moves on.

To my surprise, the surgery process has left me unusually weary. Or maybe it's the effects of the passionflower kicking in. But right now my mind's fuzzy, there's an unusual heaviness to my joints, my legs will barely support me, and I'm so drop-dead tired moment on moment that I'm shocked I made it back to my room at the *pousada* without assistance. Now that I'm here, I feel no inclination to go out again.

Convalescence lasts a day. My surgery took place at roughly 2.30pm this afternoon, meaning I'm grounded, confined to this twelve-foot square cell, until the same time tomorrow. Normally, I'd balk. I'm an active guy; I like to keep moving. But at this point it feels like pure release. As I drop onto the bed and pull the top-sheet over me, sleep is instant. Like a store rolling down its shutters for the night, the act of closing my eyes is all it takes for my mind to disengage.

Next time I surface, it's dark. The sickly smell of incense drifts under the door, most likely from Susan's room along the terrace. Occasionally, a flash of blue light nukes the curtains.

By summer's end, the weather turns iffy in Brazil. We're due for a monster storm any day now – so it must be that. On the other hand, the flashes seem unnaturally frequent and out of synch, the way they are in amateur stage productions of *Twelfth Night*. Plus, there's no thunder, making it odder still.

Despite being almost immobilized by fatigue, I manage to hoist myself to the edge of the bed, and from there to the window. To my surprise I find four people outside, standing in a line on a low wall, staring out at something in the darkened fields and taking photographs of it. Each time it's the same: one person inspects the shot, shows it to the next person, who looks closely and marvels, then hands the camera back so that the first person can take another.

If this were any other time, I'd be so overcome with curiosity that I'd rush out there and ask what they're up to. But, man, this fatigue is a bear. It won't let up. Also, we were told not to leave our rooms. So for now it'll have to wait.

Staggering back onto the bed, I close my eyes and fall into a metaphysical delirium - a round of weird fever dreams. Oddball images that tumble over each other into my mind: melons, poker players, a mineshaft, a gazelle viewed through trees, rows of Greek sculptures, people running, a bench, a lawn, lions: lions prowling, lions stalking me, lions pouncing...

I jolt awake, heart rattling around my chest, fumbling for the clock. It's 2.41am already! Where did the hours go? The voices outside have longsince stopped, along with the flashes. So what woke me up?

A few more seconds, then it hits me.

It's the pain.

A nagging discomfort deep inside my ribcage, similar to the one I felt after the doctors in L.A. removed my gallbladder, but on the opposite side. Back then, of course, I was lucky; I was dosed up with a cocktail of painkillers. Tonight, all I have is some emergency *Advil* in my bag, and that's not going to be enough to tame what began as a fairly dull ache under my right arm, but which is creeping in short pulses across my abdomen, where it starts to *really* hurt...

'Woah!' I roll over, hoping a different position will lessen the cramps, but it doesn't. Imagine a screwdriver being raked across your chest – it's like that. 'Oooh, ow.' Growing - 'Wow. Aaaaaaghgh!' - sharper by the second. For a moment I'm left gasping for air, delirious. *What is causing this?*

A few *more* seconds, then I realize.

It's not a heart attack. I'm not dying. *It's the entities*. They've started.

5

First Miracle

Coming round after what might generously be described as a rough night takes a little time. Yawning, I burrow my way up through terraces of consciousness, from fitful dozing, to snoozing, to a brief toss and turn session, and finally up and out, coaxed by spears of sunlight pricking at my eyes from between cheap curtains. By now, thankfully, brighter sensations have replaced the sweaty discomfort and stabbing stomach pains that were my companions these past few hours. That all seems to be over with now. Today, my body feels weightless, my joints are flexible and don't ache any more, and my head is refreshingly clear, almost as if...

Almost as if *I made the whole thing up*.

Ah.

For the first time this trip, pangs of doubt.

Letting the sun caress my face with the back of its warm hand, I chide myself for being so unquestioningly compliant in all of this. We humans, we're so brilliantly suggestible, aren't we? We'll believe anything if it's dressed up in the seductive colors of mysticism, presented in an upbeat way, and loaded with hope and promise.

Did you ever hear of the Baptist preacher Willard Fuller, founder of the Lively Stones World Healing Fellowship?

A man of stern countenance with shoulder-length white hair, Fuller wasn't a dentist by trade and had no formal training, though he scarcely saw this as a reason not to pass himself off as one. Over the course of his 41-year healing ministry, he claimed to have performed a staggering 40,000 dental surgeries, using as his implement nothing but the power of the Holy Spirit. In the end he came to be billed as The Psychic Dentist and regularly made splashy public displays of his skills, standing before an auditorium of captivated believers as he extracted teeth, replaced fillings, and even caused teeth that had been extracted to grow back, according to reports.

'Pandemonium broke out,' wrote a witness, 'as one person after another saw gold fillings where there had been none, and other startling changes. Nothing short of miraculous.'

'God does indeed fill teeth,' declared *The New Times* after one of his shows. And a reporter from the *Toronto Star* called Fuller, 'A veritable traveling tooth fairy.'

'We watched as cavities filled, old fillings turned to gold, crooked teeth became straight, and gums healed, right before our very eyes,' wrote a famous minister of Religious Science.

Yet according to professional skeptic James Randi, it was all utter baloney, just a clever illusion.

In his book *The Faith Healers,* he stops short of calling 'The Psychic Dentist' a downright fraud (possibly because the preacher was still alive when the book came out and likely to sue). What he does is slyly remind us that Fuller was charged in Australia with falsely advertising himself as a dentist and fined heavily, and leave us to draw our own conclusions. Additionally, Randi points out that the flashlight used to inspect people's mouths cast a yellowish glow that, on a cursory glance, would temporarily make silver fillings look gold. What's more, he maintained that the miraculous gold fillings would disappear and miraculously turn back to silver again immediately after the event. All very unfortunate.

I regret that I never got to meet Willard Fuller. Though I do wonder sometimes whether, if I had, I'd have been won over by his spectacular healing gifts the way everyone else was. The answer, I'm sorry to say, is 'yes, very probably'. Being a radio journalist, you'd think I'd know better. But, despite the inbuilt cynicism of my profession to this entire subject, I buck the trend. It's my decision, wherever possible, to err on the side of believing. Otherwise, I figure, what's the point?

The essayist Dr. Frank Crane once wrote: 'You may be deceived if you trust too much, but you will live in torment if you don't trust enough.'

That's where I'm at. You can't enjoy life to the fullest if you go through it distrusting everyone. Be circumspect and prudent, by all means; ask intelligent questions, take care to protect yourself from needless exploitation, but don't, for goodness' sake, be skeptical. Nobody's ever been able to show me a single benefit to skepticism. Basically, it's just doubt for the sake of doubting. A wall goes up, and, regardless of what comes along, or how groundbreaking it is, or revelatory, that wall just stays up. To my mind, skeptics are a flat, fun-crushing bunch. In their narrow, bleak world, there's no leeway for secrets, mysteries, or miracles: everything has to be straightforward and explainable logically. They want proof – *then* they'll believe. If they can't see it, touch it, or hear it, they doubt its very existence. Worse, they equate openness with weakness, and belief with gullibility. Skeptics are all about can'ts and why-nots and what's-the-points? I, on the other hand, take a different route. I tend to tune out any restrictions that would otherwise inhibit my enjoyment of life. And since cynicism and skepticism place futile limits on that enjoyment, I don't lean that way. I am first and foremost a believer. I believe until you prove me wrong. That's my attitude.

It's perhaps not unexpected, then, that the healing process at the Casa, as I've witnessed it so far, has me enthralled.

Nor is it too surprising that, as a direct result of undergoing a paranormal operation, I'm now bedbound, lying beneath a single white cotton sheet, incapable of movement. I was warned ahead of time that something like this would happen. It was told to me by a Casa attendant, a person I've chosen to trust, and the shaman effect of that thought took root. The idea that I would be weak and helpless for the rest of the day was firmly embedded in my open and somewhat impressionable mind during the post-operative briefing. So, quite naturally, that's exactly what's happened.

At just before 8.30am, a pretty young woman called Marianne arrives. Long mane of rusty hair, dozy eyes, and the kind of body that has sculptors reaching for a chisel.

'I brought you some dinner,' she whispers.

Marianne is not one of the sick ones. A native of Washington State, she flew to Abadiânia after discovering, quite by chance, that her husband of five years had, for four of those five, been cheating on her with the next-door neighbor. Naturally, Marianne was devastated. The moment she heard, she fled from the house, taking refuge in the peace of Brazil. Obviously, there's no operation you can have or pills you can swallow to fix a broken heart, but you do get to rest when you're here, and that's what she needed: time to get her head together and review her options. While that's happening, and since she won't be having surgery this trip, she takes care of those who do. This includes acting as room service.

Smiling warmly, she hands me a covered breakfast tray and leaves without saying anything further. Conversation is discouraged during recuperation.

As she closes the door, my mind settles into a deeper analysis of what happened overnight. Because something odd is *definitely* going on here.

I told you how trusting I can be, but I'm not a complete sucker. I know when I'm being duped, and this doesn't feel like a con to me.

If it were, how do you account for the near-paralyzed stupor I've been in these past few hours? Or the weakness in my legs? Or the freak stabbing pains that tore up my abdomen last night? Was all of that down to simple hypnotic suggestion?

As tempting as it is to attribute it to a mix of self-delusion, the power of suggestion, and my longing for something tangible to happen while I'm here, somehow I don't think that's the case. The pains during the night felt very real. Real enough at least to have me squirming and yelling out in the dark, and to get me to concede that the gateway to the other dimension that they talk about around here as though it actually exists, *actually does exist,* and entities do in fact pass through each day to perform healings at the Casa. After what just happened, I wouldn't be the least bit surprised.

Beneath the towel, the breakfast tray offers toast, fresh fruit, and scrambled eggs, which I eat at a small rickety table. That's another big difference between yesterday and now: my appetite is back to normal.

The general mood of buoyancy doesn't last long, however. Barely have I shoveled up the last few crumbs of toast and licked the fruit bowl dry, than fresh waves of lethargy begin to creep over me, but much heavier this time. It's as if a long rope has been tied to my waist and, today, I alone am responsible for making the earth spin. That's a massive responsibility. The sheer effort involved sends me back to bed, where I stay for the next five hours, bunched up into a fetal ball, not waking again until gone 6pm.

Over dinner, other members of the group complain of identical symptoms: aching bones, fever dreams, wooliness, ennui, confusion, and in some cases even 'eerie happenings'. A guy called Frank says he heard strange noises overnight. Amy insists she felt a 'very definite presence' in her room, '...like fingers touching me all over my body.'

Not to be outdone, Mary chimes up with one of her rushed station announcements. 'I felt spirits hovering over me too,' she says, before abruptly returning to her food.

Then there's Danusia, a statuesque, heavily-accented Polish fitness instructor, who claims she woke very early feeling sweaty, short of breath, and *convinced* she was drowning in a tidal wave. 'Oh, I was soooooo scared of the entities. I was - *yes!'* she squeaks. 'I am not knowing what to expect, so I am locking myself in my room. But still I felt the spirits around me.'

'Felt or saw?'

A moment's reflection, then: 'Not saw. But I *sensed* them. I *did, yes!!* Oh Cash, I couldn't sleep. And THEN....' She grips my arm, pausing for an imaginary close-up. '...I am hearing something near to my bed. Noises. Things moving. Ohhhhhhh, I am shaking with the fear, but I go, 'Danusia, you must not be scared, y'know?' So I am brave. I breathe in and turn the light on, and...'

'And?'

Another pause.

'...there is nothing there.'

'Ah.'

Her eyes are hubcaps of alarm. I'm not sure why she's subjecting herself to an experience as intense as this if it's such a nightmare for her.

Danusia came to Abadiânia suffering with acute back pain. A peril of her profession. Now, following her invisible operation yesterday, she has acute leg pain as well. I guess the agony arising from her physical problems is such that it overshadows the terror that being here clearly engenders in her.

*

Stopping by the kitchen to see what kind of cake they've prepared for us tonight - purely for research purposes, you understand - I find Dermot standing by the kettle making two mugs of tea, humming to himself. One of the things you notice about visitors to the Casa, even the sickest ones who are staring a death sentence in the face: they are remarkably cheerful. Everyone's feeling more rested, less frantic or apprehensive about the place. That makes a world of difference to our outlook. For a man with terminal cancer, the guy's spirits are way up.

'So how did the operation go yesterday?' I ask him.

'Oh, very well,' he smiles, 'very well indeed.' Two seconds later, the mask of affability cracks, giving way to sober reflection. 'I mean, you never know, of course. These are early days, like. Anyt'ing is possible. I just keep telling myself João knows what he's doing.'

Fingers crossed.

As with the rest of us, Dermot's in limbo until he knows more, making this a slow news day for the most part.

Or at least it *would* be, but for one person - his usually quiet sister, who at the last minute springs a huge surprise. Bear in mind, the woman's only here in the first place because of Dermot; she came as moral support. Nevertheless, this evening she is the first to boast a major breakthrough.

'I had a frozen shoulder,' she mumbles, her words buried beneath layers of false humility. 'For years, y'know? Terrible, it was. Painful, difficult; I couldn't feel a t'ing. But after de... .y'know, surgery yesterday, it's gone. Just like that. See?'

She rotates her arm one way with total ease, then back again.

'And how do you explain that?'

Her answer is unequivocal: it's God's work in action.

There's not a doubt in her mind. João, *the milagreiro*, produced a miracle.

'All de feeling came back at once.' And she rotates her arm all over again, then, realizing that people are staring, grows awkward and returns to her seat.

Wendy, for her part, admits to sleeping through the past twenty-four hours with little or no discomfort. I find her in the kitchen, sipping a glass of mustard-colored liquid.

'Turmeric,' she advises me. 'One of the greatest cancer-inhibitors there is. I take it every day in some form.'

'Turmeric inhibits cancer? Really? I never knew.'

Should I be writing this stuff down, d'you think?

Wendy seems to have appointed herself Chief Guinea Pig for almost every alternative cause and treatment you can name. Whenever our paths cross, she's knocking back some new potion or mix or shake or powder or tablet or homemade elixir. Yesterday morning it was a blob of vegetable fat she'd melted in a spoon ('Coconut oil – totally healthy for you; one of the best antivirals out there.'). Then, before dinner, she drank a glass of milky white water ('Bentonite clay – flushes metals out of your system.'). And now it's turmeric. Let's hope the end result is worth her almost military-level commitment. We all say we want to live longer and have strong, agile bodies, but we also acknowledge that everything's a trade-off, and if our efforts to make longevity a reality require so much discipline and application that it takes the fun out of actually living, what's the point really? Isn't it better to eat all the cake you want – just to use a random example - and die five years sooner than you otherwise might, than to deny yourself the joy that cake brings and in so doing make the days ahead so dreary and joyless that you wish you were dead right here and now?

Following British writer and polemicist Christopher Hitchens' diagnosis of esophageal cancer after a lifetime of heavy drinking and chain-smoking, he sat on Charlie Rose's TV show, his formerly fine head of hair all but eradicated by chemo, looking bloated and sick. However, asked by Rose if, given the chance, he would do it all again, he replied quite readily, 'Yes, I think I would... it's impossible for me to imagine having my life without going to those parties, without having those late nights, without that second bottle.'

I do see his point. And therein lies the dilemma.

Recently I spotted a page of intentionally bogus health tips that has been floating around the Internet for a long while. Maybe you saw it. Framed as a Q&A, it urges us to ignore the advice of health freaks and insist on doing only those things in life that bring us pleasure.

Example:

Q: What are some of the advantages of participating in a regular exercise program?

A: Can't think of single one, sorry. My philosophy is: no pain...good!

Q: Is getting in shape important for my lifestyle?

A: Hey, 'round' is a shape!

And so on. It's very funny, but with a serious sting in its tail. Scroll to the bottom of the page and you arrive at a final thought.

'Remember,' it says, 'life should NOT be a journey to the grave with the intention of arriving safely in an attractive and well-preserved body, but rather to skid in sideways, Chardonnay in one hand, chocolate in the other, body thoroughly used up, totally worn out and screaming, 'WOO-HOO, what a ride!!'

There's a lot to be said for that approach, and a surprisingly large number of people subscribe to it. 'Forget longevity,' they say. 'You're going to die someday anyhow, so quit worrying about everything and LIVE. Live every day to its fullest. Do what makes you happy, and do it now.'

The flautist Robert Cody once said, 'Have the courage to live. Anyone can die.' I hardly need to tell you that the Wendys and Sheilas of this world are shocked by such a reckless approach.

'It's a myth...,' they point out (I'm quoting almost verbatim from something Sheila said yesterday), '....that you can let yourself go like that; stuff your face with animal protein, or smoke and drink yourself stupid all your life with absolutely no consequences. More likely you'll have forty fun years, then, in your final twenty, you'll slowly fall apart as your abused body becomes backed up and stops functioning. That's why so many people, when they get old, are wracked by pain, disease, debilitation - because they 'lived for today' and gave no thought to tomorrow. How is that a good idea? Where's the sense?'

Indeed. This is also very true. Seems I agree with both sides.

The cake on the menu this evening is vanilla cream sponge, a maiden slab of which sits on a metal baking tray close to the kettle, its frosting scored obligingly into neat two-inch squares. And while I can almost guarantee that there's not a trace of vanilla anywhere in it, and the icing is just compacted chemicals, and the sponge, if it hadn't been put in a cake at the factory, could just as easily have wound up as tile cement or the padding for sofa cushions, and although I'm aware that each slice is packed with additives, flavorings, and impossible amounts of sugar, making it nasty on every imaginable level, like assaulting your body with a deadly weapon – *I still want some*. I know it's crazy and it makes me the Christopher Hitchens of cake, but I can't resist.

Unable to shake off my craving, I hatch a plan. First I bide my time, waiting on a moment when Wendy's back is turned. Then I rush in and cram three creamless, nutritionless, additive-packed, and possibly carcinogenic spongy cubes into a napkin, before quickly smuggling them out the door.

Tonight, same as last night, a small cluster of people has assembled in the walkway close by my room, chatting and smoking. Once again, cameras in hand, they're on the two-foot high wall that separates the guest quarters from the garden, taking a succession of flash photos of the field behind the *pousada*. What on earth is going on?

'Behold and be amazed, my friend,' a tall, spiky-haired guy called Joe says, squinting. He takes another picture and hands his camera down to me. 'That's what it's all about.'

Peering at it, I find the little screen speckled with transparent whitish dots. Best guess: either dust or raindrops. Or bugs even, highlighted by the flash.

'No - they're spirit orbs,' he corrects me. 'Entities.'

'But they look like bugs.'

'Well, they're not bugs, they're orbs. Orbs are the life force of spirits.'

He takes another shot. The explosion of light imprints cauliflowers on my retinas. Once again I grab the camera, and find even more white dots than before, varying in size depending on their proximity to the lens. What these dots do that bugs don't is glow. Each one has a tiny fluorescent pinprick at its center with a miniature corona around it.

'So these are the souls of dead people?'

Joe seems to think so. 'It's what a cat sees,' he says. 'Ever watched a cat's head jerk around as if it's looking at something, but you don't know what? Then it suddenly runs off, like it's chasing it? Well, those are spirit orbs. Their eyes detect them, ours don't.'

This is what the Norwegian guys were talking about that first morning, and I have to confess, I've not seen anything like it before, though I gather that if you take a camera to a cemetery at night, you get a similar experience. Orbs are certainly the rule around here not the exception, according to Joe. And they come in all sizes, apparently.

In an essay on her website *Spirit of the Mist*, Celeste Allegrea Adams, a regular visitor to the Casa during her life, wrote of once witnessing weird lights over Abadiânia.

'One evening, I looked into the sky and saw heavy, dark, long gray clouds hanging low above the horizon. There was something unusual about these clouds, because one section of cloud would light up and then go dark, then another part would light up and go dark, then another, and another — but there was no sound of thunder! This went on for several hours, and still there was no sound. An English medium in a wheelchair was told by her guides to get her camera out and film the clouds. Although she filmed for an hour, only three minutes of footage came out. Her digital footage captured three large globes behind the clouds, with small lights at various points on the globes. None of this was visible to the naked eye... On several evenings after that...the English medium struggled to film the approaching lights in the sky that surrounded us, but her digital camera kept jamming. There was a difference of opinion about the lights. Some thought they were car lights, others felt they were UFOs.'

Well, whatever the orbs are, and however implausible, I'm anxious to grab anything I can that I might show to friends back home as proof of what's going on here. So I rush to fetch my little Japanese camera, then clamber onto the wall too, where I start snapping photos of the field.

But wait...

'That's strange.'

When I come to view the picture on the little screen, it's blank. 'How come I don't have anything?'

I take a second photo. That one's blank also.

Marianne's flash goes off. Immediately, she parades the result: a shot of eight perfectly round little pinches of white, like airborne sparks from a bonfire.

Now I'm really confused. 'I don't get it. Why do they appear on your cameras but not on mine? That doesn't make sense. Is it the settings?'

'It's not the camera's settings, it's *your* settings.'

I turn around to find Marty the architect loitering beneath me. Behind thick glasses, bright globular gray eyes gleam knowingly. 'You're approaching this as a reporter would. That's why you fail. You need to get your ego and your analytical mind out of the way. Then the entities will come.'

Er...I'm sorry? How can an object stipulate who sees it and who doesn't? If there's a cloud of floating *somethings* out there in the field, then a working camera should be able to take photos of it, no matter who's manning the shutter.

But Marty is adamant. It's about belief, he insists. Belief first, proof later. That's the law. The exact opposite of how things work in our physical dimension.

Here in the regular world, stuff is either there or it's not. That's how we all stay sane. If somebody shows you something – let's take a bottle of salad dressing as an example - you know it's salad dressing because you can smell it, taste it, touch it, even hear it if you shake the bottle hard; also, you can pour it over lettuce. Straight away, you tell yourself, 'Ah, that's salad dressing.' Suddenly, despite being a staunch non-believer in the existence of salad dressing for many years, you're a believer. Unfortunately, the same rules don't apply in the spiritual realm. These orbs from another dimension insist that you fully accept that they're there even though they appear not to be. Believe they exist and they appear. Doubt them, and they stay hidden.

'Basically,' Marty sums up, looking a little smug as he says it, 'you're trying too hard. It's the law of least effort. In India, they say, 'Do less, accomplish more.' That, you'll find, is the solution to most problems in life. Surrender. Do less.'

Author Larry Eisenberg probably had it right when he said, 'For peace of mind, resign as manager of the universe.'

Marty would say amen to that.

'Step back, relax, be present,' he instructs, 'get your ego out of the way, and stop trying to control everything in every situation. Then the entities will come.'

6

The Impact of Love on the Human Cell Structure

There's a storm moving in. Abadiânians opened their doors this morning to a sky of vengeful gray, spitting warm drizzle from clouds pitched so low that, for a time, it feels like we're cowering under someone's mattress.

Thursday, the day after your surgery, you're banned from returning to the Casa grounds. Which is only right. To all intents and purposes you're recuperating, exactly the way you would after an invasive procedure received in a real hospital. When you're in as vulnerable a state as this, the many-megatonne blast of crystal energy emanating from the compound could easily blow your circuits, causing you to faint or get headaches, or even throw up. That's what you're told. Today, though, is Friday, and the danger's passed, which means you're allowed back in. Not as a patient this time, but something much lowlier – a worker bee, crewing the Incubator of Love that is John of God's current room.

By 7.00am, a fresh intake of patients is already converging on the Great Hall. Wave after wave of damp white cotton migrates along the broken road, on foot, in wheelchairs, on crutches, walkers, canes, and aboard special vans custom-built to accommodate stretchers and tables and drips, bringing a fresh tide of despair to João's door.

Anticipation is high. Too much so in a lot of cases, to the point where a reality check may be called for. Someone should stand at the main gate handing out leaflets, reminding everyone not to get carried away and expect instant cures. I mean, it can happen – look at Dermot's sister and her frozen shoulder - and by all accounts João has quite a track record of pulling rabbits out of hats - tumors gone, diabetes eradicated, even hysterectomies reversed, I read somewhere. But, just as often, nothing happens at all. At least, not right away. Case in point: my ears. How long have I been in Abadiânia? Three days already. During that time I've done everything asked of me, played it strictly by the book; nobody could have tried harder to fit in. Yet this morning when I perform my usual test - left ear...snap: 95% deaf – there's zero change. If anything, I think I even sense a mild deterioration.

'Great,' Mary announced brightly when she heard this. 'Worse is better.'

'It is?'

'At the Casa, symptoms often get worse to begin with. It shows you things are shifting on the inside.'

'It couldn't be that they're just getting worse?'

She shakes her head. Apparently not.

'The entities are fixing your soul, not your body,' Angela cuts in. 'Healing takes place on a higher consciousness level, the timeless soul level, where our usual linear calendar doesn't apply. You're being asked to take a leap of faith. It was your ear problem that brought you to Abadiânia, but maybe it's symptomatic of something far deeper. The entities are working on those deeper issues.'

This is the part many people have a problem with.

They try something and want to see results right now, and when those results aren't forthcoming in any obvious way, they start to doubt.

I pledge to myself that I won't be one of those people. I can be patient. I *will* be patient.

Late - and very damp - we shake off our coats and umbrellas and enter the Great Hall, where the rest of the Thursday crowd is already on shift, streaming into the blue doorway.

'Excuse me. Coming through!'

A loud voice outside.

On a signal from one of the attendants, the stray dogs scram and the sea of bodies parts, as...

'Watch out – excuse me. Mind your backs.'

...a young woman struggles into view, plodding up the wheelchair ramp, out of breath from pushing a mobile bed. Locked at a shallow angle, forty degrees or so to the perpendicular, it has thick tires and a clear plastic IV bag jiggling on a tall pole. The other end of the IV tube is plugged into something I don't remember seeing before: a ghoulish figure lying half on its side, its chalky features punctuated by marbled eyes and a gaping lipless mouth contorted into a Munch scream of horror.

'AAAAAAAAAAAWWWWWWWW!' it groans, trying to wriggle from its straps. 'AAAAAAAAWWWWWWWWWWWW.'

The whole place falls silent as the table jiggles between the seats, through a pall of pity. I'm not sure anyone else knows what they're looking at either. Some version of a teenage girl, would be my best guess, but twisted. Twisted and compacted into a jagged zigzag shape, her fossilized fists cocked at strange angles, punching the air as if trying to knock a cuckoo back inside its clock.

'AAAAAAWWWWWW! AAAAAAAWW! AAAAWWW!'

Though actually, it isn't the girl's peculiar disfigurement *per se* that gets to me, it's the expression on her face, the maniacal Manson stare, plus the sound that comes out of her mouth.

'AAAAAAWWWWWWWWWWWWWWW!!'

The yawning empty wail of a soul entombed.

To the common eye she appears beyond rescue. Her condition – I'm no expert, but I'm thinking motor neurone disease possibly. Same thing Stephen Hawking has – is far too extreme to be fixable. Sensibly, what can João, as powerful a healer as he is alleged to be, do in such a case to right so egregious a wrong? More to the point, knowing the near-impossibility of this task, why would a responsible, sane parent bring her child all this way to Brazil, with the immense expense and inconvenience involved, when the conclusion is already foregone and the chance of recovery slim to non-existent?

But that's the curious thing about this world we're in here, and how it differs to the one we left behind: nobody talks impossible. This is a place of miracles. Quite honestly, the impossible is John of God's low-water mark. It's the minimum he's known for: changing the odds, upending probabilities, turning sour sweet and bleak hopeful. He's done it thousands of times before - why not today?

'AAAAAAAAAAWWWWWWWWW!'

With tires shuddering, and a creamy liquid sloshing madly around the IV bag, the mother and her damaged daughter make their way to the far wall, seemingly oblivious to stares from the crowd - or just used to them – and take up their rightful position at the head of the line.

As far as I'm able to understand it, the current room functions along the same lines as a large tanning bed. So powerful is the crystal energy filtering up from the bedrock beneath the Casa, and so readily accessible the energy of the entities from above, that, just by loitering in this special spot, you are being healed. That's all it takes. Strictly speaking, *you don't even have to believe what's happening,* that's another fascinating thing. To the entities, your body is see-through, like glass. They're able to permeate it whether you acknowledge their existence or not. Though, naturally, it helps the process considerably if you're not skeptical: if your mind is 100% committed and hasn't erected barricades of doubt.

Skeptics are hardwired for failure, and that's a silly approach in a place such as this. Committing to a course of action while also doubting your chances of success, or imagining reasons why it might not work out, is enough to scupper the enterprise from the start. You wouldn't go sunbathing, then spend the entire day lying under a rug, would you? Well, then, why adopt such a calculated policy of limitation here? At least give it your best shot; *then* cast your judgments later when it's over.

Once all the chairs are filled, the gentle clamor of the Great Hall is shut out and the mediums take their place at the front of the room, facing us.

On a command from one of them, the rows of worker bees, including myself, assume the position: spine straight, hands resting on thighs palms-up, the way we saw those guys do the other day.

Amy's seated in front of me. I stare for a few seconds at the back of her Beverly Hills flip, then let my eyelids slide closed and begin meditating.

Incidentally, you're not expected to be particularly good at this. No-one's looking for professional mastery. All they ask is that you do your best. Be present in the moment and commit to the process, letting events run away with you. Even the tiniest effort from the most incompetent meditator helps bring the love turbine up to speed and will add to the healing power of the room.

This process is known as 'constructive interference.'

In his book, *The Biology of Belief*, Dr. Bruce Lipton, the renowned cell biologist, talks of quantum healing. He found that positive vibrational frequencies are able to interfere with the physical and chemical make-up of atoms in the body, lifting them to a higher state, one of harmonic resonance. Put simply, our cells are beneficially affected by positive energy. And nothing has a higher, more positive vibrational frequency than love. Love, shared unconditionally, even with total strangers, influences and even radically changes the behavior of human chemistry, Lipton discovered, which in turn can help boost immunity to disease.

He's not the first to remark on this phenomenon. Some years ago, scientists in India ran tests and found that *merely watching* documentary footage of Mother Theresa tending to the sick in the slums of Calcutta was enough to increase the level of immunoglobulin-A in *your* saliva, protecting you against colds and flu.

'All creation is the expression of love,' minister Roy Henshaw wrote in an article called *The Healing Power of Love*. 'The fear of losing love and the forms that fear takes, e.g. hatred, anger, envy, jealousy, etc., represent the stagnation or restriction of the flow of love. In a broad sense, this restriction and/or stagnation are disease. Unconditional love is the absence of restrictions in the flow of energy that creates the body. In the absence of restrictions the state of health is robust. Health problems can be seen in the energy bodies as restrictions and stagnations even before they manifest in the physical body. The restrictions of stagnation of essential energy may be seen as separation from God or the fear of separation from God.'

With that in mind, your job as a current room volunteer is simple: it's to reconnect to the Divine. You do this initially by banding together with the other current room volunteers to form a chain of love. United, the links in that chain quietly project energy at the line of patients drifting in through the door, and in so doing help shake these lost souls out of their 'stagnation', as

Henshaw put it, by increasing the flow of positive vibes around them, ready to be seen by John of God sitting next door. He will then diffuse the negative vibration of disease and elevate their bodies to the much higher vibration of good health.

Although I don't quite understand the physics of what's happening, I am not unfamiliar with the chain-link idea, or the invisible current of power that's generated when a group of people prays or meditates together.

One day, in the latter part of that Buddhist retreat I told you about, forty of us were sitting meditating one evening when the lights above us began to flicker. A minute later, for no reason, they went out and several windows high in the walls blew in. It was quite alarming when it happened, like witchcraft. But that too was a turbine of love, I'm reminded, created by focused minds. So I must accept that energy transference of this caliber not only happens, but is immensely powerful, and probably the crux of everything that goes on at the Casa. It also, I believe, stands at the very heart of a person's recovery from disease.

In the real world, you and I may not know each other. Most likely, you live many miles away. Your hair's a different color, your accent's different, and our opinions are probably world's apart. But that's all earthly trivia. In cosmic terms we are identical.

We each have two bodies - the external physical body we can see, and then an energy body. It's the energy body that imbues the physical part of us with life force, or chi or *prana*. In other words, we're not human frames with some kind of elusive spirit entity tucked away inside us somewhere that we call a soul; we are spiritual beings through and through. Sparks of immortality wrapped in mortal form. Wisps of divine intelligence encased in frail, fleshy sacks of tube and bone.

'You're not just a drop in the ocean,' the poet Rumi wrote, 'you're also the mighty ocean in the drop.'

Physically, you and I may be separated by, not only looks and geography, but also differences of race, sexuality, belief, age, culture, and religion. *Spiritually*, however, we're both playing for the same team. We hail from the Source of All Things. We're bound up and inseparable in the most profound way. And if that applies to you and me, it applies to all the patients at the Casa today too. They're no different. We're all one. There's a little piece of my eternal self inside each and every last stranger who'll be ambling by my chair today, and a piece of them inside me. That fact alone creates an invisible but powerful bond between us. What's more, it follows that any love vibes I transmit to them, though they have no idea who I am or what I'm doing – and though, coincidentally, I have no idea what I'm doing either, to tell you the truth – will harmonically resonate at a primal unconscious level, creating a positive flow that raises their vibration and helps them toward healing.

'Love and intimacy are at the root of what makes us sick and what makes us well, what causes sadness and what brings happiness, what makes us suffer and what leads us to healing.' These are the words of Dr. Dean Ornish[14]. 'If a new drug had the same impact, virtually every doctor in the country would be recommending it for their patients. It would be malpractice not to prescribe it - yet, with few exceptions, we doctors do not learn much about the healing power of love, intimacy, and transformation in our medical training. Rather, these ideas are often ignored or even denigrated.'

Better still, from a Casa perspective, the tide of love we're generating lifts all boats, meaning that, as we sit in the vortex like this, helping heal others, we're also, in some strange and very wonderful way, healing ourselves, making it a win-win all round.

---

14 *Love & Survival: 8 Pathways to Intimacy and Health* (Harper Paperbacks)

*

Time to knuckle down.

Once we're up to speed and meditating hard, the blue door opens and the crowd enters in single file. Countless feet tramp by. My eyes are closed so I can't see them, but I hear everything. Canes tap, shoes clatter, noses sniff, throats cough, wheelchair tires squeak piercingly on linoleum. At one point a baby screams, only to be drowned out quickly by whiplashes of rain above my head. What began as playful drizzle has stiffened into a steady downpour that has the thin corrugated sheet roof crackling like Christmas wrapping, making it hard to concentrate.

It's a tricky business, mentally projecting love at someone you don't know, much less hundreds of them streaming past in a long line. Everyone has his own way. What works best for me, I find, is to visualize. I need to see things in my mind's eye in order to grasp them. To that end, as the line of strangers passes - six inches, stop; six inches, stop - I picture a glowing beam of light passing from my heart into each of theirs and color it pink, for 'the pink of health'. Nobody told me to do this, I just thought it was a nice idea.

Meanwhile, I imagine my energy body uniting with theirs. I craft a sincere intention of wellbeing, visualizing everyone who's here today being perfect. Whole. Their physical bodies functioning harmoniously, the way they're made to. Then, smiling, I hug each person, but in my head obviously. As I'm doing this, I envision the lame walking, the blind seeing, tumors shrinking, heart valves mending, HIV sneaking out the back door, headaches being cured, and mysterious swellings going down. It's quite a kick. I've been a journalist for two decades, including a stint as a TV host that took me all over the world, and not once in all that time did I feel a fraction of the exhilaration gripping me now.

Maybe I'm delusional. Maybe none of these invisible care packages I'm sending out is getting through. Doesn't matter. If you've ever been to a barn dance, you know that the most fun is to be had, not by sitting on the sidelines watching others strut around, but by strutting around along with them. Well, same here today. The option's there, I guess, to abstain and not bother. But that's not my way. I'm giving it everything I've got, knowing that to do so makes it therapeutic for me as well as them. And the benefits are enormous. To the degree that I'm willing to participate with my whole being do my perceptions heighten exponentially, leaving me feeling like I'm divinely charged. My body fizzes with good works. I'm really making a difference.

So enjoyable does this practice turn out to be, that two hundred people and two entire hours disappear in a blink. Once the last patient has trotted through the current room sausage machine, I'm pooped, but entirely satisfied, and more than a little proud of myself.

By noon, the worst of the rain has eased off. Now the sky's just being foul for no reason.

Following the usual bowl of medicinal soup, I head off for a second lunch at the *One Season*. Salad, potatoes, chicken nuggets, beef stew, and watermelon, all on the same plate. Then, afterwards, and by sheer force of will, I manage to dodge a slab of coconut cake that's calling my name and make my way along the puddled main street to *Frutti's*.

Everyone goes to *Frutti's* at some point in the day. Part café, part juice bar, it's the town's chief watering hole, a cheery oasis with walls of virulent persimmon that glow like a Cambodian sunset, so bright in places that it hurts your eyes.

I've just stepped up to the counter to order a latte when Wendy and Sheila walk in. Sheila's a librarian from Kentucky,

I've come to learn. A stiff little bundle of energy that's not entirely feminine, with an above-average interest in natural health. As you can imagine, from the first moment she opened her mouth, she and Wendy became fast friends. Which basically means I'm now giving two people in our group a wide berth.

No offense or anything, because I really do like them. Sheila and Wendy are very friendly and earnest, and I love their passion. I'm just not always in the mood for a weighty monologue about disease, that's all. Or the iniquities of the medical profession, or the perils of pastry. As far as I'm concerned, doctors have their place. Just as there are times when eating junk food and drinking *Diet Coke* and gorging on muffins have their place, and, if it's all the same to Wendy and Sheila, I'd like to indulge myself as and when, without being given a running commentary on how badly I'm decimating my cell structure. I know I am; I don't need to be reminded.

After placing an order for an herbal tea, Sheila drifts over, smiling and relaxed from the morning's meditation. The smile vanishes quickly, though, when she sees me take a long, slow slurp of my delicious hot latte. The whole time I'm licking the foam moustache off my top lip her eyes are glued to me.

'Something wrong?'

Self-conscious, she looks away. 'Nothing, it's okay.'

'You don't like coffee?'

She doesn't.[15] But that's not the problem. This time it's the milk.

Sheila, it turns out, views milk the way teenagers in *Nightmare on Elm Street* view Freddy Krueger: as one of

[15] 'Coffee harms your adrenal system, which can lead to depression. Also, caffeine is a diuretic, it releases water from the body, causing it to become dehydrated. You need to drink around three pints of water to replenish what you lose by drinking a cup of coffee. Also, hot liquids, and even very cold liquids like iced drinks, damage the cells of the body. You should avoid them.' ©Sheila, dinnertime yesterday. You see now what I'm up against?

the biggest dangers to public health since typhus. Which is a terrible thing to hear, given how big a part dairy plays in my life. The exact figure escapes me, but I bet I've drunk close to five thousand lattes over the years. After banana bread, they're my next favorite thing in the world.

Alas, that's not something you say out loud around here. 'Did you not read *The China Study?*' she asks in a quite affronted tone.

'Nope.'

'I'll lend you my copy. You'll never touch cow's milk again. Or butter. Or cheese.'

'Then why would I want to read it? I *love* milk, butter and cheese.'

Worst thing I could have said! Within seconds, our little plastic table at *Frutti's* becomes a pulpit and the sermon has begun.

Quoting *The China Study*, she says that 87% of cow's milk is made up of a protein called casein, and in tests casein has been found to promote cancer of all types. *Plus*, the consumption of animal protein, including dairy, plays a significant part in the promotion of the diseases we fear most, from cancer to Type 1 diabetes to autoimmune diseases like multiple sclerosis.

'Milk does all of that?'

According to Sheila.

'Human beings were never meant to put the milk of another animal in their bodies. It's gross. But we ignore the facts; we ignore Nature. Next time you order a latte, remember: a lot of milk these days contains pus from sick cows.'

'Pus? You mean, as in...?'

Zits? Seriously?

'But...' About to take a sip of coffee, I relent and put the cup down. '...they're always telling us how good milk is for us. For our bones...'

'Who's telling you? Who's they?'

'Studies,' I reply. Because what's more reliable than studies, right?

'Studies commissioned by who? The dairy industry, possibly? Cash, marketing people in large companies only publish findings that are *favorable* to their products, you didn't know that? If milk *were* dangerous and led to long-term health problems, d'you think the Dairy Association is ever going to come out and say that?[16] There's too much money at stake. And that's not all....'

No? Oh dear. I was kinda hoping.

'....some brands of milk you buy may contain around sixty different added chemicals, including hormones and glue...'

'Glue???'[17]

'...and it's all going into your system.' She shakes her head woefully. 'A system that wasn't built to handle any of it. Did you not read *Milk – The Deadly Poison*?'

I'm stumped. 'Er...'

'How about *Child Care* by Benjamin Spock?'

'Sorry.'

I fear exasperation at my ignorance could kill this woman a lot sooner than dairy products ever would.

'Spock says that at one time, years ago, scientists thought milk was good for us, but now they're finding it's not. Milk is

---

[16] Just out of interest, an article by Mark Hyman M.D. *Dairy: 6 Reasons You Should Avoid It At All Costs...* on the *Huffington Post* cites a survey sponsored by the Federal Trade Commission into milk, and they concluded that dairy is linked to prostate cancer, heart disease, and contributes to sinus problems, Type 1 diabetes, allergies, and anemia in kids. So Sheila's right.

[17] Sadly this seems to be true too. Looking it up, I find that, according to notmilk.com's Robert Cohen, casein, the number one protein in milk, is basically glue. The stuff they use to stick labels on beer bottles. 'It's the same glue they use to hold your wooden furniture together.' And it generates vast quantities of mucus in the body. The average human body has about one pound of mucus slopping around inside it, and it doesn't sound to me like that's a good thing.

extremely mucus-forming in the body. Research has been conducted extensively, and even mainstream doctors are starting to believe that milk contributes to a lot of serious health issues, including...' Eyes gleaming mischievously, she pauses, before hammering the final nail in milk's coffin. '*...including,* Cash, *chronic ear problems*.'

It's a rule of the Casa: 'No need shall go unmet.' That is to say, if you take the trouble to make the long journey to Abadiânia, you're guaranteed free treatment when you arrive. Nobody is turned away.

In principle, it's a noble Christian philosophy. In practice, however, it can put a real strain on the staff, and especially on the worker bees.

This particular Friday afternoon, the line of Seekers seems ten miles long. Beginning at 2.00pm and for the next four hours, hundreds of people trek through the current room. Of course, in the name of being a team-player, I do what I can, continuing to dispatch pink laser beams at each and every squeaky wheel, tapping cane, and bawling child that goes by, but after two hours, the novelty's starting to wear off.

And after three I'm at my breaking point, dying of thirst and fatigue.

The chair's hard. My bones and back ache, I've lost the use of my feet, and my butt's turned to concrete. Added to which, I'm waaaaay outside my bladder window and desperately need to pee. Before too long, the love I'm sending out stops being unconditional. Shortly after, it ceases to be love at all, curdling into a mild form of resentment which I regret sincerely but can't suppress.

By the time the *four*-hour point comes and goes and we're still not done, I'm practically spasming. My neck's stiff like a mannequin's, both my legs are twitching uncontrollably, and I'm becoming highly agitated.

In the end, it's 6.15pm – a full four and a quarter hours of motionless sitting later - and already dark outside, before João finally calls it a day.

Drained and lifeless, with my motor functions and organs barely ticking over, I rush to the toilet to relieve myself, then head over to a block of outbuildings on the far side of the gardens for my crystal bed appointment.

At least I have that to look forward to.

Let me be honest up-front: the principle underlying crystal bed therapy feels a little spurious to me. It's one of the few aspects of the Casa I'm not entirely okay with.

The idea came to João in a vision from his spirit guides, I'm told. That fact alone is a gift to debunkers everywhere. Now, add to this the suggestion that, according to one website[18], crystal bed technology was devised many centuries ago in Atlantis, and you can see why I'm not inclined to take it very seriously.

Quartz crystals, the same website goes on to say, 'are capable of transmitting, storing and modulating energy... [They] are a primary source of natural healing due to their symmetrical molecular structure and their effect on the chromatic composition of light.'

Apparently, multiple benefits ensue from exposure to this energy. It:

- rebalances the frequency of your magnetic field;
- has anti-aging effects, giving a youthful glow to the face;
- triggers healing processes in the psyche;
- improves spiritual awareness, and
- harmonizes your subtle body energies.

---

[18] Crystallightbedtherapy.com.

There are even reports (unconfirmed), it says, of crystals stabilizing blood sugar in diabetics, removing arthritis pain from joints, and 'minimizing grief'.

As I rush in, the attendant, who has the weary, chagrined look of a woman for whom nothing in life has gone right since 1977, draws herself up from a chair, stubs out her cigarette, and, with smoke trailing from her nostrils, shows me to one of the cramped therapy rooms. Inside, she wearily hands me an eye-mask, turns on the machine, then leaves again to resume smoking.

Unlike most other whole body therapies, you don't have to strip off for this one. You lie down on a padded table and wriggle into place beneath a splay of large quartz prongs hanging from a metal frame. Seven of them in all, wrapped in individual black and white-striped casings, and positioned at a twelve-inch distance above your body, so as to align with its seven main energy centers, the *chakras*. The first crystal is pointed at the middle of my forehead, the second at my throat, the third at my heart, and so on.

In line with my overall spirit of open-mindedness on this trip, I refuse to shut out the possibility that crystal beds yield great benefits. Having said that, I have to admit that my first impression of the machine is: it really doesn't do very much. Then I take a closer look, and, on further inspection, find that... actually, my first impression was most likely correct.

The quartz crystals resemble chunky, blunt syringes. Syringes that flash intermittently in a random sequence like carousel lights. For all I know, they may indeed be a powerful way of focusing energy on the body and of healing illness, though on the face of it this seems unlikely. Even the automatic believer in me has difficulty buying that one. Indeed, it makes me wonder if maybe João's spirit guides were, in actual fact, handing down the blueprint for a slot machine and he just misread it.

There is one major thing in its favor, though: it's very relaxing. Once the eye mask is on, sleep overtakes me straight away.

An hour later, I emerge from the room, blinking and yawning, and feeling perfectly rested, doubtless with the frequency of my magnetic field rebalanced, a youthful glow to my face, and my subtle body energies more harmonized. Though let it be known that the contraption singularly failed to minimize the grief I feel at having spent twenty bucks to sleep on a table for an hour.

'Hey you!' Michael, a lawyer with big marsupial eyes, comes rushing over, lugging a six-pack of blessed water from the gift shop. 'Did you hear what happened to Marty?'

'No, what happened?'

'He had physical surgery today.'

'He did?' Wow, how brave. I admire that.

'He was standing around in the crowd when João grabbed him, ripped off his glasses and said, 'I told you not to wear these' - and broke them.'

'He broke Marty's glasses?'

'Scrunched them up in his hand. Marty's vision was corrected by the entities on a previous visit. The fact that he was wearing glasses again made João mad.'

'So maybe the operation didn't work out last time.'

'That's what I thought. Anyway, João pressed Marty against a wall, took out a scalpel, and scraped his eyeballs with it.'

'He - scraped - Marty's - eyeballs - with - a - scalpel?'

I can feel the color draining from my face. To think, that could have been me. I almost opted for physical surgery. 'How does he feel now?'

'That's the strange part,' Michael picks up the thread, 'he doesn't remember a thing about what happened. The entities knocked him out before the surgery, and bad energies were removed through his eyes.'

Ouch. That's gotta hurt.

Well, evidently not. He didn't feel a thing, Michael says.

On our way back to the *One Season*, we run into Susan, striding along the puddled road like the earthbound goddess she is, in an ankle-length flowing orange skirt. 'I just saw Marty,' she tells us without being asked. 'He's in a blissful state. He has to keep his eyes closed for twenty-four hours. We'll know more tomorrow.'

'If his vision improves even 25%,' Michael chips in, 'that'd be great.'

Why? How is 25% great? 'Without his glasses, he's still down 75%.' And let's not forget, the guy's a pilot. How's he going to fly his plane home?

Michael shrugs. 'Or maybe it'll be 100%, who knows?'

'There have been many incidences of spontaneous correction in vision by the entities,' Susan assures us.

For a brief moment, we lapse into pensive silence, praying silently that Marty, for the sake of João's credibility, is one of them.

7

Müller and His Miracle Healing Patch

Another storm blew in overnight, bringing with it a brutal wind and pulses of bucketing rain that thrashed Abadiânia like a Victorian orphan, then fled before dawn. At the window, I open the drooping knitted rags that pass for curtains and squint out at wet fields daubed with patches of creamy gold, hunched beneath an expanse of intimidating gray that threatens more of the same before lunchtime.

6.55am. People begin to stir. Doors to right and left creak open. My neighbors pause to admire the rain-soaked view, hang bath towels out to dry, then stride off to breakfast, wondering aloud what a lazy Saturday in Abadiânia might have in store for them.

When John of God leaves the Casa, everyone else's reason for being here leaves along with him. Usually, he'll put in a three-day week, Wednesday thru Friday, then disappear at the weekends for some much-needed R&R. Or at least he'll try. According to Angela, the Miracle Man doesn't sleep much. So strong is his connection to Source that it's more than he can do to close the portal between worlds for even a second. Result: he's pestered day and night by entities.

Not all of them are benign either. There are ghastly malefic spirits out there too. These attach themselves to João, playing mind-games with him. Because of the late nights, Angela says, and because, when he's not working at the Casa, he's more than likely busy helping heal people elsewhere, he can look a little rough sometimes.

With breakfast in mind, I grab a shower, make my bed, and leave. As I pull open the corrugated metal door, my foot catches on something propped up against the jamb and sends it flying.

It's a book.

The China Study, by T. Colin Campbell PhD.

I'd never heard of it before meeting Wendy and Sheila. It's a classic nutritional textbook, dense in facts and research, that stages an army-style ground assault on mainstream eating habits by showing the damage that many foods we routinely consume are doing to our body.

Over many decades of study, Dr. Campbell has made some phenomenal discoveries linking common foods to killer diseases. For instance, he believes he's established, no doubt to the mortified horror of the food industry, a link between cancer and the consumption of animal protein – meat, poultry, milk, cheese, and so on - and suggests that many illnesses we deem incurable these days, such as heart disease and diabetes, can be beaten, reversed, or at least held in check by a simple change in eating habits, switching from a diet dominant in animal protein to one where mainly vegetable protein is consumed.

'Other research,' he says in the book, 'shows that various cancers, autoimmune diseases, bone health, kidney health, vision and brain disorders in old age (like cognitive dysfunction and Alzheimer's) are convincingly influenced by diet,' going on to add that the truth about what really damages our health has been obscured for too long and that ignorance is killing us. 'All of these diseases, and others, spring forth from the same influence: an unhealthy, largely toxic diet and lifestyle that has an excess of sickness-promoting factors and a deficiency of health-promoting factors. In other words, the Western diet.'

But that's not all. According to Campbell's studies, cancer has an off-switch. Tumors may be turned off, he indicates, the way you turn off a reading lamp or a car engine, by simply abandoning the bodily abuse that caused them in the first place. And this doesn't just apply to tumors either. Obesity and heart disease can be slammed into reverse too. All we need do, he says, is swap our animal protein-based meals, which the body has a hard job processing, for vegetable protein-based meals, which it evidently thrives on. That will strengthen our immune system and before long we could find ourselves healthier, less prone to contracting the kinds of diseases that routinely kill us, and more able to fight off sickness in future.

I find the promise contained within this idea thrilling, but also depressing.

About 90% of the foods I was raised on, and which have served me well for many decades, or so I thought - chicken, burgers, pies, croissants, French fries, pizza, *Diet Pepsi*, and potato chips – don't fall under Campbell's heading of whole foods or plant-based protein. They're not even close. Rather, they appear on another list entirely, of foods that are utterly delicious and make life seem a lot more bearable, even as they're shortening it considerably.

'Mmm, I know it's bad for me, but it tastes so good,' I'll say, and wolf down another doughnut.

It's the kind of dilemma that faces most of us every day – go without the foods that might be killing us, OR buckle to our cravings for hamburgers and pastry and fat and butter and chocolate and cake, and allow ourselves to rejoice in the flavors, textures, and comforts they bring?

Momentary pleasure or long-term health, which is it to be?

Up to this point in my life, it's really been no contest. Now I'm beginning to wonder.

By the time I arrive at breakfast, the dining room is gripped with excitement.

Marty, it appears, wasn't the only member of the group to undergo physical surgery yesterday. Fabia, a low-key New Zealand woman struck down by unbearable migraines, got plucked from the crowd as well. One minute she was hanging out in the Great Hall, she tells us, debating which one of the poor saps around her would be John of God's latest victim; next minute it's her, and she's pinned against a wall, having a metal instrument– something called a hemostat - rammed into one of her nostrils, right up to the handle!

Since then, the results have been astonishing.

'It was, like, this total bloody shock, y'know? I mean, I'm just standing there with the others,' she says, 'and John of God holds out his hand. And I thought, what's going on? He can't mean me.'

But he did. He took a wet cotton wool swab on the end of his hemostat and jammed it up her nose, then started digging around. But evidently that's not all he did. While he was up there, I guess he must have hotwired Fabia's brain in some new way too, because since then her mind's been completely clear, with not a trace of a headache. Overnight the gloom has lifted. Her personality's gone from bite-your-head-off grumpy at the start of the trip to almost claustrophobically pleasant now.

'It's a bloody miracle, mate,' she keeps saying over and over in her strangulated New Zealand accent. 'I can hardly believe it.'

This elicits great applause, both for itself as a triumphant breakthrough but also as a shot in the arm for Lukas and Dermot, reaffirming the view that all is not lost and there may yet be hope. We're talking apples and oranges on one level, I realize that. Still, if a miracle can happen to Fabia, why not to them?

'Did you get it?' Sheila hisses conspiratorially on her way out of the dining room.

'I did, yes,' I say, thanking her for the book through a mouthful of dry toast that, if this were yesterday, would have been slathered with strawberry jam - the kind of strawberry jam that's crafted in a lab by people wearing masks, and which consists of one half sugar and one half additives, flavorings, color, and preservatives, but certainly, and by design, no strawberries.

Well, not any more. I'm a changed man.

Based on everything I've heard so far this week and what I'm learning from *The China Study*, food is starting to freak me out. Milk in particular. The mucus it causes in the body may even be a contributory cause of my deafness – who would ever have believed that? Of course, I can't be sure it's true; equally, I can't take the risk. From now on, there'll be no more dairy for me, no more toxic preservatives, and, regrettably, a huge reduction in my intake of – even though I want it very, very much indeed – cake.

In light of this, I think a period of grieving is in order.

Today is September 18th. Which just happens to be my father's birthday.

We don't speak, my dad and I. It's a horrible situation. The correct term for this impasse is, I believe, 'estranged', although I never like to admit to that, it hurts too much. Especially since the cause was so trivial. One of those silly nonsense rifts between two people that should have been nipped in the bud a decade ago and wasn't. I can't explain fully even now why our relationship landed butter side down, but it did, and as things stand, thanks to a mix of pride and indolence, and some harsh words from both sides, reconciliation seems further away than ever.

Doesn't mean I can't try, though, does it? Nothing would please me more than to find a way through the deadlock and out the other side. Which is why I made it the second of the three wishes on the list I handed to John of God last week. 'Please fix the relationship with my father,' I wrote. And what better way to kick-start the reconciliation process, frankly, than by going to the local Internet shop and sending him an email wishing him a happy birthday?

Yes, Abadiânia has an Internet shop! I was surprised too.

Brazil's telecommunications infrastructure is actually very impressive. You wouldn't think so to look at it, but it is. Having come to the table relatively late in the game, the government and a few privatized companies decided to skip the beastly dial-up nightmares that had the rest of us tearing our hair out, and plow money directly into broadband and wifi, a move that, according to the figures, has paid off big-time. Nowadays, the country has almost 70 million Internet users. 86% of public schools have a broadband connection. And 99% of Brazilians are able to file their tax returns online. As a result of this revolution, poor little Abadiânia, which seems so lacking in other ways, now has an excellent web presence.

Logging on to my email account, I suddenly find myself a little gun-shy. This will be my first real, sincere attempt at reaching out in almost ten years. What if my dad doesn't want to know? What if the old guy takes what I say the wrong way and it just makes the situation fifty times worse? That's what usually happens. Or what if I find that he died in the interim and nobody told me?

Rather than risk making a fool of myself, I decide to keep it brief. This is not the time to go digging up the tangled roots of our differences. Instead, I open with a short upbeat paragraph wishing him many happy returns of the day, then tag on some quick bullet points explaining why I'm contacting him out of the blue like this – how I'm staying at a healing center in Brazil; how it's all about love and compassion and peace here; how I felt inspired to write; and how I feel the silence between us has gone on for long enough - winding up on an optimistic note: 'Hope you're doing well. I'd love to hear your news.' That's it. As much as I can think of. Anything more might seem like pandering.

Then, before I can get cold feet, I press 'send' and watch the words vanish from the screen.

The ball's in his court now. Let's see what happens.

As luck would have it, the Internet shop is located halfway down main street, immediately next door to *Frutti's*. In no time at all this has become the group's #1 hangout, mainly due to the lack of any comparable hangouts anywhere close.

That's not to say there aren't perils awaiting those who patronize *Frutti's*. Barely have you settled into your seat some days than you find yourself targeted by members of the local *urchinati*. Street kids.

Yesterday, I noticed four or five of them congregating in the road, hatching a plan. While they were talking, one of them, in need of refreshment, bent down with cupped hands, scooped up water from a puddle in the road – a puddle swimming with oil and dirt; a puddle stray dogs had drunk from and probably pee'd in; a puddle that bikes have ridden through and pedestrians stepped in – slurped it into his mouth and drank it.

Everyone who witnessed this incident winced simultaneously.

Anyway, today they're back again. On a hand signal from their ringleader, the same team of children (minus the one that drank from the puddle, I notice, who we can assume is either in quarantine or intensive care), descends on *Frutti's* and begins circulating among the tables, begging for money, sporting their best 'Here but for the grace of God go *you*, buddy' face. A well-orchestrated shakedown that has most customers reaching for their billfolds, if only to check that they're still there.

A couple of the more enterprising boys brought merchandise. 'Very valuable,' they say. 'Very valuable crystals.' Grubby little fingers unfurl to reveal a cluster of loose stones I saw them pick up off the ground just now. I mean, jeez, they did it right there in front of us! On this occasion, however, nobody's buying.

Not that the urchins care. It was all just a ploy anyway to insinuate themselves inside the café. Making sure the proprietor's back is turned, they grab a glass sugar dispenser each from the tables and, tipping back their heads, drizzle a long slow stream of loose granules down their throats, before running off, skipping and laughing, and flinging priceless chunks of gravel at each other as they hunt for a fresh bunch of unsuspecting fools to sell them to.

Not all the pilgrims arriving in Abadiânia are sick. People come for all kinds of reasons. Many are simply annual regulars who use the Casa as a spiritual pit stop, to help repair and replenish. Others are one-offs with a well-defined agenda.

Today, during our second visit to *Frutti's* of the afternoon, a starched but personable German scientist finds his way to our table and, with very little prompting – none actually - produces a little square of material. No bigger than a Band-Aid, it's tan in color, with a texture similar to processed cheese.

'What is this?' Susan grips the strip with both hands and closes her eyes. Before the scientist, whose name is Müller, can respond, her body turns liquid. She slumps back in her chair, emitting a long, ecstatic sigh: 'Uhhhh!'

Wow.

'Zis is a reffolutionary infention,' Müller informs us in a sharp Teutonic accent. 'I call it ze new medicine. You lay it on ze bruise, or on your gums if you have ze toozache, or on a cut, and ze pain – it is gone. It vill get better in minutes.'

'But that's incredible. How does it work?'

'Enerchy,' is his straightforward reply. 'Zis substance, it balances ze yin and ze yang. It affects your body's vave pattern...'

'Vave?'

'Vaves. Like ocean vaves. Radio vaves.'

'Ah.'

'....and redistributes zem as zey come in from ze outside. Ze result is zat everyzing gets better in ze body fery quickly.'

What Müller seems to have come up with is a miracle healing balm in strip form, one that causes bruises to go down and cuts and gashes to sew themselves up in record time. How it does that is not apparent from looking at it. Appearance-wise, the strip resembles fake skin, and has the velvety texture of a baby's earlobe. What gives something so simple its healing abilities? Then again, how does a crystal bed stabilize the blood sugar of diabetics or minimize grief? According to the brochure, it just does. You're invited to take their word for it.

'Uhhhhh!' Susan continues groaning quietly to herself, absorbing a huge draft of air and sighing it out, even as Müller works at prising the strip from her fingers. 'That's...amazing.'

'You feel zis energy?'

'Oh yes. Yes. It's so strong.'

The miracle material is not yet commercially available. Everything's at the research and development stage. But yesterday, as part of his R&D initiative, Müller stood in line at the Casa, eager to get John of God's input, and if possible endorsement. To his relief, the Big Man was very impressed. He felt it for a few moments, no doubt delighting in the velvety texture, consulted with the entities about the commercial possibilities, and promptly declared that this material would have a significant impact on all of mankind. The news made Müller very happy indeed. And it's just the beginning. I gather he and his team are currently making a coat of the same material that will wrap around the body, forming a shell of constant healing.

'Does it heal everything?' I ask when my turn comes to be seduced by the two-inch square patch. Mmmm, so soft. I'm not lying about the baby's earlobes.

'So far, yes,' Müller advises me. 'But at ze different speeds, you understand? Depending on ze grafity of ze problem.'

'Well, my problem's pretty grave, so let's see, shall we?'

And, leaning my head to one side, I place the strip over my left ear, letting it sit there for several minutes while the others stand around, waiting and watching.

'Some people notice a difference right away,' Müller prompts me.

I'm sure that's true. Sadly, I'm not one of them. Though that doesn't mean it's not working. Praying for a breakthrough, I give it a full quarter of an hour.

'So?' Danusia leans in. 'What is happening?'

Customers at other tables lean in too. Even the staffers behind the counter stop mixing smoothies while I do my usual all-systems check.

Right ear – snap. Clear.

Left ear – snap. Still 95% deaf.

Aww.

The test is a flop. As disappointment punctures the balloon of anticipation, the whole café joins me – and Müller - in a collective sigh.

8

A Serious Threat

'Oh my gosh. *Look there!*'

I follow Danusia's finger to the opposite sidewalk, where a casually dressed elderly man with brown hair, glasses, and a fleshy face the color of unbaked dough is engaged in a gentle altercation with a younger, smaller man in coveralls.

'Cash, it's him. YES! You see?'

'Who?'

'*John of God.*'

'Are you sure?'

I stood close enough to João in the Current Room the other day; you'd think I'd be able to recognize him. But he's so different in person. If you've ever visited the Louvre in Paris and laid eyes on the real Mona Lisa, you'll recall the sense of anticlimax you felt when you realized how small and unimpressive it was. I met Dustin Hoffman in a restaurant once – same thing. Viewed in a street setting, wearing ordinary clothes, and without the usual team of acolytes fussing over his every move, João is unusually un-deity-like, a mere shadow of the miracle-making superbeing we're familiar with.

Danusia doesn't care. She's all a-flutter. 'I want a picture with him. Also, what about your book? You want to talk with him, yes?'

Weirdly, I hadn't considered that. I read a couple of interviews with John of God before I came here and it always amounts to the same few ideas: 'I don't heal people, it's God working through me; love is the answer; love is all powerful....' etc etc. He sticks very tightly to the story. For that reason, I'd already decided not to bother. Though I guess if the chance arises naturally in a juice bar, for instance, or a street setting...

We're still debating what to do when the Big Man makes a move, shuffling out of sight into a nearby boutique.

'Come!' Danusia is on it. 'We go in after him. Follow me.'

Too late. Almost immediately he re-emerges, heading off around the back of the building into a dusty side street.

Now we have him! My finger hovers over the red shutter button. Danusia adjusts her rakish flop of dark hair ready for a pose. 'Come! Come!'

'Yes, yes, I'm coming.'

But we hesitated too long. By the time we turn the corner, João's gone. There's no sign of him anywhere. A man of his age and in his condition is hardly going to be fleet of foot, so logic tells me there had to be a car waiting back here.

'Come, Cash, we go in anyway,' Danusia says, retracing her steps.

The store João walked into is a fashionable jewelry outlet, where emerald and ruby rings and necklaces shimmer enticingly on spotlit shelves, tended by Cora, the owner. In her late 30s, I'd say, and pleasant, but looking slightly worried, she stands behind a glass counter while her husband flits about the room, making minor adjustments to the displays. Neither seems particularly comfortable owning a jewelry shop.

'John of God told me to buy this place,' Cora admits in a tone suggesting that running a store hadn't necessarily been on her bucket list up to that point.

'But if you didn't want it, shouldn't you have said no?'

Beginning at resigned, her mood turns wistful, then settles at plain glum. 'I was volunteering at the Casa. I have known John of God for many years, and one day he turned to me and said he thought I should run a store in town. So with his help and the guidance of the entities I bought this place.'

João is always doing that – telling people to do this, go there, work at such-and-such. I've heard whispers that he has fingers in the pies of many of the local businesses around here, including the hotels that profit from his spiritual hospital, but these are just rumors. I've asked several people if it's true, but they stop short of giving a direct answer. All they'll say, and this while smiling glassily, is that João is very proactive in the community and a compassionate, generous, caring, and attentive soul.

'What is he really like, this man?' Danusia asks. 'Is João the nice person?'

'He is a *great* person,' Cora exclaims. 'A wonderful person.'

'But if he's so great and he has all these powers that everyone claims,' I put to her, 'why am I not healed? How come my left ear is still blocked?'

I quickly rehash my story: about what a downer it is for a radio guy to be half deaf. Her answer is not comforting 'It takes time. You might not be healed for six years, nine years. You might not even be healed for what you came for. There might be something else, something you didn't know about, and you caught it just in time. The entities are everywhere. Your job is to let them do their work. All I know is, John of God changes your world.'

'Is he married?' Danusia steers her back on-topic.

This earns a nod. 'He has had some wives.' His current one is called Ana and she's a sweetheart.

'And children?'

'Oh yes. Elev...'

The word is wrenched from her lips by an unholy howling racket from outside. A battered station wagon loaded with loudspeakers thunders by the door on squeaky suspension, loud music blaring, with several highly vocal youths hanging off its fenders. One of them waves a homemade white flag with the number 22 painted on it.

I cover my ears. 'Good grief. What's that about?'

Cora's husband knows. A particularly fierce mayoral race is being fought in the neighborhood, he tells us. Many candidates are on the ballot, but really it's a two-horse race, between the incumbent: referred to as Number 11, Dr. Itamar - 'Nobody knows his first name.' – of the Hope, Renewal, and Work Party, and Number 22, a local lawyer, Wilmar Arantes.

To the 13,000 inhabitants of Abadiânia and its surrounding districts, which of these guys becomes mayor next week is crucial to the future of their town and their economy.

'Arantes,' Cora tells us, becoming emphatic, '*must be defeated.*'

'Why? Who is he?'

Short answer: The Devil, it seems. A troublemaker running on an anti-John of God ticket. According to her, Arantes takes exception to activities at the Casa on religious grounds. She fears he'll not only seek to shut it down asap., like within ten minutes of the polls closing, but his followers will want João chased out of town, taking his hordes of followers with him, never to return.

'And Number Eleven?'

'Dr. Itamar? He is a friend of John of God. He's often seen at the Casa. John of God is a big supporter and he attends all of his political rallies. He loves politics. Just last week I saw him campaigning for Dr. Itamar on the back of a truck. It was dangerous, very dangerous. I thought for a moment he would fall off!'

Behind me, adjusting a sparkly bracelet, Cora's husband sports a strange smile. Maybe he's a secret Wilmar Arantes supporter.

Just guessing, but something tells me that, like his dear wife, this man probably never envisaged being stuck with a jewelry store either, and rues the day he let João talk her into it. Most likely, if Arantes wins next week and the Casa is forced to shut its doors, it will spell freedom for both of them. With John of God out of the picture, they can finally return to a way of living they're more suited to. If I'm right and that happens, I suspect their cries of jubilation will be audible from here to Ecuador.

Returning to the *pousada* for dinner, I meet Angela in the kitchen and decide to raise what, for me anyway, has become a tricky issue this past couple of days. A test of faith, you might say. My session on the crystal bed.

'I'm not doubting the existence of the entities,' I tell her. 'All I'm saying is: maybe, viewed out of context, and looked at objectively in the cold light of day... the crystal bed concept is ...y'know...'

She looks up from her protein shake: 'Is what?'

'....a rip-off.' The words are out before I can stop them, and I instantly regret it.

'Cash! It is NOT a rip-off! It's *energy.*' Dark clouds cross her face. 'You're at the Casa – the entities are healing you everywhere you go, okay? The crystals focus that healing power. For goodness' sake, what do you want from this place? You came here for a treatment; you're getting the treatment. Surgery, herbs, meditation. It works, but you have to be patient. Give it time, okay? *Give it time.*'

Basically, what she's saying is: it's a two-way street.

Here's my theory of how it happens.

When you submit to faith healing, you're communing with spiritual forces. A divine partnership is created, one that can be very powerful and in some cases produce miracles, but only if you let it, and only if you are convinced that a transformation can happen and don't go erecting barriers to your greater good by questioning everything. Healing at this level is intention made manifest. You have to be a willing participant or it won't work.

Think of the last time you went down with a bad cold. Very probably it lasted a few days and was horribly uncomfortable, but did you doubt that you'd get well? No. Perhaps you took Vitamin C, lay in bed for a day, and basically sat it out until you didn't feel sick any more. The same would apply if you'd broken your ankle or sprained your wrist. In those instances, it might be months rather than days before they healed, but in each case you'd take it for granted that your body had the power to mend itself. This is a simple act of faith. And faith, as one-time Harvard chaplain Elton Trueblood pointed out, 'is not belief without proof, but trust without reservation.'

However, when it comes to serious diseases - the real heavy hitters - finding the level of trust necessary to pull off a healing is rarely easy. Somehow, greater leverage is needed: a stronger dose of conviction that can be sustained over a longer period, perhaps years, while the body is slowly bringing itself back into balance. That, in my opinion, is what the Casa is for. It exists to provide leverage.

10% of what goes on here, I'd say, revolves around the idea of entities and vortex energy. The other 90% - the herbs, the ceremony, the dressing in white, the operations, the blessed minestrone soup, etc – they're just tools. Ways of jacking up your expectations, helping to convince you that you're not doomed, stuck being sick for the rest of your days, but that a healing is possible. You're being lifted from the low-level state of despair and defeat you were in when you arrived, to a far higher altitude, one where you, the patient, actively start to believe you can get well. It's a simple switch in approach, but one that can make a world of difference.

Believing firmly that you will recover seems to be a significant component in the actual recovery itself, and one of the ways you get there is through meditation.

Meditation, prayer, and forced relaxation over many days are powerful remedial exercises. They help still our busy minds. In that point of emptiness, a new dynamic comes into play. Of release and surrender. Suddenly, with our guard down, we now find ourselves able to tap into the forces of Divine Mind, or Source energy, where we couldn't before. By sidestepping the ego - our internal doubter and saboteur - and plugging directly into the eternal Source, we quit sitting back and waiting for help to arrive. Instead we are actively engaged in the healing mechanism. In so doing, we make ourselves lighter to lift.

How does João get us to that point?

Simple. With carefully-orchestrated acts of showmanship.

I mentioned earlier that the bottles of water on sale at the Casa gift shop are 'blessed' – that is to say spiritually energized - before they're put on sale.

In 2007, there was an investigation into John of God's commercial activities by skeptic Joe Nickell and the National Geographic. As part of their research, they had the so-called holy water tested by the Washington Suburban Sanitation Commission.

'It was found to have no unusual properties,' Nickell wrote later, 'and to be entirely unremarkable.'[19]

Normally, that would be disconcerting. Even if you overlook the issue of exactly how the Washington Suburban Sanitation Commission would go about testing water for

---

[19] *Skeptical Inquirer*, 2007

'holiness' anyway, the fact that it appears to be in every other respect just ordinary spring water is enough to sow serious seeds of doubt in even the most resistant minds.

But this, I'm now beginning to see, misses the point.

The 'blessing' of the water is a very clever idea. If you can bring yourself to believe that the blessing helps, then, each time you take a sip, you are subconsciously connecting two dots: one telling your mind that what you're drinking is divinely charged, and another that says, 'If it's divinely charged, then God must be healing my body from the inside.' This single act of self-justification might be enough in some cases to sure up, on a very deep level, the belief that a person is going to get well.

Peter Popoff and His Holy Table Salt

Pastor Peter Popoff was the genial host of something called The Miracle Crusades in the 1980s. Another showman, like John of God, he incited wonder and awe in his congregation at Sunday church meetings by randomly calling out the names and ailments of total strangers.

'Alice Gould,' he'd shout, 'God is touching that thyroid condition right now. It is banished in the name of our Lord, Jesus Christ!'

And dear old Alice Gould, baffled as to how the preacher could possibly know who she was, much less that she had a painful thyroid problem, would burst into tears.

Sometimes Popoff would even call out people's home addresses. It was astonishing stuff. And if ever he was challenged, as would occasionally happen, he'd simply shrug and say what João says: 'I dunno how it works; it's all God's doing.' The Lord was speaking through him, he insisted, giving him information.

Except that...well, not really. Apparently, it was his wife Elizabeth at the back of the church, speaking to him through a secret wireless earpiece. For which he was duly exposed on *The Tonight Show* by skeptic James Randi.

Other allegations claimed that Popoff would plant stooges in the audience. Key people he could call on during his performance. So there might, for instance, be a disabled guy there sitting in a wheelchair. At some point, the pastor would approach him and issue a command from God to 'stand up and walk'. The man would then rise out of the chair and take a few tentative steps, his first in years. Naturally, this made for captivating theater.

Popoff's critics, though, wouldn't let up. They derided his act as flimflam, claiming that the disabled guy was a plant and that he'd been able to walk all along. 'You just put him in a wheelchair before the show, so that, when he stood up, it would look like God had granted a spontaneous remission.'

Despite this, Popoff remained as popular as ever, bouncing back later with a new, equally ingenious plan.

He sent to each viewer of his TV show, free of charge, a vial of what he called 'miracle spring water,' plus a sachet of 'holy' table salt. Both water and salt had been charged with Christ-energy. Over the following months, thousands of people received the gifts. As I understand it, the idea was this: the instant the miracle water arrived, you would make out a check for $27 to Peter Popoff's ministry. Prior to sealing up the envelope and mailing it in, though – and this was the important part - you had to sprinkle the check with the holy salt. That was it. Five days later - bingo! You'd be inundated with riches.

'It's not the water that releases the power,' the good reverend insisted to his wide-eyed audience, 'it's your obedience to the instructions of the prophet of God.' And if riches didn't come, he added, then it was your own fault. You simply didn't believe enough.

Luckily, in most cases riches did come, though mainly to Reverend Popoff, in the form of thousands of $27 checks.

Clearly, the man's a genius, as much to be admired for his marketing skills as he is to be scorned, his critics might say, for preying on his parishioners in this way. Like many other evangelists, Popoff made extraordinary amounts of money with his divine schemes, and debunkers begrudge him that. But why? After all, he was only providing a service. Wasn't he in the business of raising people's consciousness? Escorting them from the valley of doubt and fear up to the mountaintop of hope?

Seen from this viewpoint, having a disabled guy suddenly get out of his wheelchair is not a con-trick, but rather an inspiration to others who might be in the same condition. Similarly, it's entirely possible that the salt and holy water scheme helped some people overcome their doubts about ever achieving abundance. If I'm right, it means that, when skeptics set out to slam faith healing as a corrupt exploitation of gullible minds, very likely they're missing the point. What if Popoff, John of God, and many other healers in the world are, by their actions, assisting Seekers to tap into dormant spiritual forces that are very real, and which could, if belief is strong enough, bring desires into reality?

That's what I'm starting to wonder, based on what I've seen at the Casa.

When I first joined the long lines at the gift shop and watched people hand over cash to buy bottles of 'blessed' water, or wooden triangles, or booking crystal bed sessions, I found myself pitching in with the doubters, wondering if João's operation wasn't just an extremely clever ruse to milk thousands of pilgrims out of their hard-earned money. But now I'm starting to doubt my own doubts. John of God, like Popoff, has been branded a conman more than once. But is he?

Or is he, by his gift for showmanship and presentation, merely infusing desperate minds with new possibilities? Bolstering up their faith. Instilling in them a firm conviction that a healing miracle is just around the corner. Because, as noted earlier, it says in Scripture, 'All things, whatsoever ye shall ask in prayer, believing, ye shall receive.' Perhaps João is simply helping people unburden themselves of negativity and fears, so that they can embark on a new path, where at long last they begin to believe that they can be healthy.

Very possibly, that constitutes 90% of what happens here.

When I put this hypothesis to Angela, she rolls her eyes. Her rationale of this place is far more straightforward. Entities are doing the healing, thanks to John of God who channels them from the other side of the ethereal divide. That's the top and bottom of it. 'He is not a bloody televangelist.'

She raises her hand as if to clout me for even mentioning Popoff and João in the same breath. Then I realize she's just showing me her finger.

'See this? I came here years ago with a septic fingernail. It was really bad. *Festering*. Horrible. I thought it was going to drop off or something. Then I showed it to João one day. He touched it, and that was it. It healed at once. No fuss, no magic tricks. Within hours it was good again. I was blown away. Totally convinced.'

Ah. Now, *that's* something else. It falls into the remaining 10%. The 10% of the 12-day Casa process that's covered by the inconveniently vague heading of 'other-worldly', and which can't be explained away so easily.

'So why is my bad ear not healing?' I ask her finally. 'I mean, I'm doing everything right. I believe John of God has the power to make that happen. So why is it not happening?'

Glancing up from her drink, she replies with a smile: 'Ah yes, but do you believe *enough*?'

9

Will Doctors Ever Find a Cure for Cancer?

I can't help but be intrigued by these little wooden triangles people carry around under their arm at the Casa. On further inquiry, I find that they're modeled on three larger originals nailed up in various parts of the compound. The main one hangs on the wall behind the dais in the Great Hall and is said to have been blessed by Dom Inaçio himself when the place was being built. Two feet by two by two, it's gotten to be quite grubby, with a vertical skid mark down the middle, left by countless heads bent in countless hours of prayer.

'That spot,' you're told on your orientation, first night, 'is at the very center of the vortex.' Think of it as an interface between the spirit world and the mortal one, between you and the Source of All Things, as well as a conduit funneling the power of the vast geological plateau beneath Abadiânia directly up into the Casa complex like a geyser, from where it radiates out in all directions.

To make use of it, you must let yourself relax. Stand in stillness with your head down and both forearms resting on the wooden frame, then close your eyes and allow your mind and spirit to connect to Source. Like the three wishes, it's a powerful and intriguing idea that exerts a strong pull on the imagination.

What you're looking at is a hotline to God,' Angela told us. 'It's a powerful place and He's listening. So be careful what you pray for, alright?'

Each time I pass through the Great Hall, I see visitors doing this - praying to the triangle. Some bring letters or written requests from home and tuck them into the gap between wood and wall. Others leave photos of loved ones, or of distant friends too ill or too poor to make the journey, but who nevertheless seek something called 'remote healing' – energy projected at them in their absence.

It's one of the more touching elements of the trip, actually: the degree of trust people are prepared to invest in this process. Their unquestioning faith. The lengths they'll go to, when they're at rock bottom and all other options have run out, in their quest for salvation or rescue or whatever else they're searching for. I confess, I'm moved. You'd have to be a real hard nut not to be, and I promise myself I'll look into this further, and maybe even pray to the triangle myself at some point, if I can summon the nerve.

Amusements are few in Abadiânia. On the main drag, for example, you can do one of two things: a) walk up it, then walk back; or b) walk up it, stop off at *Frutti's* for a bit, then walk back. Most people opt for b.

Today, I'm halfway there, thinking I'll grab myself a quick smoothie before lunch, when I spot a striking figure in the middle distance bustling toward me at great speed.

Danusia is always a vision. Today, her tight white Capri pants and primrose yellow shirt, knotted playfully at the waist, inject a welcome shot of summery loveliness into an otherwise dour world of studied monochrome. As she passes, heads turn and mouths drop open, something she's only too aware of normally and plays up to. Though not this time. Today, she's clearly in a panic.

'Oh my goodness, Cash!' she collapses onto me, breathless. 'A strange thing, it is happening just now.' She seems genuinely shaken up. Her hands are trembling and she has goosebumps up both arms. 'I must tell you. Come.'

Obviously it's a long story, and long stories call for a safe harbor. So we hurry along to *Frutti's*. Barely through the doorway, I spot Wendy sitting in a corner. Ordering a slice of quiche – ingredients: eggs, cheese, wheat, and milk. Verdict: delicious but probably deadly - at the counter, I take my plate to a far table and turn my back to her. That way I don't have to watch her scowling playfully at me for my pathetic human weakness.

For once, however, she's otherwise engaged, dispensing wisdom, the way a Tibetan guru might, to a delta of disciples fanned out around her.

It's amazing the following she's accumulated in just a few days with this homespun heresy of hers. Most of it is too heavy-handed to write down in a book, but when you're here in person, listening, it's enough to make even a borderline-dependent cake-eater and latte-drinker change his lifestyle for good.

Naturally, her audience is lapping up every word. Sheila's there of course. And Dermot has made an appearance. Lukas too.

'The real problem is the way we handle the disease,' she says, talking about cancer again. 'Instead of tackling the *cause* of the tumor - by correcting the core problem: cleansing our bodies, improving our lifestyle habits, our diets, our attitude, and generally supporting the immune system, helping it do its work - we just keep on moving down the same old road: same diet, same bad habits. And what happens? Of course the cancer continues to thrive. So we're drawn into submitting to harsh medical treatments that only compromise our body's ability to repair itself. These may force the cancer into remission, but often it's only a temporary reprieve while it regroups, waiting to come back – which it's likely to do if we keep abusing ourselves the way we always did and don't address the core issue. Truthfully, the *real* problem in most cases is laziness and lack of discipline. People don't have follow-through. Often they could begin to heal if only they'd change how they live their lives. But they won't. The question I ask them is: how much do you want to live? Where's the desire to survive your disease? I find that most of them, even when they know they're facing a death sentence, would sooner die than change. They'd rather end their time on the planet than give up burgers or cigarettes or candy. And so they....'

Okay. Enough.

These things concern me, but I swore to myself I wouldn't be drawn in again. Back to Danusia, who's close to erupting in a vesuvian way over her news. By the time the drinks finally arrive - coconut smoothie for Sir; tea for Madam – her eyes are wide and she's jabbering superfast in her singsong Polish accent.

'It is crazy. I am on my way to the Casa this morning for the crystal bed, and I pass him in the street.'

'Who?'

'Marty! He is walking by me and he is not wearing the glasses. So I wave and he stops. And he says out of nowhere: 'Oh hello, Danusia. What is it, the date today?' And I am not sure, so I think a bit. Then I am saying to him, 'Well, Marty, it is September 21st.' When I say this, he is looking at me strange. 'No, Danusia, what *day* is this?' he is saying again. And I am thinking, 'Are you deaf, Marty? I am just telling you this thing.' So I go, 'Okay,' and say again, 'September 21st.' Only this time he frowns, you know? And then he smiles and says, 'Exactly.' And he walks off.'

Trusting dark brown eyes sweep my face, as if seeking confirmation that she's not nuts and that this is Very Strange Behavior Indeed, which I agree it is. But I'm wrong, that's not what she wants from me at all.

'Because you see, *he's correct!'* she trills.

'Okay.'

'Today, it is September 21st.'

'So?' Clearly, I'm missing something here.

The answer lies with a piece of paper she brought with her from home. A letter from a sick friend in Arizona - another guy dying of cancer! - along with a photo. His name is Alberto. Couldn't make the trip himself. Too sick. So, as a last ditch effort, he entrusted Danusia with a mission: ask the entities to direct their energies long-distance to tackle his disease.

''Well, sure, *of course*,' I am telling Alberto before I leave. 'I promise this. You are my friend. I will do this thing. I will place your letter and the photograph in the triangle while I am here.... and I will do it on your birthday.'...'

'Okay.'

'*...which is September 21st* – yes! Today!'

Ah, now I get it. 'But wait, how did Marty kno...?'

'*Exactly*.' She wriggles excitedly in her seat. 'This is what I am saying. How does Marty know this thing, Cash? How does he know this is the important day for Alberto?'

'Maybe you told him and you forgot.'

She shakes her head. 'I mention this to nobody. I am sure of it. It is odd, yes?'

Very odd indeed. But also *very Marty* as well. The man's a total enigma. I have yet to figure him out.

'Anyway, this is the really good news, no? I run to the Casa straight away, just now,' she says, holding back tears, 'and I place the letter and a photograph of Alberto in the triangle and I am saying a prayer for him, for his cancer. So all is good. I keep my promise, I am happy. But imagine! Imagine if I am not meeting Marty in the street today, oh my....' For a moment or two she chews on the consequences of failure. 'This cannot be a coincidence. It is the entities – yes! They are the ones who direct Marty to tell me this.'

The best I can offer is a vacant hitch of the shoulders. No idea.

At this point, I am more open to the idea of paranormal happenings than ever before. Abadiânia seems to be the kind of place where the inexplicable happens more often than it doesn't. But who's to say what's going on for real? How can anyone be sure?

Danusia hurries away, eager to tell others about her weird experience, leaving me sitting at the table staring beyond the café's little terrace into the street, where people drift aimlessly about, sometimes in groups, but very often alone, their distracted eyes gazing contemplatively into the middle distance.

When you see a guy push himself by in a wheelchair, at least you're offered some hint of what the problem is and why he came all this way, whereas for the rest of them – who knows? A strained face, a hollowness in the cheeks, a faltering step...all clues to something, but truthfully they tell you very little. A person may have been strapped to the mast of his or her suffering for twenty years, and you'd never know it. Nobody here goes around advertising that they have cancer or diabetes or back pain or whatever else. Pain and despair are handled in private, with as much dignity as they can manage.

'Why d'you suppose,' a voice pipes up behind me, 'there's never been a cure found for cancer?'

Wendy, done with her mini-lecture by now, has opened up the floor to a Q&A.

'Nobody really finds a cure for anything,' she says to the group with resignation in her voice. 'You must have noticed that. Colds, M.S., AIDS, diabetes - they say they're searching, but they never seem to come up with the goods. Look at Jerry Lewis and all the money he's raised over the years with his telethons on TV? All those hundreds of millions of dollars plowed into researching a cure for muscular dystrophy, or whatever – and where is it?'

'Yeah, but why is that? There has to be a reason.'

A lot of the time I'm able to tune out Wendy's little speeches as white noise. Problem is, as you've heard already, she delivers her truths with so much passion and such a sense of moral rectitude that it's not always easy to ignore them, particularly on an issue as troubling as this, with so many question marks hanging over it.

Why *don't* doctors find actual cures for things?

Forgive me if this seems like a bit of a digression, but if you know anyone currently living under the cloud of serious disease, especially cancer, or who died from it, then you too have a vested interest in learning more about this, for your own sake as much as theirs.

In my case it's a mystery I live with daily, ever since my otherwise hardy, unflappable mother took to the couch with kidney cancer in the '90s.

One year she was vibrantly well, the next she was sick. The year after that she was gone. 'Nothing,' her doctors told us afterwards, 'could have been done to save her life.'

In my mom's case, the Shaman Effect played out to its fullest extent. She believed the doctor's word 100%. He told her she'd die, so she obliged by sitting around and waiting until she did. It's the same grim knell heard by Geena and, as things stand right now, by Dermot and Lukas too. Their physicians called it quits and said there was no hope; it was a done deal.

'Nothing we can do.'

Why, though? Why is there nothing they can do? We know that some of the finest minds in the scientific community have had this demon in their crosshairs for decades. As far back as 1971, President Richard Nixon promised the American people that a cure for cancer would be found within five years. Four decades later, nobody's seen even a glimmer of a breakthrough. Why is that?

Well, Wendy believes she has an answer.

As I noted earlier, she doesn't view cancer in a lot of cases as a disease to be cured, as such, more as a protest vote. The body's way of getting our attention, telling us, 'It's time to change the way you've been treating me, or else I'll get sicker and sicker until you do.' But because doctors and drugs companies make a mountain of money from suppressing our symptoms or simply cutting them out, they're in no hurry to find the root cause of the problem or to develop a way to cure it.

'If tomorrow everybody suddenly got well, the system would collapse. It'd be over for hospitals and cancer charities and everyone connected with them. They depend for their financial survival on us being ill and needing treatment after treatment. Return business – it's what all industries thrive on. Otherwise they'd be broke, and all that expensive medical equipment they bought would go to waste. The more prescriptions physicians write, the more hospital visits they arrange, the more profit they make. So they need you to be sick and to stay sick and to keep coming back. It's simple economics.'

I admit, I'd never looked at it that way before. We forget sometimes, I guess, that healthcare companies are in the profit business, not the people-helping business, the way their name suggests.

'But what if someone came up with a real cure for cancer, one that worked?' I ask, walking over to gatecrash the group.

'What would happen then?'

At this, Wendy pushes the hair out of her eyes and cracks a smile. 'Ever heard of Rene Caisse?'

Rene Caisse and Her Amazing Cancer Cure

There used to be two competing branches of medicine: empiric and allopathic.

Empiric doctors were kindly and wise and favored gentle natural remedies that supported and empowered the immune system to help the body do its job of getting and staying well. With that end in mind, they would prescribe not only herbal remedies, but lots of rest, sleep, positive thinking, laughter, optimism, deep breathing, exercise, topped off with a sensible nourishing diet. Altogether, this kind of care brought the body back into harmony and balance, producing highly beneficial results and some very happy patients.

Early allopathic doctors, on the other hand, were no fans of herbal treatments. 'Ridiculous!' they chortled. 'How do you verify your results for a start? And more importantly, how do you make a boatload of money from selling herbs?'

Good question. Because, of course, you know what did make a boatload of money? Cutting people open. Or bleeding their disease away, which was also very popular at the time. Or simply administering poisonous minerals to their body. All quite barbaric practices that came at a premium price. Allopathic doctors took the view that you have to show a disease who's boss. You did this, they figured, by attacking it, carving out chunks of tissue, and medicating the bejeebers out of the patient until their illness quit. In those circumstances, and since allopathic treatments generally made a huge profit, the last thing doctors wanted was for impostors to come along with their cheap alternative remedies and homespun ways, and start muscling in on their territory. But that's what happened with

Rene Caisse.

Caisse was a Canadian nurse in the early part of the 20th Century. A robust and determined woman who, apparently, quite by accident, chanced upon a formula for ridding the body of cancer.

One day, a patient came to see her. The wife of a gold prospector. This woman was in the advanced stages of breast cancer and on the brink of lengthy, debilitating surgery when something quite extraordinary happened. While out traveling in northern Ontario, she journeyed across the reservation of the Ojibway Indian tribe. Here, a medicine man treated her disease using simple, tribal methods. Not only treated it, but healed her of it, no less.

'It's a miracle. My tumor has gone down,' the prospector's wife informed her very perkily, 'and I feel on top of the world.'

In light of this, Nurse Rene set off for northern Ontario to track down this mysterious medicine man for herself, and found to her astonishment that his formula was embarrassingly simple. It consisted of four herbs: burdock root, sheep sorrel, Indian or Turkish rhubarb root, and slippery elm inner bark, ground up, mixed together in a specific ratio in hot water, and drunk as a tea.

'That's it?' she cried. 'That's all it takes?'

Soon after, Rene's own aunt fell ill with stomach cancer. Sensing that death wasn't far off, and figuring the old dear had nothing left to lose, Nurse Rene administered the Indian tea formula every day for the next few weeks. And guess what: this poor woman, who'd been handed a death sentence by the medical profession, made a full recovery. Not only that, but she lived for another 21 years.

By all accounts, Rene pulled off a similar miracle with her mother too. She happened to be dying of liver cancer. After administering a program that combined the miracle herbal formula with a regime of healthy activities: deep breathing, exercise, positive thinking, good nutrition, and so on, the tumors once again disappeared.

That's when Rene decided to market her secret formula openly so that everyone could benefit. 'Essiac Tea,' she called it - Essiac being Caisse spelled backwards.

Well, naturally, news of this wonder remedy spread far and wide. As it did so, Rene's usual steady dribble of cancer patients exploded into a full-blown multitude, same way it did with John of God. Many were even referred to her by medical doctors who'd given up on their patients. Until, in the end, the influx forced Rene to open a clinic. She took over the three-story British Lion Hotel in Bracebridge, Ontario, where, in the years that followed, she saved thousands of lives using only a mug of hot tea, strict diet, discipline, rest, positive thinking, and lashings of common sense. The more patients she treated, the more she came to understand this killer illness and its causes.

'There is no specific entity called 'cancer',' she is quoted as saying[20]. 'There are only people who have succumbed to the process which creates cancer cells...those whose bodies have lost the ability to neutralize and get rid of all the chemicals, poisons and carcinogens which damage cells.' She went on: 'Diseases are messengers from the soul demanding us to...change. Cancer is a disease of civilization - the vindication of all the abuses we perpetrate on ourselves and what the abnormalities and hazards of chemicals, of our environment and external world do to our bodies. Over many years, we each build our own cancer tombstone.'

The truth of this statement struck a chord with many people.

---

[20] *Bridge of Hope* by James Derners.

Before long, Nurse Rene Caisse became a legendary name in alternative healing circles. So it was perhaps inevitable that eventually her spectacular record in seemingly being able to reverse cancer would come to the attention of the regular medical establishment. The instant it did....well, sadly, that's when things started to go wrong for Rene. And this, I think, is the part Wendy is referring to when she talks about why nobody has yet discovered a cure for cancer.

'What's this?' the authorities huffed. 'A clinic curing people of cancer? Outrageous. Cancer can't be cured. Stop this nonsense at once!'

But Rene wasn't about to yield to a few self-serving bullies. She stood her ground and continued treating hundreds more people.

Doctors were again outraged. Seeing she wasn't going to give up, that's when they began playing dirty.

First, they launched a rigorous campaign to undermine the reputation of Essiac Tea. 'Expert' scientists were drafted in to conduct tests on the formula in labs, from which they concluded categorically that the tea was useless. A hoax. No way did it cure cancer. And members of the Canadian Cancer Commission went even further. In 1938, they rubbished the tea comprehensively, claiming its effects were very limited and any success Rene had had in healing cancer thus far was due to a misdiagnosis: her patients didn't have cancer in the first place – so *of course* she was able to heal them. But, just in case, they insisted that Nurse Rene hand over her formula at once, so that they could ~~destroy~~ analyze it.

Very wisely, she refused.

Next, they tried to buy her out, offering to pay a large sum of money if she'd divulge her formula. Once again she refused. And that's when they snapped. What an impossible woman! Under no circumstances could they have some renegade, albeit well-meaning old biddy out in the sticks achieving better results than they did – it could undermine the entire medical industry. So, in desperation, they marched in with warrants and affidavits and all manner of accusations and threats, made her close down her clinic, and forced her out of business. They also had her arrested. Twice.

Rene, however, was a canny and singular woman, as you've probably gathered, with the fortitude of a goat. Shrugging off all attempts at bribery, intimidation, and sabotage, she set up shop in her basement at home instead, where she continued making and administering her Essiac Tea until her death in 1978.

What the Rene Caisse story seems to show is that, under attack, if its profits are threatened, the medical industry makes a mean enemy and will stop at nothing to protect its own. So perhaps it's not surprising, in light of this, that John of God, too, often comes under fire.

He has quite a history of being rounded on by folk who disapprove of his methods. In times past, he was even beaten up and imprisoned. Then there are the ongoing investigations by debunkers anxious to undermine his track record of healing disease and prove him to be a charlatan. Not forgetting the Church, and local politicians like Abadiânia's possible future mayor (if things go wrong in the elections next week) – each of them seeking to have the Casa shut down and João run out of town for practicing medicine without a license.

'It's not all that different today,' Wendy tells her little group of acolytes. 'Anyone threatening the status quo the way Rene did, by coming up with a natural rival to pharmaceutical drugs, one that even *hints* at curing cancer, would be prosecuted.'

They'd also be maligned by media companies, she says, who reap much of their advertising revenue from drugs companies. After which the discredited 'cure' would never again see the light of day. Not because it's dangerous and doesn't work necessarily, but precisely *because it might work* and could pose a threat to the income of the medical profession and pharmaceutical companies.

While it's tempting to dismiss this as the skewed viewpoint of an overwrought and overzealous health-nut, it seems there is some evidence out there to support her.

Example: in 1974, the Medical College of Virginia, which was funded by the National Institutes of Health, was charged with investigating the damage done to the human body by marijuana. The whole thing was designed as an anti-drug initiative, stressing the potential harm of smoking cannabis.

'Imagine their surprise,' journalist Steven Hager wrote in an article in 2009, 'when the results came back indicating the opposite: instead of hastening the death of mice implanted with brain cancer, marijuana dramatically slowed the growth of their tumors and extended their lives. The DEA quickly shut down this promising research... [T]wo years later, President Gerald Ford would put an end to all public cannabis research and grant exclusive rights to major pharmaceutical companies to develop synthetic THC.'[21]

THC is the shortened version of delta-tetrahydrocannabinol, a chemical found in cannabis. In 2007, in Novia Scotia, Canada, a guy called Rick Simpson was claiming to have cured dozens of people of their stage 4 cancer using simple homemade hemp oil. In fact, that same year, the Division of Experimental Medicine, a scientific study group at Harvard University ran tests on mice, using THC, the way the Medical College of Virginia did, and discovered that it cuts tumor growth for lung cancer in half, as well as reducing the cancer's ability to spread.[22]

---

[21] *High Times*, November 13th 2009

[22] It took until March 2011 before the National Cancer Institute would issue a statement announcing that in tests conducted on diseased mice, the cannabinoid compounds in marijuana had been shown to inhibit the spread of cancer and reduce tumor size. It

'[W]e are showing that a substance of abuse, if used prudently, may offer a new road to therapy against lung cancer,' one of the researchers, Anju Preet, Ph.D., said in an interview.[23]

And that was that. Nothing more has been heard since.

Rick Simpson, though operating outside of the law, backs up their research. He claims to have had a 70% success rate with his homemade hemp oil, which, if true, seems like a staggering achievement, one that must surely make the medical establishment sit up and take notice. But evidently not. His reward was to be rounded on by the Canadian authorities in an effort to shut him down. His home was raided by police. He was prosecuted several times and jailed, forcing him ultimately to become an exile in Europe. All, he says, because the medical and pharmaceutical industries don't want a natural product they can't patent to hit the market. Not while they're busy behind the scenes trying to figure out a way to replicate THC in pill form in order to cream off the profits for themselves.[24]

In the end, it probably comes down to who you believe: the Rick Simpsons, the John of Gods, the Wendys, Sheilas, and other free spirits of this world who say they just want to see people healed of their diseases by as natural a means as possible; or big business and the governmental agencies regulating healthcare, who say they're just trying to keep quack operators of all kinds from exploiting the public by running dangerous or untested remedies on innocent patients.

Whatever side you come down on, at least we can agree on one thing: that as patients we need to be smart. We may not be granted access to some of the more innovative cancer cures for

---

would be an irony indeed if, after decades of damning marijuana as a gateway drug and danger to society, society was now forced to embrace it as the cure for one of its greatest killers.

[23] *Science Daily*, April 17th 2007.

[24] If you're interested, this discussion is taken further in the documentary *What If Cannabis Cured Cancer?*, by Len Richmond.

several years yet. In the meantime we owe it to ourselves to take care of our own interests. To ask more questions, get second and third opinions, seek out reliable information, and if at all possible avoid the surgery, radiation and of course drugs – lots and lots of drugs - that doctors recommend all too frequently as a first, not last, resort, as they did when I had my gallbladder taken out. The question: 'Might there be another way?' never came up. But, of course, I was naïve back then. In future, it'll be the first thing I ask.

Wendy carries a little notebook. From it she reads a quote from Bruce Lipton's *The Biology of Belief*. 'The trillion-dollar pharmaceutical industry puts its research money into the search for magic bullets in the form of chemicals, because pills mean money. If energy healing could be made into tablet form, drug manufacturers would get interested quickly.'

With that, the meeting winds up. The small knot of disciples, their heads by now filled with thoughts of conspiracy and revolution, drift out of *Frutti's* into the street, leaving their guru picking thoughtfully at a bowl of cantaloupe with a plastic fork, and me staring across the café at her, wondering what's going on in her head. What could possibly have lit such a massive bonfire in this woman's belly, to the extent that she feels compelled to keep punching home the same message day after day to anyone who'll listen, and with such passion?

It's a question I've asked myself more than once on this trip. Maybe one day soon I'll pluck up the courage to put it to her.

10

Prayers and Revelations

Close on the heels of the Shaman Effect I mentioned earlier comes something more nebulous - 'the Casa Effect,' which kicks in around day five of your stay. I've heard people speak of it from time to time, without fully understanding what it is.

Today I'm beginning to.

The usual steady downpour has chased almost everyone from the compound. Across the deserted grounds, sodden gardeners shrouded in mist continue working, digging holes for plants whose names I probably should know but don't, each man seemingly oblivious to the weather and how wet he's getting. Far off, sheltering beneath a tiled canopy, a creamy white poncho sits facing the valley, its wearer adrift in contemplation. And I think I saw Marianne just now weaving along one of the pathways in search of solitude. Doubtless they're feeling the Effect too.

The longer you stay in Abadiânia, the more necessary these periods of alone-time become. Normally I'd do anything to avoid the kind of peace and quiet that has me hearing the blood pulse through my ears or my neck crackling as it turns. Back home in Los Angeles, I can be confident that no such thing will ever happen. Hollywood is in a whole different universe. The air buzzes non-stop with traffic copters, private planes, police and ambulance sirens, and of course people there are comets.

They move fast, drive crazily, schedule too many meetings in a day, then arrive late for them all, pulled every which way by duties, errands, appointments, deadlines, and a hundred other diversionary tactics. It's common in L.A. to confuse enthusiasm with ability, activity with achievement, and 'having a nice day' with being fulfilled and happy. Why? Because without the diversion, the relentless bustle, the faux-happiness, the self-absorption, all the effort and struggle, what's left really? Nothing. A vast gulf of emptiness opens up, driving them to introspection, and introspection is dangerous. None of us wants to be lulled into thinking dark, disturbing thoughts about life and its purpose, do we? That kind of information can really mess you up.

But it's what happens in Abadiânia. Here in this rural isolation tank, where diversions are non-existent, at some point your mind, because it's not preoccupied by trivialities, turns inward and begins feasting on itself. Suddenly you find yourself stuck in what feels like spiritual rehab.

Everything's fine for several days; all systems are go, nothing to report – then out of the blue you wake up one morning feeling strangely light-headed, with your emotions in a tangle, aware suddenly, without understanding the specifics, that an unseen hand has been at work, tinkering with your psyche, stirring things up. I'm tempted at first to blame it on the soothing effects of the passionflower tablets I've been taking each mealtime, but something tells me it's not only that. This is more than just drowsiness or a change of pace. At times, it feels almost molecular, as shifts take place at a deep, deep level.

Around about now, if you haven't already, is when you start to believe those things you've been hearing about the Casa, and figure they might be for real after all.

You find yourself questioning things. Overthinking things. Doubting stuff you thought you knew for sure. From time to time you even taste a slight tang of worthlessness on your tongue. Troubles that merely simmered gently at the low temperature of ordinary living, when exposed to a high spiritual heat boil right over, leaving you vexed and muddled and broody. And, worse, unable to snap the lid back on.

That's how I am today – broody. As well as a little disoriented, where I wasn't yesterday. I feel sensitive, vulnerable, a little nauseous.

'Pah! How is that possible?' doubters would say. 'Show us proof that the energy from this so-called vortex is screwing with your senses like this.'

But how do I do that? How does one demonstrate a subtle inner shift under test conditions, or something as vague and subjective as mild nausea brought on by entities from another dimension? You can't.

'For those who believe,' St. Ignatius de Loyola is famous for saying, 'no words are necessary. For those who do not believe, no words are possible.'

You hear this quoted a lot at the Casa, but it's really what it's all about.

The Parable of the Damaged Daughter

Feeling disturbingly fragile, I take shelter on the terrace alongside the kitchen, at one of the communal tables we use when we eat our blessed medicinal soup, and slice open my journal, thinking I'll scratch down a few notes.

But it's impossible to concentrate. My mind, a vacuum to begin with, quickly fills with dark, disturbing thoughts. About my father mostly, and that dumb email I sent him. What a mistake that was. I had to go and poke the hornets' nest, didn't I, when the wisdom of hindsight dictates I should have left it well alone? What, I wonder, will be his reaction to receiving a message out of the blue from a son he acts like he despises, and whom he pretends to have forgotten? I imagine his first re...

'AAAAAAWWWWWWWWWWWW!'

My train of thought is derailed by a yawning noise behind me. Up the pathway through the teeming rain comes the young mother from the other day, shunting her padded leather table on wheels with the IV bag jiggling on its pole.

'AWWWWWWWWWWWWWWW!'

Strapped in, still flat on her back, is her daughter. Grotesque bloodless face, permanently screaming mouth. Someone had the idea to dress the girl fashionably this afternoon. Gray cardigan over a cool black Metallica T-shirt, bearing the logo: 'Ride the Lightning.' Oblivious, she lies rigid, her praying mantis hands shuddering in time with the tires as they jubber-jubber-jubber over rough concrete.

Passing by, two dark chasms of confusion scan my features with great alarm. 'Who's that strange man, mommy?' they seem to be asking. 'How does he get about? Who pushes *him* around?'

'Who? Oh, everyone,' I want to tell her. 'Everyone pushes me around.'

See? Didn't I tell you I was feeling broody? The Casa Effect. I really need to get a grip. This place is starting to bum me out.

'AAAAWWWWWWW. AAAAAAAWWWWW.'

The mother sighs wearily, her spotty complexion framed by graying yellowy hair yanked back into a fierce ponytail. Her clothes laugh at style. I get the sense that she was probably attractive once. Now, like the rest of us, she takes what she can get.

The table rolls to a stop just shy of a dripping gutter.

'Wait here,' Mother orders. Once the parking brake is engaged, she drags her collar up about her ears and squelches off across the grass. Suddenly, the girl is alone, making distraught noises, watching her caregiver and sole provider disappear around the rear of the toilet block.

Two minutes go by; still no sign of the mother. Then five more.

In her absence, another woman appears, independent of the first. A slim redhead in a Burberry raincoat. Her features are benign but horsey like Princess Anne's. 'Hello. How are you?' she asks softly, approaching the padded table. The accent is generic European. Czech possibly; Dutch would be an outside bet. 'Are you enjoying the rain?'

'AAAAAAAWWWWW. AAAAAAWWWWW. AAAAWWW.'

The girl twists in her straps, rocking violently from side to side. Squeaky wheels override the brake and inch forward into the wet. Rain splashes her face.

'AAAAAAAAWWWWWWWWWWW! AAAAAWWWWWW!'

'Yes, it's great, isn't it? I like that feeling too. Very warm.'

It's rare, I should think, that anyone stops to chat. Few are sufficiently self-assured to look past the ghoulish carcass for long enough to find the real person trapped inside. But this woman has something extra. She seems to have found a key that the rest of us have not. We dwell on the prison bars; she focuses on the soul locked up behind them.

'How about the energy?' the woman continues. 'Do you feel it? The energy at the Casa? The love?'

Hands flap and wave all ways. Feet kick feebly. 'AAAAAWWWWWW.'

'Love is all around you. It's God's blessing. God sees you as perfect. You are perfect. A perfect spirit, made in His image and likeness. He sees you, you know that. He sees you doing His work and He loves you for it. With God's help, you will be....'

Mid-sentence, she's interrupted by a large gray SUV that comes splashing toward her in reverse, swerving over a bush and crushing it, before rejoining the pathway and squealing to a halt where the woman would have been standing had she not just leapt out of the way.

'AAAAAAWWWWWW. AAAAAAWWWWWW.'

Out hops Mother, and, with a bustling efficiency born of routine, unstraps her daughter from the table - 'One, two, three, uhhhh!' - hoists her into her arms, staggering a little at first for balance, then....

'Please, allow me.' The redheaded woman rushes to help her.

'No, no, it's fine. I got it. Really.'

After steadying herself, she makes for the truck.

'Here....' If she can't help carry the kid, the stranger can at least grab the rear door handle and be useful that way.

Well, this is one kindly gesture too far.

'I *said,'* Mother snaps, raising her face to the weeping heavens in despair, 'NO – THANK – YOU!' A couple of the gardeners look up from their shovels. '*We don't need any help*. We're fine. Understand?'

The woman flushes red to match her hair. 'I'm sorry. I was just....'

Not interested. Fighting the elements, Mother drags open the door herself and transfers her life's burden into the back seat.

A pause for breath, then it's onto Phase II: dismantling and folding up the table, which, handily, is designed to collapse in on itself like a first-time ice-skater. Finally, after the slam of several doors and the growl of the engine, the SUV, stair-rods drumming on its roof, inches back onto the path, rolling over another bush and flattening it – that's two bushes and one heart crushed in the space of four minutes; not bad – and sloshes slowly off toward the main gate, tail lights blinking between buildings, staining the puddles the color of annoyance.

*

By the time I enter the Great Hall and find a seat at the back, my cheeks are wet and I have dewdrops dripping from my nose. I'd blame the weather, but that would be a cowardly lie. Something about the excruciating drama that played out on the terrace just now has touched me at levels I'd normally not acknowledge.

As I noted earlier, part of the Casa Effect is that your emotions become sharpened sticks. Sometimes they turn on you. It doesn't take much. Anything can set you off. This particular weak moment today was triggered by - not a dark, disturbing thought exactly, more of a profound question.

Is it possible, d'you suppose, that the mother in that situation - although quite clearly the primary caregiver – is, in spiritual terms, *actually the one receiving the treatment*?

I know, it sounds crazy, but what if?

Healing can take all forms. You come here for one problem, but an entirely different one gets treated. The former just gave you reason to fly to Brazil; it's the latter, though, that really needs attending to, and you may not even have known it. Healing begins first and foremost with awareness. That's why you simply have to relax and trust whatever comes. Be open. Be willing. Be.

So although the mother thinks, and would no doubt insist, that she traveled to the Casa solely for the benefit of her damaged daughter, perhaps that's not the case - it's the other way around. The daughter is the ticket. In fact, could it be that the birth into that particular family of that particular problem child, which must be like living with a fire alarm that keeps going off every three minutes, was no accident at all, but happened for a much larger reason?

What if the daughter is not flawed, the way we assume? I mean, visually, by our usual standards of normal, she is. But I'm talking on a higher level. What if, in her own way, she's absolutely perfect just as she is? Perfect for the job that's been assigned to her in this lifetime, which is twofold: i) to create for her parents a rough road to travel down, throwing up an immeasurable number of daily challenges; and, by virtue of that, by virtue of rising to those challenges, ii) to help them learn how to become more rounded, open, loving people. More aware, more compassionate, more understanding, more in touch with the Divine.

The disease is the teacher. Not only in this case, but in every case. It's not a curse. It's not bad luck. We're not victims. God hasn't singled us out for more pain than anyone else. The disease is there to teach us something about ourselves that we need to change.

In the case of the girl on the table, the pupil is not the patient, as we might be forgiven for thinking, it's whoever's charged with supervising her. That's the one that receives the healing. *By her very existence,* the girl carries out her life's purpose to the fullest extent, triggering a dramatic learning curve in everyone who comes into contact with her, but primarily in her mother.

More interesting still, what if this same scenario isn't unique to that family, and we all have a damaged daughter in our life? Perhaps more than one. Somebody whose job it is to educate us in the ways of love, tolerance, patience and compassion, or a hundred other troubling lessons. But we're not grasping the opportunity. Instead, we get caught up in the struggle, the fight – the daily grind of having, owning, winning, getting to where we want to be, all that superficial stuff, and, in so doing, fail to recognize the vital contribution those people are making to our growth, much less acknowledge it.

Author and medical intuitive Carolyn Myss calls these relationships 'sacred contracts'. We arrive in this lifetime with specific points of growth to reach, she believes, and a roster of fellow souls who've tacitly agreed to help us reach them. And they do help us, though not always in the ways we'd like - by being agreeable and making things easy for us. Rather, they present us with problems and challenges. They make the road ahead that much steeper and the going a lot more difficult.

It could be anyone, I guess – a child with Motor Neurone Disease, a disagreeable boss, the rogue landlord, the angry ex-wife, bullying classmate, awkward co-worker; that careless driver who rear-ends us on the freeway; the lazy cop who unjustly writes us a parking ticket just to make up his quota; the aloof, impossible-to-understand father who...

...hasn't spoken to us in more than ten years...

Sweet Jesus, no! Not that.

For me, a man feeling anything but stable today, this rapid download of information hits me like a bus. Wendy promised me as much right at the start, but I didn't take her seriously.

All those arguments we used to have, my father and I. The ceaseless criticism he showered me with when I was a kid. The deliberate withholding of love, approval, hugs, affection, sympathy; all the shouting and slamming of doors...on and on and on, creating so much grief and anguish that it put me in therapy for years. Now you're telling me that it was nothing? Just a sacred contract? All that stuff I took so seriously. Stuff I lost sleep and tortured myself over – nothing but a pre-arranged series of lessons to help me grow as a person in this lifetime? *That's it?*

And I'm not alone in this. It's the same for everyone. I bet you have many examples of your own. Unfortunate clashes with troublesome people who, now that you look back, taught you so much. They weren't really there to make your life miserable, which was how it seemed at the time, but to educate you in higher principles. You came away wiser, better equipped for the next step.

Perhaps the same is true for nations as well. What if our enemies, whether they be terrorists or whole countries, are not our enemies at all, merely sentinels of truth?

For thousands of years, we have engaged in costly, wasteful battles driven by ego or greed, justifying our campaigns with, "They are our enemies, they are bad people, we must fight them." But really, they're not bad people. They're mirrors, reflecting back at us an image of ourselves and information about where we fall short, so that we as a nation can communally grow on the spiritual level. Fighting a problem is senseless and only makes it worse. Instead, we need to lay down our weapons and observe our enemies closely, not to find their weaknesses, but so that we can see our own. "What is it," we should be asking, 'that you are trying to teach us about ourselves?" Because that's why they're there. Not to kill us, not to terrorize us, not to rob us of our freedoms, which is what the political machine would have us believe, but for a far grander purpose: to be our damaged daughters and educate us. To give us lessons in love, compassion, patience, acceptance, and forgiveness. And to let us know how far we have yet to go.

In the end, it's about us, not them.

Seen from this same standpoint, it means that my father has done no wrong. My ego doesn't want to hear that, but it's true. All along he was just fulfilling his role as a teacher. For years I thought, 'If only I could change him, make him understand...,' when, really, it was I who needed to change and understand. This was my lesson, not his. The old guy is innocent of all charges. He was simply acting out the role he was put here for. Yet, that whole time, I kept on resenting him for it, hurting him for hurting me.

It's all a major revelation, and needs some absorbing. Reframed in this way, our 'problem people' take on an entirely fresh sheen.

They're teachers, not tormentors, I now realize. Allies, not enemies. We should be showing enormous gratitude for their sacrifice, not resentment. After all, they are unwitting instruments in our betterment and in our slow development as spirits while we're on the planet. 'Forgive them – they know not what they do' – right? They may indeed know not what they do, but what they do is entirely for our greater good.

Inexplicably, I have this...this....odd burning sensation beneath my lower ribs, as though someone's pressing a lit cigar to my heart.

Before I can think of a reason not to, I'm on my feet.

A moment later, I surprise myself by scampering along the side of the main hall, face turned to the wall to hide my tears, heading for the triangle at the far end.

This is it. My moment. I need to talk.

Show up

Say yes

Take a deep breath

Dive in and get it over with

You've heard of the Western Wall in Jerusalem, also known as the Wailing Wall? One of the holiest sites in the world. Jews flock there by the tens of thousands each year to pray, and to wedge personal notes to God in the cracks between the giant limestone blocks, a tradition dating back centuries.

The temple was built in 1000 BC, at the geographical point where, according to legend, Heaven and Earth meet, making the wall a Hotline to God too in its way. Those who congregate there often admit to feeling a divine presence. They weep, they mourn, they wail, they beg for favors. In fact, it's said that if someone prays at the 105-foot wall for forty consecutive days, then the Lord will answer his or her prayer. An intoxicating idea, and one that João may well have drawn on for inspiration when he decided to hang a giant triangle on the wall of his healing center and invite people to pray to it.

By comparison, and as hotlines go, João's emits only limited mystique. And that's from far away. Close up, it's even less impressive. For a start, it could use a squirt of *Pledge*. It's scuffed and scruffy, the grain sullied by thousands of hands and elbows rubbing up against it.

As with the Western Wall, there are a handful of handwritten notes and a splay of photographs tucked into the crack behind it. Flicking through, I find a grinning Hispanic kid in a wheelchair. A middle-aged couple standing arm in arm on a seaside pier, doubtless taken in better days. A guy on crutches. A blond boy about five years old, with puffy eyes and a broad flat forehead, squinting goofily at the camera. Down Syndrome, obviously. Each picture constitutes a request for remote healing. An improbable illusory notion on the face of it. How can anyone be healed 'remotely' across thousands of miles? On the other hand, if you believe that we are all one, which is the premise on which the love-based healing at the Casa is founded, why would distance pose any problem? What's five thousand miles to divine intelligence? Nothing.

Furthermore, according to author Josie RavenWing, those who receive this kind of treatment definitely know something's happening. Wherever they are on the planet, when the healing energy reaches them, they experience 'a powerful wave of love', as she calls it.

This afternoon there are seven other people in the Great Hall, meditating. Nobody's paying attention to me. Good, because this is already feeling embarrassingly awkward. But the urge is strong and I need to get it done. So I take up my position on the dais, rest my arms against two sides of the triangle, let my head drop to the wall, the way I've seen others do, and... wait.

Now what?

Not sure.

I thought I'd feel something, but I don't. No rush of excitement. No chills. Even a slight breeze would have been okay, like when you stand over a vent, only from above this time. But there's nothing. Nothing to differentiate this spot from any other in the compound.

The best thing I can do while I'm waiting, I figure, is restate my three wishes. So: 'Please unblock my ear. Please fix the relationship with my father. Please open up my life and help me change career, take me away from public radio.'

There's no way of explaining to rational people what the benefits might be of praying to a wall. But who cares what anyone else thinks? What's the point of praying in the first place if you're going to devalue the process by asking frivolous questions or holding back? Why would God take your prayers seriously if you don't take him seriously? Nobody cares how you pray, I'm told, or when, why, or where, only that you do.

'Please unblock my ear. Please fix my relationship with my father. Please open up my life and help me change career, take me away from public radio.'

That's it. That's all I have. I'm fresh out of ideas, and unsure how to respectfully wind up our little one-sided exchange.

I decide to end with the Lord's Prayer.

'...the power and the glory, forever and ever. Amen.'

The words have scarcely left my lips when something weird happens. My stomach, which has been feeling rough all day, now does something like an acrobatic backflip, so violent that it makes me even more nauseous.

Good grief, what's *that* about?

Deciding that it's better not to wait and find out, I scurry off the dais toward the exit. By the time I emerge into the steady downpour outside, the original queasiness has compounded severalfold and I'm dizzy.

From the Great Hall to the main gate is no distance at all; I've crossed this same messy patch of gravel many times since I got here. Today, though, for some peculiar reason, walking poses a challenge. It feels like a mile and a half, with the gate slipping further and further away the closer I get to it, in a strange telescoping sensation I've seen in movies but never personally felt before. Every footstep is leaden, my balance pitched. Worse, my stomach and chest are grumbling. Ominous spasms ripple inside my ribs.

With the rain pounding my back, I force myself to a low wall and bend over it in readiness. But nothing happens, and after thirty seconds of retching emptily, I figure out why. My body is playing tricks. There is no physical vomit, is there? These are *feelings* I'm regurgitating. The triple-whammy of: a) the fossilized daughter; b) a Down Syndrome kid whose foolish despairing parents don't recognize him as perfect in his own way and who want João to fix him up, as if they're returning a faulty ironing board to *Target;* not to mention: c) the violent memories of the years and years my dad and I wasted pointlessly fighting – all of this converges and comes crashing down on me at once. Until...

Holy cow, this can-*not* be happening.

...I'm crying!

I am. I'm actually *crying* on a public highway.

Left unchecked, my feet plot their own path along the main street, stumbling down the middle of the road.

A reminder of what a terrible idea this is arrives seconds later in the form of a battered flatbed truck that comes up the hill, headlights ablaze, thundering straight at me, honking its horn. It whips by so close that its rusting fender scuffs my coat, missing me by *this much* - a hair - before it splashes away in bouncing lurches through half a dozen potholes, heading in the direction of *Frutti's*. Blinking after it, I notice that the truck has a pole stuck on the back at a 45-degree angle, with a large white bedsheet tied to it, snapping perkily in the wind.

The sheet bears an ugly motif, the way pirate ships do. *A big black Number 22*.

Arantes!

Scrambling to safety, I flop down on the Casa wall in a pool of water. My shoes are squelchy, my raincoat is just a bucket with sleeves, my hair's glued to my head, and the tears are refusing to quit. What a horrible, bedraggled mess. I must look like I'm melting.

'Excuse me.'

'Hh?'

A gentle hand touches my arm. The hand of a woman. An old woman in a cheap blue gaberdeen, the hood expelling thin rivulets all ways across her shoulders. God only knows where she came from, but apparently she was out enjoying the storm, saw some bozo almost get hit by a truck, and rushed over to see if he needed help.

'Are you alright?'

I keep my head down. Don't want her to see me crying. 'I'm good, thanks,' I say, even though it's clear I'm not. 'Oh, and by the way,' I want to add, 'I never cry in public places. Just so's you know. This is....well, I have no clue what this is, to tell you the truth. A compassion attack possibly. Forty years of misery all releasing at once. But in any case, I never cry, okay?'

'Do you need a doctor?' she asks calmly.

'Oh n-no. Not at all.' *Definitely* not a doctor!

After a couple of seconds' pause: 'This happens a lot here, you know.' Her soft Irish lilt speaks to my good ear.

'What does?'

'What you're going through. Happens all the time. You should be glad. It means something's stirring. The entities are doing their job. Don't give up, it'll all work out. It usually does.

Now - sure you're okay?'

'Yes. Th-thank you. I'm great. I really ap-preciate your concern.'

'Don't mention it. That's what we're here for.'

With that, she walks off, sensible rubber boots sloshing through puddles, only to stop ten paces further on with an afterthought. 'Get indoors,' she calls out. 'Dry off. Have yourself some hot tea. You'll be fine.'

I dismiss her concern with a wave. 'Will do. Thanks again.'

This time the Samaritan leaves for good, taking her extraordinary loving kindness with her. Secretly, I'm glad she's gone. Otherwise she'd see me flop back into my puddle and break down all over again, and that wouldn't be good. Word might get out: there's a guy wandering around the main street who's just realized he can no longer manage his own universe and is learning to give up control and to trust. How would that be then? What would people say?

11

Physical Surgery

Last night before dinner, our group assembled in the reception area of a neighboring *pousada* to watch some video footage shot by Angela of João performing his miracle healings. She'd told us ahead of time that the contents were graphic. I wish I'd taken the warning more seriously.

In a scene that I only dared glance at through my fingers, João positioned a small, frail-looking woman up against the big wooden triangle in the main hall. The commentary said she was suffering from chronic fatigue. With little or no ceremony, the Big Man yanked her left breast out of her shirt, plumped it up a little as if kneading a pie crust, then carved a pocket into it with a knife. Observers squealed as the blade sliced through bare flesh like a spoon through crême brulée, then again as fingers reached inside and extracted a blob of deep red tissue. The hole was promptly sewn back up again.

Worth noting: the patient herself remained eerily impassive throughout. No anesthetic was administered. She just stood against the wall and took it. Didn't resist or scream or faint, as I fear I would do in the same situation.

In *The Book of Miracles*, Josie RavenWing reports that she has stood alongside regular allopathic doctors, mostly emergency room medics visiting the Casa, as they studied at close range one of John of God's surgeries. Always, she says, the reaction was the same: the doctors said they couldn't have done a better job of operating or suturing than João. It's details like this that make his work so convincing. There's no sleight of hand or fancy fumbling. Nor is there a pivotal moment of deviousness when he could have pulled a bag of duck guts out from under a table, or attempted to pass off one thing as another. It all plays out right there in front of you: straightforward surgery, performed, João claims, by the spirits of long-dead doctors working through him.

'[E]ven though an incision is being performed in a way and location that we can see,' Josie writes, 'the real surgery is still taking place invisibly within the body and energy system of the patient through the work of the various entities.... [T]he entities always work on the source of the problem. That source could be mental, emotional, physical, or spiritual...and because the entities work at the source, true healing takes place, not just the curing of symptoms.'

On the video: 'I don't cure anyone,' João launches into his usual disclaimer before an awed crowd. 'I don't operate on anyone. He who operates is God and the good spirits.'

He then incorporates as Dr. José Valdevino, a frequent commuter through the vortex. Every spirit has its 'thing'. One will tackle diabetes, another blindness, and so on. Valdevino is responsible for restoring paraplegics and those with dire physical infirmities back to health. In the surgery room, there's a photograph of João, taken while he's performing an operation, only in place of his actual physical form is a white-robed ghost with totally different facial features that, quite honestly, look photoshopped, though we're told they're not. *That's* José Valdevino.

Up next in Angela's film was a close-up of a woman having her right eye scraped with a metal instrument, the way you scrape ice off a windshield, which is *beyond* ghoulish, let me tell you, and elicited a long, slow 'yeuuuw' from the *pousada* audience, many of whom turned their heads.

A petite middle-aged blonde was then summoned up to the dais. 'She has a liver problem. It is cancer,' one of her friends said, to which João replied bluntly, 'I know.'

Raising her shirt, he pressed his thumb deep into her fleshy abdomen and rummaged around vigorously for several moments. Once he'd found the spot he gave it one last compacted push that obviously hurt a lot because the woman winced and started to cry. Then she was escorted away. Healed, presumably.

After this we got to see the procedure Fabia went through, in which João rams a wetted cotton wool ball on the tip of a metal surgical instrument called a hemostat up someone's nose. A new woman was brought onto the dais. We watched the hemostat go up, and João wriggle it around with short, strong strokes until he found something suspicious, whereupon he pulled a gob of tissue from her brain. Bleeding, the still-stunned patient was maneuvered by one of the many attendants into a waiting wheelchair and pushed away.

The whole thing was very difficult to watch. Real people, real incisions, real blood – and no anesthetic.

At dinner, later, I sat myself next to someone new, as is my policy: this time a jovial guy called Frank. I mentioned him briefly earlier. He's Canadian. Late '50s. Upbeat. Well-educated. Arrived in Brazil tanked up on medication to counteract the pain of his sciatica. So on the one hand I guess he's motivated to believe in John of God's powers. On the other, he's not a fool, and the instant he heard about Fabia's surgery his B.S. meter flew into the red, he says. His suspicions were only compounded by the video.

'Hemostat up the nose – that's a variation on an old carnival trick. It dates back to the twenties. Traveling freak show magicians would hammer five-inch nails up their own nose as a stunt.'

'You're kidding me. And it didn't kill them?'

He shakes his head - 'There's a long cavity just here.' – jabbing an index finger at the skin above the bridge of his nose. 'It leads straight up to the pineal gland. That's how it's done. It doesn't hurt. Quite the opposite, actually. The pineal gland is stimulated and it gives the sensation of pleasure, contentment, or relief. That's why she felt good. But it's not what you could call 'surgery'.'

Big-time John of God doubter Joe Nickell, author of the book *Secrets of the Sideshows*, backs up what Frank is saying. '[H]is procedures are a sham,' he writes harshly on the website *Skeptical Inquirer*. 'The twisting of forceps up a pilgrim's nose is an old circus and carnival sideshow stunt.... Looking far more tortuous than it is, the feat depends on the fact that, unknown to many people, there is a sinus cavity that extends horizontally from the nostrils over the roof of the mouth to a surprising distance—enough to accommodate a spike, icepick, or other implement....'

Oh dear.

To prove his point, Nickell found himself an old carnival performer called Stephon Walker, and asked him to demonstrate the eye-scraping trick. Walker apparently used 'a blunt knife to scrape the white part of his eyeball and acknowledged that such stunts look more risky than they are.'

So is that it, then? Are John of God's treatments really just a series of clever stunts? Are the Seekers who arrive here believing something is going on simply being duped? That would be very disappointing if so. It would also, I might add, fail to explain a whole raft of winning eyewitness testimonials included in Angela's documentary. She interviewed many former Casa patients whose claims that they were healed seem thoroughly genuine. These are not actors or stooges.

- A woman who was suffering severe degenerative spinal injuries said she was now 80% better and off her medication;
- An older guy, who for nine years had suffered from severe back problems, arrived at the Casa in a wheelchair and left walking, he said. 'I'm now able to get about and life is much improved.'
- Tom, diagnosed with incurable throat cancer, who was told by his doctor, 'Get your affairs in order.' Two years later, after seeing John of God, he was fine and apparently completely healed[25].
- A man with ulcerative colitis and Menière's Disease, affecting his inner ear, both of which had been designated incurable by doctors, had nevertheless recovered. According to his testimony, he was 95% healed, if one can put a percentage on such a thing.

Yet none of these testimonies, as convincing as they are, would appease the skeptics, I'm sure. They'd still smell something fishy.

Indeed, Nickell concludes his article by saying, 'A surgeon who commented on John of God's incisions stated that they were superficial (little more than skin deep, apparently) and would not be expected either to bleed very much or even to cause much initial pain.... The bottom line regarding the procedures is that they are pseudosurgeries that have no objective medical benefit other than the well-known placebo effect.'

If he's right, then that's the end of it. The Casa and its workings are a disgraceful sham, and a lot of good, trusting people have been thoroughly conned. Problem is, it's easy to dismiss this stuff from afar, but less so when you're here, especially when you see the results João achieves and listen to

---

[25] Although later on, according to Angela, the cancer came back and Tom died, so not every one's a home run.

the accounts of those whose lives have been changed forever by coming to Abadiânia. Sure, under scrutiny there are aspects of the Casa experience that leak a little water in places, and maybe there is flourish of gimmickry and fancy showmanship involved, but even taking those into account, there's still, I maintain, a font of spiritual power within this compound, beyond, and greater than, what we see in everyday life. It's not all hocus pocus or woo-woo nonsense. Nor is the case against João as cut and dried as the debunkers would have us believe.

There is *definitely* something going on here.

12

Secrets of the Sacred Waterfall

Today is Revision Day. That's when the previous week's patients – us, in this case - return to the Casa for a final evaluation. Then, tonight, if we pass the inspection, and if we've shown an improvement, spirits from the Casa will stop by our room while we're sleeping and remove our stitches.

How they do this or if it will hurt doesn't bother me at all. You'd think it would, but it doesn't. As inclined as I have been to resist the more questionable aspects of this operation – like the crystal bed therapy, for instance – as time goes by, all my concerns seem to be slowly evaporating in favor of raw excitement. I can't wait for tonight to come around. For me, this is the best part of the trip, when we finally get to meet the entities.

Inching through the current room for the final time, I find John of God sitting on his little throne as always, looking irritable. Eyes, tired and watery, peer out at me from behind frameless spectacles. The weekend's R&R has done him no good whatsoever, it would seem.

Once again, he ignores me. I tell myself it's nothing personal. He's a vessel, that's all. Grumpy old José Valdevino and the other spirits are flitting along the line, scanning everyone for signs that the treatment is working and conveying their verdicts to him. In my case, it seems I'm doing okay, because João lets me pass by without comment. Next thing I know, I'm stepping into bright sunlight again, heading to the kitchen for lunch.

'So?' Danusia asks over our medicinal soup. 'What is with you?'

'Well, it seems my operation was a success. I'm good to go for tonight. Most likely I won't get my hearing back until after the stitches have been taken out.'

At this, she makes little applauding motions with her hands. Seems she got an all-clear as well. 'It is going to be great, yes? I am very exciting,' she coos, then suddenly realizes what that means – spirits from beyond the grave will be visiting her in her room in a few hours' time. The very thought of which causes her to go extremely quiet.

Naturally, the others are 'exciting' at being visited by the entities too. All, that is, except one: Dermot. He stands at the kitchen window, bowl in hand, looking more than a little deflated. Did he not pass the inspection, then?

While he's out of earshot, his sister leans over to share a confidence. 'John of God told him he has to go back for more surgery on Friday.'

'More surgery? But why?'

His problem runs deep. Deep enough that just the one operation won't be enough to chase it off.

You see? It's little details like this that, to my mind, speak volumes and cement John of God's credibility, reassuring me that his work really isn't a scam after all. Because why on earth would he put himself out that much? At his age, as sick as he appears to be, worn down by sleepless nights and malicious spirits, and with thousands of new pilgrims passing through here each week, draining him still further, why would he eke out more work for himself than he has to? Unlike allopathic doctors, he makes no money from putting in overtime. Everything he does is done for the good of the patients. Call me naïve, but that, right there, is enough to convince me that we're in good hands.

There's a small amount of prep work to be done before you can be visited by entities. Certain ground rules need to be followed, or else nothing happens.

After dinner, and following an inspiring meditation session by Susan in the hotel's recreation room, we're given instructions on how to derive the maximum benefit from the stitch-removal process. Angela has a list. We must, she says:

- 'Be in bed by midnight. The entities will stop by your room sometime before 5am.'
- 'Wear white. It creates good healing energy.'
- 'Place a glass of clean water by your bedside, bless it with a prayer, then, when you wake up tomorrow, drink it.'
- 'Keep your eyes closed until dawn. *Do not open them*. The entities cannot work on you effectively if you're looking at them.'

'What happens if I'm caught short and need to go to the bathroom?' someone with a 90-minute bladder window interrupts.

'Keep your eyes closed as much as you can, *even when going to the bathroom*. Don't turn on the lights and under no circumstances must you peek, okay?'

'Got it,' I smile at her. 'Thanks.'

As the group breaks up, Joe, the tall, spiky-haired guy I saw taking photos of the entities in the field, calls out, 'Hey, don't forget tomorrow morning, Cash.'

'I won't,' I reply, even though I have no idea what he's talking about.

'Be ready at 6.45am and bring money for the cab.'

A cab - why? Where are we going in a cab at a quarter to six in the morning?

'Leave all your valuables in your room. And bring a towel.'

'A towe...?'

Ohhhhhhhhh. *Now* I remember. The *cacheoira*.

Did I mention this to you earlier? I meant to. There's a sacred waterfall on the outskirts of the Casa grounds. It's called the Cachoeira de Lázaros. According to legend, the vortex energy is stronger there than almost anywhere on the compound, attracting hundreds of entities, and making it a powerful spiritual and healing experience for visitors. Earlier in the week, I'd committed to going down with a small group of guys, though admittedly this was before I'd taken into account how bitterly cold a forest waterfall is going to be first thing in the morning. I don't think anyone's factoring that in.

'It'll just be the four of us,' Joe says. 'Me, you, Dermot and Frank. We're meeting in reception. Don't be late.'

'Great. I can't wait.'

10.05pm. Prior to going to bed, and for my peace of mind, I execute a quick search of my room, check my door is locked, then undertake a systematic and thorough recce of the whole place top to bottom, tapping ceiling tiles, pushing at walls, making sure there are no hidden entrances or compartments anywhere, and that all windows are either secured from the inside or nailed down. Once I'm satisfied that nobody can get in while I'm asleep, I slip on a white T-shirt and a pair of white trousers over my *Fruit of the Loom* white underpants, pour myself a glass of water and place it by my bedside, the way Angela told us to, then switch off the bedside lamp, slide under the sheet and wait for midnight.

It's now 10.37pm.

Once again, to a world of entrenched doubters, *the very notion* that a grown adult would believe he's about to be visited by apparitions as they cross over to this dimension from behind the ethereal divide is beyond ludicrous. And as I lie in semi-darkness, bristling with anticipation, I am not unaware of what you must be thinking. But here's the thing: I've been recalling the stories. About those people who, upon returning home, were shown X-rays and found they had internal scarring, even though there was no corresponding wound on their flesh. I don't know about you, but to me that's fascinating, and highly exhilarating.

Josie RavenWing cites a case in which a young woman decided to avoid future pregnancies by having her tubes tied. Then, when she got back from the Casa, an X-ray 'showed that the tubal ligation had been undone and her fallopian tubes were now connected again.... Several months later she was pregnant.'

Many visitors over the years claim to have laid eyes on the entities. An ageing photograph on the wall of the Great Hall - this one taken by a tourist, I believe - of João performing one of his physical surgeries, shows a thick shaft of light plunging diagonally across the frame. Evidently, that's an entity too. Spiritual beings can take any form they want, including a yellow streak, or orbs - as they did in Joe's photograph - or even a human shape, the way Rita appeared to João in that creek fifty years ago. That's what I'm hearing and I couldn't be more intrigued. I've noted before the similarity between this experience and waiting for Santa when you're a kid. It's really no different.

I wonder what form my entity will take tonight.

10.55pm. For the next several minutes, I watch flickers of light cavort spastically across the ceiling and down the walls. The whole while, my good ear is pricked for clues, anything to indicate that the process might be under way. Unfortunately, there's nothing, just the usual racket from outside. Laughter, calls of 'Goodnight', followed by assorted bangs as my neighbors slam their doors and turn in too.

At 11.10pm it starts to rain.

11.13pm. More laughter from neighboring rooms. More metal doors. For about the hundredth time I roll over and check the bedside clock.

11.21pm. Not long now. Almost there.

Dressed in white, eyes closed, lying still – I'm braced and I'm ready.

The stage is set for a miracle.

The next seven hours flit by at cartoon speeds. Before I know it, it's 6.41am and the alarm clock's going off, jolting me awake.

With eyes so blurred they feel like they're coated in Vaseline, I drag on yesterday's clothes, then bumble around to the *pousada's* reception area, ready – if ready is the right word at this ridiculous hour – for our ride to the waterfall.

It's twilight out. The temperature's dragging its knuckles through the low fifties. At the front door of the hotel, I find the other three guys making light chitchat beside a taxi. Joe, who's managed to bum a *Marlboro* off the driver, stands contentedly expelling toxic geysers into the crisp morning air, happier than any healthy habit could ever make him. Everyone's disconcertingly upbeat.

The cab, a dusty, clapped-out old banger with windows that won't close, is a tight squeeze for five. As I'm wedging myself into the back seat alongside Dermot, he asks, 'So? Anyt'ing happen last night at all? Were you visited?'

'Nope,' I admit, sadly.

Not that I know of anyway.

After all the build-up, and despite being supercharged with adrenaline for most of the evening in anticipation of my first supernatural experience, I passed out around 11.25pm and stayed out for the full seven hours. Out and gone. So if Dr.

José Valdevino did happen to stop by in the dark and take my stitches out, then God bless him for tiptoeing about the place, because I missed his grand entrance completely. And his exit. And everything in between. The sense of anticlimax is crushing.

'How can you tell if you've had stitches removed? What are the signs?'

Joe cranes his neck around from the front seat. 'Here's how you tell. You go inside of yourself.' He rolls his eyes up into his lids, flares his nostrils, breathes in. 'Feel your body. Do you have an ache anywhere today? Inside, outside...?'

'As a matter of fact, yes I do. The area around my lower ribs feels tender.'

'Well, there you go.'

'But that could be anything. Maybe I just slept in a weird position.'

'How about your ears?' Frank asks. 'Any improvement there?'

Of *course* - my ears! That's the real test.

Snap right – clear.

Snap left – *still 95% muffled,* practically deaf.

Nope. Still the same.

So there you have it. Eight days into the trip, and not the teeniest inkling of a breakthrough to justify the level of faith I've shown so far. Much as I hate to admit failure, this is my second disturbing wake-up call of the morning.

'What about the rest of you guys?' I ask. 'Anything?'

Three heads shake. Turns out that they felt nothing either.

As always in these situations, the disappointment is palpable.

'Here we are, boys.' The taxi rumbles to a stop.

The sun, responding to our silent prayers, begins to beat a little warmer as we follow a muddy groove through the grass.

We're on the far fringes of the Casa now, out of sight of the main compound. The *cachoeira,* tucked away below us in a gulley, is reached by trekking down a steep incline to a gate. Beyond the gate, the same pathway continues into the trees.

'Okay, follow me,' Joe says, with a whispered reminder that we have entered a mystical sacred place and must be quiet and respectful at all times. 'There are dozens, perhaps even hundreds of entities down there. We need to honor that, okay?'

Sure.

A hairpin twist takes us out of view of the world above and into a steep trough, its walls cast in leafy semi-darkness. Ribs of wet rock are overhung with numerous species of tropical plants. The cold air makes my nostrils tingle. Ahead of us, I can hear an echoing rumble. Ten paces more, and the rumble grows into a splashing sound, its origin a sunken grotto filled with bubbling mossy-green water.

'This is it. We'll wait here.'

The meeting comes to order with a group hug.

'Men....' Joe has prepared a short invocation to recite before we bathe. '...we have come together...' His voice deepens to a growl and he closes his eyes. '...as *men.* When we give our spirits up to the sacred task ahead, the word we attach to our manliness today in this place is...oho.'

Oho?

A symbolic codeword he just made up. Spoken beforehand as one, then again by each of us individually later once we complete our excursion into the waterfall.

'Oho,' he repeats gravely.

'Oho,' we chant, before breaking the circle and stripping down to our underpants.

Several feet further along and down a bit, etched deep inside the gulley, a sparkling boa of water spills in a steady churning torrent into a natural rocky hollow, clouding the pool a foamy white. Boy, does it look cold, though!

Up to this point, the choice was all ours, I guess: stay or go back. Any one of us could opt to sit out the whole ordeal; nobody's making us do this. But it's not that easy, is it? Now that we've hugged and said 'oho', the process has acquired a deal more gravitas. Suddenly we're a club. A tribe.

Dermot has invested his whole heart in the possibility that there really are entities floating around down here and they're going to help heal him. In the face of such profound need, fleeing is out of the question. For his sake alone, we have to stay, in case by not participating we are putting a life at risk. None of us wants to take that chance.

So who's going first?

I think we're all very relieved when Joe kicks off the clunky leather sandals he's wearing and launches himself gamely along the path, hopping from stone to stone 'til he arrives at the water's edge, where, with a cavalier flick of his arms and not a speck of hesitation, he plunges into the pool up to his waist, wades to the middle, and stands there motionless.

Evidently it takes a few seconds for the shock of being almost frozen alive to wear off. Once it has, he submerges beneath the surface and disappears.

Moments pass. Enough moments for a guy to drown. But no, he's up again, exploding in a foamy column of spray and soggy leaves. Arms raised, head skewed up at the dawn sky, he lets rip a yodel of such primal ferocity - 'Aaaaaaa-eeeee-aaaaa--eeeee-aaaaaaa!' - that it sends exotic birds scattering like buckshot from the tree canopy above our heads, caw-caw-caw-caw.

Upright now, his thin rasher of a body plows against a small current to the foot of the *cachoeira*, a thrashing torrent that threatens to swallow him whole. Allowing his shoulders to absorb the impact, he sinks into a cross-legged meditation position. For the next half-minute or so at least, while we watch from the bank, he lets the water pound his skull, keeping his eyes closed, neck outstretched, nostrils flaring, as he communes with the entities, while the rest of us await our turn, gazing around distractedly.

If you ignore the bugs and the damp and the mysticism, this hollow would make a really picturesque picnic area, I'm thinking, with its arc of trees, the fans of dewy gossamer slung between blades of grass, and of course the *cach*...

Hang on, what's that over there? I've just spotted something.

A small detail about the waterfall that isn't entirely obvious at first glance, or from every angle. Indeed, I dare say that, if you're entirely focused on the bathing ritual, as the others are, you might miss it altogether. Specifically, it concerns the speed of the water flowing over the ledge. And *more specifically*, how controlled it is. Almost as if...

My thoughts are hijacked by a glistening blue streak sprinting toward us. 'Oho!' it yells. Joe's back. 'Okay, Frank – go for it.'

Frank's a no-fuss, seen-it-all kind of guy. There's no melodrama with him; no posturing, no theater. He kicks off his shorts and flaps away down the slope into the pool, throwing himself under the falls, where he stays long enough to realize that any longer might kill him, then leaps out. I doubt the entities even got a chance to say hi, he was so fast. Quaking violently, and fit to expire, he spits out, 'O-ho!'

And the next one goes. Dermot.

He's quite an attractive man clothed. Half-naked somewhat less so. His love of beer and good food means he probably wouldn't look out of place among the background characters in a Botticelli fresco. In fact, given the education we've received from Wendy this trip, I can't help speculating if Dermot - had he taken greater care of himself over the years, eaten better, exercised, stayed off the alcohol, meat, fat, and processed foods loaded with chemicals, and whatever else - might have avoided getting ill in the first place. It's a valid consideration, though not one I'll be vocalizing to him.

His time in the pool is little more than a perfunctory splasharound. I didn't bring a watch, but by my best estimate he lasted ten seconds. Now he's back, gasping up the hill, salt and pepper hair plastered, glistening, to his forehead. 'Oho.' Whereupon Joe turns to me. 'Alright, Cash. Get your clothes off.'

I've kept my T-shirt on 'til the very last minute. Now I peel it off and hang it neatly on a spare branch, then descend into the gloomy basin, though with less gung-ho enthusiasm than the other three, I must say. Immediately, I feel the frigid hands of a Brazilian dawn close in around my bare buttocks. By the time I reach the water's edge, it's practically winter. I can see my breath.

'Quit being a baby.' Joe heckles quietly.

'You can do it, Cash.' Frank and Dermot. 'Go on, mate.'

If making a global TV travel show in adverse circumstances taught me anything at all, it's this: in a horrendous situation, when you're faced with no choice at all and if forward is the only way to go, then go forward. Don't waste time debating what'll happen if you do, or thinking of excuses why not – just go, do it. Follow the risk-takers' protocol: show up, say yes, take a deep breath, dive in and get it over with. So there'll be no dithering here. Snorting in a draught of air to steady my nerves, I close my eyes, suspend all thoughts of fear, and, edging out across the pool, chest first – 'Three, two, one...' - fling myself at the pillar of water.

'AAAAAAAAAAAAAAAAAGHGHGHGHGHGHGHGH! OHHHHHHHHHH!'

Entering the *cachoeira* is like being waterboarded. Like ten thousand panic attacks crammed into one, fifty for every gallon.

'AAAAAAAAAAAAAAAAAAAAAGHGHGHGHGHGHGHGH. AAAAAAAAAAAAAAAAAAAAAAAGHGH.'

My pulse accelerates. My heart's a gong. The hammering on my head....

'AAAAAAAAAAAAAAAAAAAAAAAAGHGHGH!'

...causes my knees to buckle, even as it's extending freezing tentacles into every crevice.

I made up my mind in the taxi coming that I would use my brief time down here to restate my three wishes, the way I did before the triangle. So that's what I do, but at high speed.

'P-p-please unblock my ears,' I mumble through violently chattering teeth. 'P-p-p-p-lease unb-b-block my c-career. P-please unb-b-lock-k my relationship-p with my f-f-f-father. But mostly p-p-please unblock-k my ear.'

As I chant, I cling onto the rocks with my fingertips to prevent myself from being washed away in a sudden surge. Then I realize how silly that idea is. How could there be a surge? That's what struck me as odd before. In case I'm wrong, I step back into the pool away from the waterfall and begin inspecting at close range the ledge it's pouring over, because, as I said, something about the perfectly steady flow of the *cachoeira* feels unnatural to me, almost as if it's a...

Good grief, I'm right - *it is!*

It's a hose!

Or a pipe or a conduit, hard to say precisely. *Something,* anyway.

Now it's all beginning to make sense. One of the rules of the Casa is: you can't just show up at the falls. Being a 'sacred place', the entities must vote on whether to let you down here or not. In effect, therefore, you're being granted permission to grace their presence. But of *course* you need permission - I see it all now. But it has nothing to do with entities, does it? Or with honoring sacred places, or making the gods angry. It's because, if you get here too early in the day, there's no waterfall to sit under. Not until someone – probably one of the gardeners from the Casa – climbs in his car, drives over here, flicks a switch, and turns it on.

I'll be darned.

If any consensus can be drawn at all about the *cachoeira* outing, then it leans toward it being a very potent healing experience. Frank and Dermot are not just feeling invigorated as a result, but are infused with greater faith in the process, they say. And Joe's the same way, declaring the ceremony to be a magical liaison with spirit that affected him at a deep level.

I'm only sorry that I don't feel like that.

Joe and I are the last ones to arrive at the breakfast table. By the time we sit down with our plates of scrambled eggs and fruit, everyone else is deep in conversation, not about how bummed out they are at the entities' failure to show up last night, the way you might expect, but about nutrition. Angela's itemizing the contents of her morning protein smoothie for Amy. Judy, a realtor from Wales, is describing to Mary how for years she was debilitated by a mystery illness that caused extreme fatigue and dizziness. 'Turned out to be an infestation of parasites.' And Wendy's explaining with a deep furrow in her brow how wifi is the new asbestos.

'Seriously, in five to ten years' time, when people are dropping like flies with malignant tumors, it's going to be one class action suit after another against the wireless companies. We have no idea how bad this is going to get. It'll be big tobacco all over again.'

Meanwhile, at the other end of the table Danusia sits alone. Distanced from the chatter, she looks frangelic – a combination of fragile and angelic – dressed all in white ready for a morning at the Casa. Eager to reveal my big scoop - that the sacred waterfall is *manmade*, can you believe that? Or at the very least artificially augmented by man, which is just as bad – I shunt up alongside her. 'Guess what!'

But she doesn't want to know. The Casa Effect is upon her and she's lost in dark, disturbing thoughts. 'Do they come, Cash, the entities?' she asks limply. 'To your room in the night?'

'Er...you know what? I'm not sure. I'm still deaf in one ear, so I suppose not.'

Across the table, Angela hears this. Emitting a sigh long enough to hang me with, she breaks off from itemizing her drink ingredients. 'How - many - times – are - you - going - to - say - that? And how many times do I have to tell you - *this is just the beginning?* It's an ongoing process. You don't know what the entities did. What if you had a tumor or clogged arteries and they found the problem and sorted it out? For all you know, they may have saved your life this week. But instead of being grateful, all you can do is complain about your bloody ears.'

'Oh yeah? Well, if it's all the same to you,' I snap at her, 'I'm in radio. I happen to think my ears are important, thank you very much.'

Exasperated, she grabs an armful of admin junk she always carries with her – a clipboard, a pen, a stack of forms – and bustles out.

'How about you?' I ask, returning to Danusia. 'Did you see any entities?'

She shakes her head. 'But I *feel* them - yes. I know they are there. I lock my door and I hide, like this...' She pulls a napkin over her face. '...in bed. Oh gosh, I am so scared. But then....'

'Then what?'

'...nothing. I am falling asleep. And today – nothing as well. It is very...'

Inconclusive.

And that's the problem. You can never put your finger on anything tangible at the Casa. There's no point at which you're able to go, 'A-ha, yes, *there* it is. That proves to me that John of God heals people.' Or that there are invisible beings here. Or that praying to triangles has any effect whatsoever. Or diving into waterfalls. I mean, of course, we *wish* it were that way, and wishing, like prayer, can be a potent force in and of itself. Just because we're not kids any more, doesn't preclude us from dreaming that magical things will happen. In fact, when we hear stories about Fabia being set free from an oppressive pattern of migraines and the story of Dermot's sister and her unfrozen shoulder, or listen to all the testimonials on Angela's video, it's tempting to forget that there's something called the Shaman Effect and believe 100% that invisible spirits were behind it all, demanding no further proof than John of God's word. But seriously, when you get down to it, apart from hearsay and some loose talk, where's the real evidence?

Danusia's suspicions aren't as pronounced at this point as mine are. In pain still with her back, and praying for a breakthrough, she's determined to give John of God the benefit of the doubt to the bitter end.

'It is time, we must go,' she sighs. João's back at the Casa today. Several more hours of sitting in current lie ahead. 'We will be late.'

Hm.

To be honest, I don't know if I have it in me to face this. These long meditation sessions are brutal; they sap my strength. Far more appealing would be to eat a leisurely breakfast, hang out in *Frutti's* reading the book Sheila gave me, go for a walk, explore Abadiânia, something I've not had time to do yet, and generally enjoy my last couple of days in Brazil. Indeed, I've just about made up my mind that that's what I'm going to do, when who should walk in but Marty the architect. More elusive than any entity since his eye operation, he drifts around the kitchen area, picking up a mug of tea and some toast, then comes on through and joins us, saying hello to the staff and waving at faces he recognizes, which may not be many, given that he doesn't have his spectacles on. Though I admit, his eyes do seem to be in tip-top condition, gleaming a glorious bluey-gray today.

'So the operation worked, then, you think?'

'My vision's not 20/20 yet,' he replies, 'but it's getting there.'

'Excellent. Good for you.'

Since this might be the only chance I get, I quickly raise the mystery of Danusia's friend last week and the way Marty came up to her in the street and reminded her that the 21st was the day she'd promised to put that photo in the wooden triangle. How did he know to do that? It's bugging me too now.

But apparently there's no mystery. At least not to him. He left his private plane sitting in an airport hangar in Rio de Janeiro, he says. When he departs Abadiânia, he has to fly back there to pick it up. 'That day, I was thinking about confirming my flight and wondering what the date was, that's all.'

'Yes, but you said exactly the right thing to her at the right time. I mean, that's too freaky to be a coincidence.'

'Why is it? Maybe it's the reason I came on this trip. I had to be here, so I could say that precise thing to Danusia at that precise moment.'

'Oh come on, now! You honestly believe that?'

'*You mean you don't?'* His eyes become bulgy, mocking me. 'Isn't that what life is, when you get down to it - a matrix of crossed paths and coincidences?'

I hadn't thought of it that way. Just sacred contracts, that's all. Spiritual agreements being played out as prearranged.

'We are all angels for one other, Cash. We have no idea how a random word, a gesture, or something we do might affect a stranger, or help him overcome a problem, or turn a corner in his life, or see the issues he's facing in a fresh light. That's not for us to know. We just have to trust and get on with it. We all have responsibilities and we all have a job to do. All it takes is openness. We have to remain authentically present, aware, and willing to participate. Sometimes we're angels for others, other times they're angels for us. The trick is to let it happen. Everybody tries so hard all the time. So much more would be achieved if we'd quit trying, relax into life, respond with trust to events instead of willfully and anxiously trying to control them, lower our resistance to believing that good things will happen, and let them develop in their own perfect way.'

As he speaks, his eyes never leave my face, not even when the conversation lapses while I'm thinking through the logic of what he's telling me.

'And...' I return after a while, 'when you say 'we' in all of this. '*We*' should quit trying so hard....you're talking about me, right?'

My question garners no reply. Without another word, but wearing a wicked smile, he takes a seat alongside Fabia and digs into his toast.

13

Amy's Story

Once again, today's session in the current room seems to last forever, as John of God works his way down a long, snaking line of pilgrims. There have to be three hundred Seekers in here this morning at least. For me and the rest of the worker bees, that means reprising our roles as energy donors, projecting loving thoughts at a procession of crutches, canes, tears, pained faces, expectant smiles, and endless need. When it's over, feeling woozy, and with my resources severely depleted, I grab a bowl of soup from the kitchen window and go join a chunky cream-colored poncho sitting at the farthest table.

After a spirited start, the Poncho Diva has been noticeably subdued of late. The Casa Effect, for her, is at the root of a profound awakening.

'I seem to be going the opposite way to everyone else,' she sighs, eyes fixed dreamily on a distant past. 'I was born a grown-up; now I feel like I'm getting younger all the time, finding what it's like to be a child.'

Apparently, her stay in Abadiânia has helped consolidate that. The longer Amy's here, the more beguiled she becomes by John of God and his entities.

'I had a miracle healing once,' she admits. 'That happened in a vortex too.'

'Oh yeah? What was wrong with you?'

'Multiple sclerosis.'

Without meaning to, I do a comedic double-take. 'You're kidding. You're telling me you were cured by a vortex – of *M.S.?*'

Nodding: 'I was diagnosed in 1990. Worst news I'd ever had.'

'Of course.'

'I remember being so stressed out at the time – there was a lot going on, with my kids and my marriage, and everything else. And of course stress only makes M.S. worse. In the end, I was in so much pain, there were times when I couldn't even get out of bed. The doctors said they couldn't do anything. It was a terrible time. Then, one day, we were going away on vacation and I had this inspiration out of the blue that I needed to be in Arizona. Don't know why, but I knew I had to go, just knew it. So we packed up the car and the whole family drove to Sedona. Ever been?'

I hadn't, I said.

'Oh you should, it's beautiful. Surrounded by these amazing red rock mountains – absolutely stunning. You'd love it. It's famous for having six vortexes, like the one here in Abadiânia, only smaller. The one we chose to visit was up a steep hillside, under a juniper tree. Cash, I'm telling you, I don't know how I made it up there. I had my cane with me, and this hill was – I mean, it was *impossible.* But something drove me on. A feeling, a compulsion. With my daughter's help, I fought and clawed my way to the top, and kept on going until I reached that damned juniper tree.'

Have you ever seen a juniper tree, by the way? It's not much to look at really; all twisted into and upon itself, like a wrung-out towel. Hardly the place for a miracle, you might think.

'Anyway, I sat under the tree at the center of the vortex and prayed. 'Please God, I don't want to be sick any more,' I said.

I kept repeating it, over and over. 'Please God, I don't want to be sick any more.' Then I continued meditating about all the wonderful things in my life and how I so wanted to continue living, but in a healthy body. When I was done, I took a long, deep breath in, and...that was it.'

'What was?'

'I knew instantly, Cash. I *knew* that, from that day forward, I was going to be well. That I *was* well. After a few minutes, I stood up, and – I swear – I felt this surge through my entire body, followed by an overwhelming feeling of being at peace, a feeling I'd never experienced before.'

'So what happened then?'

It's traditional in journalism for good news to be followed by a 'but'. There's always a catch.

'Nothing. I was cured.'

Oh.

'I didn't use my cane again. I left it there on the hillside under the juniper tree. Went home without it. When I met my husband at the bottom, I told him straight, 'I'm healed.' And I was. It was a miracle.'

What an incredible story.

Incredible, because I happen to know a little about M.S. I shared a house once in London with a middle-aged guy in the latter stages of the disease. When we met, Peter was already in the drooling, uncoordinated phase and unable to walk. The last time I saw him, he couldn't get food from the plate into his mouth without dropping it in his lap, and only two days earlier had set fire to a couch when his lips lost tensile strength and let go of a lit cigarette. Soon after, he died.

What I took away from that difficult experience was that there's no reasoning with M.S. at its worst. Left unattended, it can be an unrelenting and insidious tyrant, one that may be held at bay for a while with medication and other treatments, but not vanquished, and certainly not in simplistic ways - by dreaming, or positive thinking, for example, or making happy wishes under bushes. That's just not how it works. Or so I thought. I guess an aggressive state of denial might help. And I've read about instances where a radical change to a raw vegan diet has made enormous inroads for some M.S. patients. But those are rare. In most cases, unless I'm mistaken, the condition marches on through the nervous system as it did with Peter, like Rotor-Rooter, slowly decimating it.

So in Amy's case – well, actually, it's hard to know what to say. Perhaps it was a misdiagnosis, has she thought of that? Not M.S., but something like it? The medical profession is not infallible; it wouldn't be the first time a doctor got something wrong.

But she won't hear of it. To her mind, this was spontaneous remission. She's convinced she tapped into a greater energy. Divine intelligence, the universal life force, took control of her disease, helping her replace an old idea – that she was sick - with a new one: that her health was perfect and disease-free. Basically, that day on the mountain, she focused the power of her belief so unshakingly on getting well that her mind essentially strongarmed her body into compliance. That's what it seems like. If so, this opens a door on something very important in terms of healing.

According to author Alan Cohen, '[T]he only reason that miracles do not happen, when they do not, is that our minds are shut airtight against the possibility. We simply know too much and are well fortified with reasons why our good cannot come. In such a case, we are literally our own worst enemy, for in that moment we close the door through which our success could arrive.'[26]

---

[26] *A Daily Dose of Sanity*. Hay House, 2010.

What this means, if he's right, is that for a sick person to fully harness the power of the universal life force and conjure up a healing miracle, the first step has to be to align himself with the idea that he can be healed, *and be utterly convinced of it*. The secret is in believing.

Someone who proved this technique very convincingly, and created a small revolution in the process, was a spiritual trailblazer called Mary Baker Eddy (1821-1910).

I should say at this point that, when I was young, my parents were rookie Christian Scientists, my dad especially. So I know a little about Mrs. Eddy.

I know, for instance, that she was one of the late 19th century's greatest spiritual rebels. Mark Twain called her 'the most interesting woman that ever lived and the most extraordinary,' while simultaneously being convinced she was insane. When later she launched her own spiritual movement it was labeled a cult, not a religion.

As a very sickly and difficult kid, Mary suffered from what were discreetly referred to as 'hysterical illnesses', the doctors' way of saying she was quite mad. For instance, she regularly heard voices in her head, and at the age of eight would grab a sick dog, shout to her friends, 'Look what I can do, everyone!', then claim to heal it with her bare hands.

Things didn't improve any as she grew up: Mary was always ill with something and constantly searching for a solution. In 1862, she fell in with a healer from Belfast, Maine, called Phineas Parkhurst Quimby, a self-styled medical clairvoyant who'd formulated a technique for 'convincing' sick people back to health. It was a very clever idea, and I mention it only because I feel it may have a direct bearing on how John of God executes his own healings.

Here's Quimby's protocol. It's a little hard to get your mind around at first, but see what you think.

The material world we live in, Quimby asserted, is nothing more than a consensual illusion. Within that illusion, sickness doesn't exist. Despite appearing real, it's not real. It's merely a hoax, a fanciful indulgence of mortal mind, born of ignorance, erroneous thought, and the sinful neglect of our highest good. We believe illness exists and can harm us, and because we do, because we affirm it in this way, we give it the power to do just that – to bring us down. However, he went on, if man could somehow bypass the workings of his conscious mind, and all its troubling mechanism of personality, ego, doubt, fear, control, and insecurity, and tap instead into the pure, loving, universal energy of divine intelligence, which is eternal and all-powerful and knows nothing of disease, then this divine energy, suitably harnessed, could be channeled into the body and used to cancel out all signs of physical illness.

In short: mind over matter.

'Christ was the first practitioner of this science,' he told Mrs. Eddy. 'Anyone who masters this technique will be able to do what Jesus did: lay hands on the sick and heal them!'[27]

Now, to some, I'm sure, this seemed like a preposterous idea. Though not to Mrs. Eddy. She grasped its potential at once.

'Divine energy heals!' she cried. 'I see.' It was a life-changing proposition, but one that still required backing up with hard evidence.

---

[27] Mark 16, verses 15-18: 'And He said to them, 'Go into all the world and preach the gospel to every creature. He who believes and is baptized will be saved; but he who does not believe will be condemned. And these signs will follow those who believe: In my name they will cast out demons; they will speak with new tongues; they will take up serpents; and if they drink anything deadly, it will by no means hurt them; they will lay hands on the sick, and they will recover.'

Returning home, her mind on fire, she took Quimby's healing principles, reworked them, simplified them for the common audience, wrapped them up in Scripture, sprinkled in a few ideas of her own, and put it all together into a universal theory of healing she called Christian Science, which had one simple, sustained theme at its core. Boiled down to basics, it's this:

Everything in existence is a branch of divine energy. Everything we see and everything we are. Even the most apparently solid object, such as this book you're holding, or the car you drive, or the spot you park it in, or even the guy who gives you a parking ticket for leaving it there for ten minutes longer than you should, is just a bunch of matter vibrating at different frequencies, and it's these that give them the appearance of substance. And since divine energy vibrates at the highest frequency of all, it's not possible for it to get sick. How could it? It's God; it's perfect. Whereas disease, on the other hand, is a mortal affliction and therefore, almost by definition, a low vibration phenomenon.

It follows, then – and this was the root of Quimby's and, later, Mrs. Eddy's theories – that if you could somehow raise the frequency of a sick person's physical body and return it to a higher-vibration and more harmonious state, one that's closer to the perfection of divine intelligence, then the patient should, by rights – if all goes according to plan - get well.

'Health,' she wrote, 'is not a condition of matter, but of Mind.'

Well, Mrs. Eddy's critics – Mark Twain among them – had a field day with this. They thought it was the biggest load of nonsense they'd heard in a while.

But then something strange happened. Soon after she arrived at these breakthrough conclusions, she had an accident. On February 1st 1866, Mary Baker Eddy slipped on a patch of ice, taking a cataclysmic tumble that damaged her spine, as well as causing all kinds of internal injuries. Just this once, rather than subject herself to the whims and guesswork of a conventional allopathic doctor, as she normally would have done, she decided instead to put her new Christian Science principles to the test. She used the power of suggestion to stoically stare down the terrible pain she was in, denying it any power over her, telling herself she was fine and getting better with every passing minute. For the next few days, it was touch and go, but she carried on affirming her perfection, focusing solely on raising the vibration of her body by reminding herself of her unimpeachable status as a child of God, a satellite of divine love.

'God is perfect,' she told herself over and over. 'And since I am one of his children and therefore made in his image and likeness, I must be perfect too. In which case, how can I be sick? Perfect and sick are mutually exclusive concepts.'

Again, the debunkers quarreled with her hypothesis. 'But disease is real, Mary,' they told her. 'People suffer and die from diseases every day. How can something as ephemeral as mere thought heal a damaged spine and internal organs? What impenetrable gibberish is this?'

Maybe you were thinking the same thing.

Well, mock all you want, but the fact remains that, within days, Mary Baker Eddy was up and about as if nothing had happened. Her belief in her own wellness had apparently elevated her vibration to a wellness frequency, taking it from a state of 'I'm ill, poor me' to 'God is love and I'm perfect', and her body responded obediently. All trace of the spinal problems vanished, same way Amy's multiple sclerosis vanished when she sat praying under the juniper tree, and Mrs. Eddy recovered completely.

'In the degree,' author Ralph Trine once wrote, 'that you come...' into a vital realization of your oneness with the Infinite Spirit of Life...and in the degree that through this realization you open yourself to its divine inflow, do you set into operation forces that will sooner or later bring even the physical body into a state of abounding health and strength.'

Perhaps that's a clue to how faith healing of any sort works in the end. First comes your unswerving belief that healing is possible for you, even when common sense and your power of reason say otherwise. Only then do you receive proof of that healing.

Viewed from this level, it's suddenly much easier to understand where John of God is coming from, I think. Maybe when he says repeatedly and categorically in interviews that he doesn't heal anyone at the Casa, it's not to avoid prosecution for practicing medicine without a license, the way some of us first thought; no, it's because *he really doesn't heal anyone*. His role as a faith healer is primarily to invoke *a potential* for healing in the patient by creating an environment and conditions in which, not healing per se, but *the belief that restored health is achievable*, can occur.

Stay long enough at the Casa, re-connect yourself with the eternal flow of divine consciousness, submit wholeheartedly to the process, even the most far-fetched parts of it that rather test your patience, bathe in the waves of love and positive energy that fill this place, and inevitably, inexorably, things begin to change. They must, because your thoughts have changed, and when your thoughts change, the circumstances around you change. In time, the erroneous idea that is sickness, a low frequency vibrational state, is replaced in the patient's mind with a higher-vibrational expectation that he is going to get well.

Healing happens at the point where expanded expectation meets raised consciousness. It's not the faith of the healer that creates a miracle in the patient, it's the faith of the patient that a miracle can occur that does it.

'What did your doctor say when you arrived home?' I ask Amy as we make our way back to the *One Season*.

'Nothing, really. He had no clue how it happened. But that's okay. Sometimes you just have to accept that there's no explanation. It really was a miracle.'

'And this was when?'

'Fifteen years ago. I've not had a single symptom since.' Her little head shakes from side to side. Even she can't fully believe it. 'As far as I'm concerned there's a lot more going on here than we realize. I know it's frustrating to have a blocked ear. But we each have to find our own path. Maybe the Casa isn't the one for you, that's all.'

This is not a night to be outside. By 6.30pm, another fierce, blustery frontal system has bulldozed into Abadiânia. It's been this way our whole stay, with barely a let-up. For the next few hours, temperamental squalls chase each other along muddy alleys, lashing the rickety metal rooftops and sending stray dogs rushing for cover, lest they get beaten unconscious. For that reason, most members of our group have decided to return to their quarters, either to pack, ready for our departure Saturday morning, or just to get an early night.

At my end of the terrace, though, sleep proves elusive. There's too much going on, as always. Neighbors laughing and chatting. The loud grinding of gears from trucks splashing along the main street. The rhythmic tapping of a leaky gutter, in between pulses of seething wind that thrash the tin roof so hard you'd swear someone was throwing chandeliers at it, followed by distant rumbles of thunder.

Then closer rumbles of thunder.

Then closer still, until....

GABOOOOOOOMM!

...loud enough to rattle shelves in my bathroom, making the toiletries jiggle.

A good hour goes by at least before my mind can be persuaded to relax its grip and drift into dreams. Once again, they're the restless, turgid kind. The kind I've only ever had in Abadiânia, or during a flu epidemic. Collapsing buildings. An ocean liner with a horse's head and tail. There's singing I can't hear and faces I don't recognize, driving me toward a brown drawbridge. Folks inside the castle are tiny; they come up to my knees. Their pets are taller than they are. They drag me to a precipice. At the last minute, the ocean below surges up and, amid a suffocating terror, washes the precipice away, as a wave comes crashing over me, flinging me into a pit of –

Into a pit of what?

No idea. The sheer horror of dying wakes me up.

When I do, I'm sweating, and totally immobilized. I want to use the bathroom, but can't move. How strange is that! I tossed and wriggled so hard during the night apparently that I somehow got corkscrewed into the sheets and mummified myself. Unfathomably, the bedclothes are latticed across my body into a straitjacket, with one end hooked around my throat, tying me up like an old garbage sack. Facedown in the pillow, I'm stuck. My legs are stuck and my hands are stuck. In my semi-conscious state I can't figure out how to unravel myself.

It has to be gone midnight. Except for the occasional lingering growl of thunder, all's quiet outside, meaning there's nobody I can call on to help me.

'Calm down,' I instruct my panicking body. 'It's just a sheet - you'll figure this out.'

Working methodically for several seconds, I manage to wriggle half an arm free, enough to lever my face off the pillow.

Which is when I notice the light.

A bright orange light out of the corner of my eye.

A light that has never been there before and shouldn't be there now.

HOLY COW, THERE'S SOMEONE IN MY ROOM!!

'Aaaaghgh!' Hurtling off the bed to the floor, I drag everything with me - sheet, pillow, blanket - and collapse into a corner.

No, wait, it's not a someone – it's a someTHING. An orangey yellow blob hovering over the bed. You'll think I'm making this up, but I'm not. Big and bright and spherical, it floats in the air for a split-second more, then, in a blink, is gone and the room goes dark.

What did I just see?

What did I just see?

I know I'm not telling it right. Not in a convincing way. 'It was just a flash of lightning,' you'll say. But no. We've had a lot of those this trip, but for once it wasn't. 'Or a car passing by your window.' *No, it wasn't.* The road is not even close to my window. Or perhaps you're thinking, 'Oh, how convenient. A last-minute, souped-up thrilling twist to the story to round off an otherwise uneventful week. How neat.'

Well, I don't blame you for being skeptical, but you have my word on this. I swear on the life of my partner, whom I value more than anything else on this earth - I *vow* I am not making this up or lying to you.

There was a ball just now. A fluorescent ball of energy floating in my room. Size – arguable. But large. Larger than I am. Enough to almost fill my entire field of vision. A marmalade-colored orb drifting *this close* - two feet, maybe less - from my face, looking down on me and....well, I'm not sure what: sitting there, observing me.

As the full impact sinks in, my face turns hot, then cold. I'm shaking. Shivering. I just saw my first entity. My only entity. I SAW AN ENTITY!!!!!!

I should call somebody, but who? And how? My phone gave up on me in Rio and hasn't worked since. I don't believe this. Here it is, my big moment, and I have nobody to share it with.

But wait. It's not over. I thought it was, but now something else is going on too. Still sitting here hunched on the floor in the dark, back pressed against the wall, with my flimsy cotton sheet draped around me like Queen Nefertiti, I begin to notice a new sensation. A tingling that gradually expands into a slight pressure on both sides of my head, as if someone's forcing their thumbs against my ear canals. Not hard, but deliberately, for a second or two.

While this is happening, my left ear makes a rustling sound, then two more. As it does so, the room begins to swim. All of a sudden up is down. Bracing myself against the chair, I'm just starting to wonder if this is what an aneurysm feels like when - whoosh, I'm gripped by a renewed sense of spatial awareness, bringing everything closer - raindrops on grass, distant thunder, the drip-drip-drip of a drain, wind howling through treetops; the monotone chirrup of woodland creatures I should probably be able to name by now but can't. All of it comes crashing into me with extraordinarily crisp Dolby clarity, until my skull feels a thousand feet across.

I pivot my head delicately – can this really be happening? - scared that the effect may be momentary and one wrong move will reverse what just happened. But as far as I can tell it's permanent. As recently as yesterday I was convinced I would someday go the same way as Beethoven. Now look. And, more to the point, *listen*. It's all there. Everything I've been missing. The world.

Snap left – perfect. Snap right – perfect.

Oh lord.

Oh lord.

Oh Lord.

Maybe you still don't believe me. You think I'm imagining this. But these are my ears. I know what's true and what's real, and this is very real and very spectacular and it's *definitely* happening. Five arduous years of inner torment and everything being lop-sided, and muffled frustration, and having to pretend that I can tell what people are saying to me when I can't and I lost the conversation twenty minutes ago – it's all history. The ordeal is finally over. I can hear again.

14

A Day of Many Miracles

Sun-up finds me curled in a deckchair on the walkway outside my room, knees scissored to my chest, still cocooned inside the bedsheet, which I've slung over and around to make a toga. It's cold out here, though not enough to drive me back indoors. *Nothing* right now would drive me back indoors.

Today, I own the dawn. I own the landscape and everything in it, from the darkened fields at my feet to the distant hills, their snaggled crest scuffed by a lattice of clouds that partially hides the sun, which right now resembles the orb that paid me a visit only a few hours ago. Unlike the glowing pinpricks in Joe's pictures, or the photographs on the Casa wall that show a ghostly shaft of brilliant orange operating beside João as he works, my entity wasn't a shaft or an orb, it was a disc. Large and dense and perfectly round. I'm not complaining; I'm just grateful it showed up at all. Even if, by doing so, it shattered every theory I'd formulated thus far about the Casa being one giant placebo, the grand, cunning invention of a peasant boy's imagination. Now I'm forced to concede that it's a lot more than that.

There's a silhouetted knoll half a mile away. After a few minutes, a set of headlamps comes bobbing through a cleft in the hillside and disappears into a copse of trees. A car or truck. But here's the thing: for once I can not only see it, but I hear the rasping growl of its engine too. A year ago, last month, even yesterday, a vehicle like that would have had to travel the full half mile across country, swerve off the road onto this terrace, and probably plow right into my chair before I'd even know it existed. Now, it's right there, a subtle vibration rippling out through the morning air for the sole purpose of allowing my ears to acknowledge it. Instead of the blanket mush and howling tinnitus that haunted me before, I now have pitch, depth, clarity, nuance - same way you do. The car-engine, a husky rustle of leaves, the far-off grinding of someone's generator, a door slamming on main street, dogs - I can hear it all.

Inevitably at times like this you begin asking yourself the obvious questions: so did I dream it, then? Was there really an etheric orb in my room – because that takes a pretty huge leap of anyone's imagination - or was it simply a gigantic ball of wishful thinking? A last-ditch attempt to lend a layer of sense and meaning to this experience? Or maybe someone did in fact pass by carrying a flashlight and shine it through the window. I'm not ruling anything out.

Then again, if I did imagine the orb, which I'm 95% sure I did not, but *if I did*, how do you explain the fact that I have my hearing back? I wished for it last week – and this week it's here. The very thing that several doctors told me was impossible has happened anyway. That, to me, is simply a miracle. The kind of miracle that happens in profusion here in Abadiânia.

Fergus Tighe's 2010 movie, *John of God: Spirit Doctor of Brazil*, features a tall, thoughtful guy with a bald head and glasses called Jeff. He attends the Casa for an invisible operation. No physical invasion of the body takes places. Yet as he's strolling back along the street to his *pousada*, speaking as he goes about 'understanding the phenomena in his head, but not accepting them in his heart,' he's alarmed to see red spots on his sweatshirt. Lifting it up, he finds a single dribble of blood oozing from a small nick in his chest beneath his left nipple. When the blood keeps on coming, and coming, to the point where he has to mop it up with a tissue, he's left with no choice but to suppose that the entities may, after all, have performed an operation on him invisibly.

Now, what are we to think? Is it a set-up? Is Jeff acting as a P.R. stooge for the Casa and this is just a cleverly engineered stunt for the film?

You'd be forgiven for jumping to that conclusion. Until you realize that 'Jeff' is actually Dr. Jeffrey Rediger, a doctor at Harvard Medical School. He came to the Casa in his capacity as a conventional medical practitioner to investigate the interface between faith and medicine and to cast a genuine and fascinated, if somewhat wary eye, I'm sure, over what was going on here. He even helped out with some of the physical operations, though without ever being able to explain much of what he saw John of God do. So when his heart began bleeding that day, he was thrown for a loop.

'I feel afraid,' he admits in the film. 'I don't feel violated, just not in control.'

That says it all. Come to the Casa, and you surrender control to something far greater, whether you have a full understanding of what that something greater is or not. When you have one of the heads of Harvard's prestigious medical school bleeding inexplicably *for an entire hour* from the pores in his chest and being genuinely mystified by it, you know you've crossed a threshold. Different rules apply now. Where once this might have seemed like a bunch of clever hypnotic trickery dressed up in layers of ceremony and faux religious significance, now, suddenly, a major shift has occurred. You have tangible proof that something extraordinary is going on here.

*

To my right hangs a small hand-mirror, dangling from a nail on the wall. As the sun exploits widening cracks in the clouds, a hummingbird darts down from above the hotel roof and flies beak-first into the glass. Mistaking the land beyond the mirror for somewhere it can actually go, it begins pecking at its own reflection. Tap-tap-tapping, moving on, tap-tap-tapping again, moving on; this angle, that angle, up, down, every which way. This time yesterday the bird's pointless endeavor would have been lost on me. It would have come and gone and I'd never have known. Now, I swear I can hear every flap of its tiny wings, in the same way that I can pick up every whispered word of a very private conversation that an elderly couple is having in a nearby room, unaware that somebody in a chair outside is eavesdropping on them. Somebody who hasn't been able to eavesdrop on people's private conversations for almost five years.

'Yes, it is morning. Yes, it's almost time for breakfast,' I want to answer them. 'And yes, one of the showers in this block has been known to electrocute people, we just don't know which one.'

Oh, it feels so good to be back.

Your final day at the Casa is little more than a routine wrap-up for the week. An opportunity to go before John of God one last time and let the old boy look you over to approve the spirits' handiwork before sending you on your way. That's his job. Yours is to stand there, say thank-you, hand him any flowers you may have left over, then step aside.

Still gloating massively over having an entity visit me last night - 'Yes, *an entity!* Plain as day. It hovered above my bed. Seconds later, bingo, I got my hearing back. I know, I can hardly believe it myself!' - I quite naturally consider myself a very satisfied customer indeed, one who owes John of God a hefty slice of gratitude for what he's done. Or, if not done, facilitated. I know the non-believers remain unmoved and will continue to insist that he's a quack. That his silly homogenized herbs are bogus and simply a reminder of how gullible a person can be when he's desperate; that his physical surgeries are a cruel and barbaric hoax, and the crystal bed therapy one more way of persuading visitors to part with their money, on top of the bottled water, on top of all the crystals, CDs, knickknacks, and other merchandise they bought from his shop. I take all of that on board. Usually, though, those who are the most skeptical about something are the ones who haven't experienced it firsthand; they enjoy the luxury of standing back and, when the so-called healer turns out to be a charlatan after all, laughing heartily at those who fell for his trickery, and saying, 'I told you so.'

I understand the risks of being a believer.

All I can tell you is this: after years of frustration, my hearing's pristine again in both ears – snap: 100%; snap: 100% – and I'm as good as new. Quite honestly, I can ask for nothing more. Let the debunkers think what they like.

With more than a touch of euphoria in the air, breakfast today at the *One Season* felt like Mardi Gras: a non-stop chorus of vibrant sounds: the rattle of cutlery, people shouting and laughing and singing, flipflops clopping over tile, the toaster popping up, the sizzle of eggs on a griddle, a dozen conversations overlapping each other. I rejoiced in it all.

'This is your last chance to ask John of God something,' a smiling Marty told me on our way to the Great Hall for the last time. 'So be ready with your questions.' As he peeled away, he called after me, 'And don't forget to buy a triangle.'

'As a souvenir, you mean?'

'No. Get João to sign it, then it becomes a sacred item. A

connection is formed and you take the power of the entities home with you.'

'I do?' Well, who can resist that?

Ten minutes later, gripping my triangle to my chest, I trek into the Great Hall and get in line. Noticeably, on this occasion, the pace is leisurely. The old hands who were so frantic a week ago are now happy to wait their turn; nobody scrambles to be first. That's the Casa Effect at work, or maybe the passionflower herbs. Either way, twelve days in Abadiânia will rob you of most of your silliest impulses. By the end you're so calm and your ego's been so disarmed by compassion, not to mention daily infusions of unconditional love, that your heart's a swamp of vulnerability, leaving you way too relaxed to fight for anything, much less something as meaningless as being at the head of a line; you're just happy to be here, among friends, similar minds, basking in the wonder of the healings going on all around you.

Easing through the blue door again, I tiptoe into the current room – six inches, stop; six inches, stop - past this week's new intake of worker bees, and around the corner to where João sits, flanked by his usual bank of attendants as they guide people to left and right, translating where necessary, and occasionally stepping up to seize a gigantic bouquet thrust at João by another satisfied customer.

The Big Man is in a good mood this morning, I can tell. Glasses off, he leans back in his seat, wearing a sky-blue jerkin that really makes his eyes pop. I've heard tell that sometimes they change color to match those of the entity he's channeling. A week ago I'd have laughed at the very idea. Now I'm not so sure.

As the line dribbles by, he graces each beseeching face with a broad smile, muttering occasional prayers to people if he feels the urge, even reaching out his hand now and then to comfort and reassure.

When my turn comes, the male attendant beckons me with a whispered 'Please.'

'Hi, I'm Cash...' Beaming like a lunatic, I hand him my triangle and a pen. '...you may remember me from the other day.' The attendant translates my words as I go. 'I had the ear thing going on. Well, I just wanted to say what an amazing breakthrough experience it's been. And...'

As I talk, he scribbles his signature onto one side of the triangle. Such odd handwriting he has. You know when a button's about to come off your coat and all the threads are hanging loose in little hoops? It looks like that.

'...before I go, though, I have one last question....'

Handing it back, he beckons to the next person in line.

'Wait - I'm not done.' As *per* Marty's advice, I'd thought of a question: would it be possible to arrange an interview with him for the book I'm writing?

He's the star of the show, after all. And although I know he's bound to trot out the same bullet points he does to all journalists, at least they'll have been trotted out to me directly, they won't be lifted from a DVD this time, or a book by Josie RavenWing.

But my plan backfires. The instant I start to put this to him, he becomes visibly irate. 'No questions!' he snaps.

'But I was told th...'

'No questions!'

Scowling, he flaps me away with his hand and moves on to the woman behind me, a young, buxom creature in a tight white blouse and shorts. At this point, his smile returns.

Spotting how hurt I am, the sympathetic attendant leans over. 'John of God does not answer questions this day.'

Er, yes, I kinda gathered that. So why would Marty tell me he does if he doesn't?

Only as I step outside the door into a fresh splash of warm

morning drizzle does it dawn on me that I've been set up. Aaah, yes, I see now.

It was a playful reminder, wasn't it? Marty's way of saying let go, quit trying so hard, quit wanting to know, accept the proof of your eyes and ears and stop asking why and how. No interview, no awkward probing about the workings of this or that. Just leave things as they are.

Acknowledge, accept, trust.

Be.

Thanks. I get it. I was a little slow on the uptake, but it's starting to sink in.

Our goodbye party, held at a pizzeria on the main drag, is a wonderfully relaxed celebration of what has been a groundbreaking week. Most of us are declaring it a success on some level. Fabia is rid of her migraines. Dermot's sister's shoulder remains unfrozen. Then there's Marty, who had his eyesight restored – a major, *major* coup, that. And let's not forget my ears; big kudos to John of God for pulling off such an amazing breakthrough. Only Dermot has nothing to report. Mainly because he's not here. On João's instructions, he was rushed in for his second surgery and is holed up in his room once again, recuperating.

Even Danusia, the Polish fitness instructor, has made welcome headway. The pain in her back has eased considerably.

'Look how I am going - yes!' she squeals, stretching her torso in all directions before calming down. 'But still, I am worried. In the current room today, I am asking João the question: what is right to be doing in my life?' She's been debating for a while if she should stick to being a personal trainer or follow a new passion – photography, which she's also very good at. 'I don't know which of the ones is right. So I ask João and...'

'Wait,' I interrupt her. 'João let you ask him a question?'

'But of course.'

I don't believe it. 'And he gave you the answer?'

'He said the photography. Which is what I am wanting – yes! Why you say that?'

'Oh, no reason.'

A week or so in Abadiânia works its magic in more subtle ways too, producing many low-key transformations, the kind that don't make headlines.

Amy admits to being replenished - feeling younger and freer than she has in a long while. Marianne, whose husband cheated on her with the next-door neighbor, has already decided which lake he can go and jump into. Her mind's made up - she's divorcing him the moment she gets home. Angela's heading off to film school in London. Mary has made a resolution: she's going to find herself a man when she returns back. No more singleton status for her. With any luck, he'll be a railway station announcer; that would be a perfect match. And Lukas – amazing, perky, brave Lukas - is taking a huge step forward in his life. He's setting up a health foundation, a move predicated on the idea that he will survive long enough to do so, as a way of bringing other people to see John of God.

'So what happened to you today?' I ask him, first chance I get. 'Anything?'

'Oh yes. I'm cured.'

'NO!' His snap announcement elicits a small round of applause. 'You're *kidding* me. Just like that? Completely?'

He nods. Completely. 'João says the surgery worked. My cancer is gone.'

'And you believe him?'

Shoot! Not the right thing to say *at all*. As far as Lukas is concerned, the death sentence has been lifted. He believes he's cancer-free because John of God says he is. And belief is 90% of it. Let's not go planting seeds of doubt.

'My goal now,' he concludes, 'is to help someone else do what I've done. Many people would benefit from visiting the Casa, but they don't have the means to get here. I think it should be open to everyone. So that's what I'll do. I want to help as many as I can to fly to Brazil for treatment.'

Others in the group are considering a similar initiative. In Lukas's case, however, the gesture strikes me as particularly noble, given that he is a doctor of many years' standing. A very smart man; certainly not the type to be bamboozled by conjuring tricks. What he's been through these past few days represents a tectonic shift in his understanding of how healing works and how miracles can happen. Having played the role of laboratory rat back in Switzerland for years, witnessing first-hand the epic and ghastly bungling of his own profession, it's like a window has opened on a whole new landscape of possibility. In the absence of categorical proof that regular physicians have the faintest notion what they're talking about when it comes to treating disease, he was finally driven to extremes, turning away from allopathic medicine toward a road of faith and natural healing. I'm only sorry he didn't do this earlier, before they removed half his organs.

Of course, I can't offer you any credible proof that Lukas is cancer-free. We only have John of God's word for it. Yet there's something about that word that, when you're here, is very convincing. It essentially takes up Mary Baker Eddy's basic principle and runs with it, supporting the idea that with a strong mental conviction, an unyielding *determination* to achieve perfect health, and a readiness to put doubt aside and allow yourself to be open to a miracle, you're already well on the way to recovery. Lukas believes 100% that John of God has the power to execute a healing and rid him of his cancer. With such an extreme, unwavering belief, it wouldn't surprise me if this was enough to raise his vibration from one of sickness to one of good health, enough to keep him alive.

15

Returning Home

Our final morning in Abadiânia dawns gray and cold, same as usual. Above us, a doom-laden sky sobs fitfully to the very end.

Traditionally, tour groups get a bit sentimental on the last day, and ours is no different. Having started out as total strangers, a marvelous kinship has built up between us based on our shared experience. The enlightening conversations we had together, the camaraderie, the adventure, the tears – it made a world of difference, and I'm going to miss it.

Between loading up the minivan, hugging each other, and exchanging phone numbers, we cluster into twos and threes for photos. Not everyone's leaving today. Frank's staying on until Tuesday. Others head out tomorrow first thing. Including Dermot, who had to switch flights at the last moment after João sprung the whole second-operation thing on him. Because he's confined to quarters, we won't get the chance to wish him well, and are forced to send supportive messages via his sister.

'T'ank you all,' she says, accepting hugs for two. 'Oil tell 'im.'

Good. Let him know that we'll be thinking of him.

As I'm lugging my bags onto the bus, Wendy comes pushing through the crowd last minute, and presses a sheaf of notes into my hands. 'Here, take this with you.'

'Why? What is it?'

What it *is* is a document. A bunch of handwritten notes listing many of the things she told me these past few days, about ways to cleanse, protect, and heal the body. Out of the corner of my eye, I see her watch eagerly as I give it a cursory glance. There's no time to read it now. It does, however, bring to mind a question I've been meaning to ask her all along. This may be the one chance I'll get.

'Forgive me,' I say, cramming the papers into my already-overloaded backpack. 'Not to put your work down or anything - I love your passion - but, I mean, why? Why is it so important that I know this stuff? What's in it for you?'

At first, she's taken aback that anyone would think of asking such a thing. Then she realizes I'm serious and, lips churning, toys for a while with how to answer, settling in the end for the blunt truth.

'I've lost almost everyone I loved to cancer,' she says. 'They went..,' – snapping her fingers - '...like that. In a few short years. My parents. Both my brothers, my sister, two grandfathers, two cousins - all gone. There's a predisposition toward cancer in my family, and I could be next. That's all. But you know what? Nothing is set in stone. For previous generations, it was down to a lack of information. They were victims of ignorance. They didn't know what we know: that their food and environment and thoughts and medication had the power to kill them. They took their chances. Ate what they liked, smoked, drank, took baths in chlorinated tap-water, they didn't think to exercise, and they trusted doctors to be acting in their best interests. So it's not exactly a surprise that they got sick. But I'm not them, am I? That's what I figure. I have a chance to break the pattern. Maybe there's no such thing as predisposition. Maybe it's just a choice: a healing path or a destructive path, and I don't need to go down the same route they did.'

She turns away, pondering the wisdom of her own words. When she looks back, she surveys me with moist eyes. 'I keep telling myself: there is another way to do this. There has to be.'

Exactly! Echoing what Geena said.

'You're on the radio, Cash. You can get that message out to people.'

A nice idea, I tell her, but it won't happen. There's little appetite on primetime TV or radio for her brand of heresy. Not any more. Everything's spin and politics these days; handshakes and back scratching.

She, more than anyone, understands that broadcasting companies rake in big bucks from food and drug advertising. This puts them in the pockets of their major sponsors, the very corporations that have the most to lose by allowing the truth about their products and services to leak out on news and magazine shows. And even when drugs and medical practice do come under scrutiny, it's always done in a deftly political way in the name of 'balance', when really they're just dodging the real issues. To that end, an 'expert' doctor will usually be hauled in, even though this person is all too often, by tradition and training, a lapdog of the pharmaceutical or food industry, paid to attack anything remotely alternative or groundbreaking.

Given what happened to Rene Caisse, and given that the system is, today, more severely rigged in favor of the medical giants than ever, and that it's illegal in America for anyone to even *suggest* there might be a cure for any of our major diseases, does Wendy honestly think that alternatives to mainstream medicine, say, or a small *China Study*-style exposé of how the casein in cow's milk may lead to cancer in some people, even if they're proved to be valid, are going to be allowed to reach the minds of average Americans? There's too much money sloshing around the system for that to happen.

She looks hurt. 'So put it in your book, then. Let people find out that way...'

Er...

'...but *whatever happens...*' She drags the split ends out of her face with both hands to expose a rebellious grin - '...look after yourself, alright? Remember, you're all you've got.'

'Thank you. I will. You too.'

Still grinning through faint tears, she gives a fond little wave, then steps out of the way just in time for the driver to slide the door of the bus closed.

But as it slams, something odd happens. Something bad.

The sudden compression causes an unexpected shift in my left ear. First I get a grating noise, like crackers, then what sounds like a muffled thud that resonates throughout my head. For a second or two it feels like I've been shot. With that single slug to the brain, the whole world around me is sucked into itself. Shortly after that, half of it disappears altogether, as if I just put earmuffs on, taking with it, in an instant, any hope I had of hearing clearly ever again.

During the first few days that followed my return to Los Angeles, I came in for a surprising amount of flak about the Brazil trip, as unsympathetic and doubting friends challenged almost every story I told about the Casa.

'Soup empowered by divine energy, eh?'

'An orb floating over your bed, eh?'

'You got your hearing back, eh?' they scoffed. 'But wait - then you went deaf again just before you got back? Hm, yes, I see. And by the way, where are your photographs of those orbs in the field?'

Ah.

Not only that, but, invariably, conversations would run into impenetrable barriers of logic. For example, when I mentioned to an elderly academic friend, someone who's a slave to conventional medicine and doesn't make a move without her internist's permission, that I'd had an operation in Brazil, she not only didn't believe me, but became quite agitated.

'On which part of your body?'

'I really don't know for sure,' I told her.

'How can you have an operation and not be sure? Where was it?'

'On my liver, I think. That's where the pain was the day after.'

'What was wrong with your liver?'

'Nothing. The operation was for my ears.'

'You had an operation on your liver to fix your ears?'

'Yes.'

'Show me the scar.'

'There is no scar.'

'I'm sorry, but if you - had - an - operation...' She smacked the table insistently in time with her words. '...you'd - have - a – scar.'

'No I wouldn't. It was an invisible operation.'

'Ohhhhh, an *invisible* operation.'

'The entities went in through the back of my head.'

'How do you know?'

An excellent question, and one I have an answer to, as it turns out. But only because something else happened to me during my time at the Casa that I haven't told you about. Something equally as bizarre as finding a glowing orb in my room, but which I didn't discover until after I got home. I was having my hair cut one day, when my hairdresser blurted out, 'What's this on your head?'

Of course, I had no idea what he meant.

It turned out to be a circle. A perfect circle, completely white, about two inches in diameter, etched into my hair, but around the back where I couldn't see it. I'd swear on a stack of Bibles – and so would my hairdresser - that it hadn't been there when I left for Brazil, but, by the time I came home, bingo, there it was, and it became quite the talking point. Everyone commented. Strangers stared. I have countless witnesses. Like crop circles, its beauty lay in its mysteriousness, I suppose, just sitting there, perfectly round with no hint as to what might have caused it, but looking as if I'd carefully bleached that one spot, doing so merely for effect, to get attention.

Later, most alarmingly, it started to grow, forcing me to wear a hat for weeks, until it spread around the back and began to look a little more natural, the way it does today. All the same, it was one of the most peculiar things I've seen. Angela's best guess was that the white spot indicated the point where the entities went in.

'So these spirits entered through your head,' my skeptical academic friend said again, 'to perform an operation on your liver.'

'Correct.'

'To heal your ears.'

'Correct.'

'Even though it made no difference whatsoever and you're still half-deaf?'

'Correct.'

'Pah!' she snapped, dismissing me with a thorny glare. And the subject was never brought up again.

Other things my friends found hard to believe: the fact that I insisted on sticking rigidly to the Casa's forty-day protocol, for example, abstaining from sex, from eating pepper, from heavy lifting, and other activities that tend to hijack the body's energy and divert it away from healing. Most people found this funny. The 'no sex for a month and a half' rule alone turned a lot of heads. But what the heck? I'm an all-or-nothing guy. If you're going to do something as extraordinary as this, why not give it your best shot? That's how I see it.

Second of all, they were shocked at the drastic changes I'd made to my health regime after Brazil, in the sense that I didn't have one at all before I left, and now I did.

Gone was the cake-a-day habit, the burgers and fries, pizza, sausages – all the stuff I love, basically – to be replaced with a predominantly vegetable protein-based diet of leafy greens, fruits, nuts, seeds, sea vegetables, and sprouts. All Wendy's fault, of course. For two straight weeks she'd scared the bejeebers out of me with her endless warnings and lectures, recommending websites I should visit, studies I urgently needed to see, authors whose books I must read. In the face of this constant barrage, how could I not take notice?

So I did as I was told: I read the books (some of which I've quoted from in this one) and dutifully surfed the Internet for helpful research, until I was substantially less ignorant than before. I began to exercise more as well; I bought a trampoline because Wendy said it was good for cleaning toxins out of my lymph nodes, even though I have no idea what my lymph nodes are. I started drinking organic fruit and vegetable juices. I quit putting harmful soaps, shampoos, sunscreens, and other chemicals on my body. We had a water filtration system installed throughout our entire house to cut chlorine and other potentially unsafe chemicals from our water. I cut down on my exposure to electromagnetic radiation. I organized cleanses to flush out my tubes and organs. But above all I began picking the foods I ate using my brain, not my emotions.

'Just because something tastes fantastic, doesn't mean I have to eat it.' That's what I kept telling myself.

My love of refined sugar and junk food would have to be curtailed for the greater good. No more fun trips to the coffee shop for a latte and a slice of banana loaf - up to that point one of the staples of my day, *every day*. I also organized a massive spring clean of my refrigerator and cupboards, tossing out any products that contained chemicals and corn sugar (high fructose corn syrup), which, I discovered in horror, was almost all of them, from supermarket bread to sodas.

Everything that might make my body too acidic, thereby contributing to inflammation or degenerative diseases, went in the trash.

Goodbye, ketchup (corn sugar was the third listed ingredient on the label); farewell, bottled barbecue sauce (fourth listed ingredient); adieu, delicious-but-probably-because-they-contain-so-much-sugar *Rice Krispies* (corn sugar fourth listed ingredient), and so on.

At times it seemed like a bitter divorce. The love affair was over; we were dividing up our things and going our separate ways. Sad, but, since fructose, according to research, promotes the growth of tumors in the pancreas[28], cake in the end didn't have a leg to stand on. Henceforth, white flour and refined sugar would be relegated from starring roles in my diet to occasional minor walk-ons.

After this, I crammed Wendy's document in a drawer and forgot about it.

But then, about a month later, something happened that put me in a tailspin and sent me running off to find it again.

Going to my computer one morning, I opened my inbox and found an email from my father. 'Hi there,' it began.

My whole body tensed up.

Dad's emails are like hand grenades with the pins taken out. Harmless enough on the face of it, but liable to go off in

---

[28] University of California Los Angeles study, published in Cancer Research Journal, August 2010.

your face when you least expect it. A line or two of pleasantries, then - BOOOOM! - it blows, leveling your self-esteem and ripping the still-beating heart from your chest.

One time, for a dare, I sent him a message of three simple words: 'I love you.' That's all it said, just to see what happened. Well, I tell you, the fall-out from this one gesture was almost thermonuclear in its intensity. His response ran to three pages and dripped with vitriol, beginning with, 'You don't know the meaning of the word love...', exploding from there into great fireballs of rage and disdain. So you can see what I'm dealing with. I'm mature enough now, after Brazil, to know that he is simply transferring the anger at his own father and the frustrations of his life onto me. It's not personal. The guy's pissed at the world in general and needs a scapegoat. 'I am here to learn from him,' I tell myself. 'He is my damaged daughter.'

Even so, it can be daunting when it happens. At a bare minimum, I was half-expecting to be hauled over the coals for *daring* to break a blissful twelve-year silence.

But that just shows how wrong you can be.

Remarkably, there was nothing of the sort. Instead, he seemed glad to be back in touch. Not overjoyed – let's not go crazy; this is my dad after all - but glad. His words were upbeat and almost lavishly kind, making no mention at all of the deep, dark bog our relationship had been wading through for more than a decade, except to agree with me that twelve years of silence between father and son was outrageous and indefensible. Life is short, was the message, and although we wouldn't always see eye-to-eye, we should at least try to swallow our differences and start a new chapter.

Incredible.

Angela, I'm sure, would attribute this dazzling turnaround to behind-the-scenes string-pulling by the entities.

'There – you see, I told you so,' she'd say. 'They helped bring about a long hoped-for reconciliation. How can you possibly doubt their existence now?'

And on the face of it, it certainly seems like a miracle. But how will we ever know? For that reason, I'm forced to reserve judgment.

In any case, the rest of his message was chatty and filled with the minutiae of life in a north of England village: the state of his garden, the plight of the friends he meets each week in the pub. All pretty routine stuff, and politely innocuous. For the first time in more than a decade, an overture from me had landed butter side up, and all was mellow and rosy between us once again. That is, until I reached the last paragraph, where, casually, almost as an afterthought, I found he'd slipped in an update on his health. At 84, it wasn't holding up too well, he said. 'The past three years have been rough.'

This was followed by a shock announcement.

He'd been diagnosed with cancer.

My god, not him as well!

Naturally, his doctors had leapt into action at once, the way doctors do, performing multiple operations on his bladder, removing tumor after tumor - six in all – never once stopping, I suspect, to question the cause, or how he might have arrived at the low-vibration state that caused him to become diseased. Was it the eighteen cups of strong black tea he drinks every day perhaps? Or the sugar and milk he puts in each cup? Or the various kinds of meat he eats for dinner every evening? Or the thousands of cigarettes he smoked over a lifetime? Such issues never came up. It was straight to the operating table with him, followed by a course of heavy medication. Medication that had given rise to some dire side-effects, apparently, including severe breathing problems, which then required further medication to suppress them.

The news came as a terrible blow, especially in light of everything I'd learned in Abadiânia. First my mother dies of cancer; now this beastly condition was trying to claim my father too.

Big flashing neon warning signs started going off in my head, enough to propel me upstairs to dig Wendy's health formula out of the drawer. Maybe there was something in this eccentric thesis of hers that could nudge my dad in the direction of good health, but the natural way this time, without resorting to further surgery and harmful drugs.

Sifting through, I cherry-picked a handful of relevant tips. I sent him information about Essiac tea, for example. Sounding very knowledgeable, I'm sure, I also emphasized the apparent benefits of drinking nutritious organic green juice each day for its beneficial cell-building enzymes. I advised him to cut back drastically on anything he was putting in his body that might be making his system too acidic and possibly promoting disease, and told him that he should switch to a vegetable-based diet, as this, according to *The China Study*, had an inhibiting effect on cancer. This, and some other stuff was packed off to him without delay. It's the least I could do.

A week later, I heard back.

He was grateful for my concern, he said, sounding genuine enough, but he wouldn't be adopting any of the suggestions I'd sent him. For a start, he didn't believe they'd work. Also, he'd prefer to take the advice of a qualified medical professional about the state of his body over that of a journalist. Which is a fair point. He'd fallen back, he added, on the teachings of Mary Baker Eddy and Christian Science, and was working daily to affirm the erroneous nature of disease, replacing thoughts of illness with reminders of his divine status as a child of God, born in His image and likeness, and therefore perfect.

Just in case, though, further surgery had been scheduled for later that month. Yes, the side-effects might be debilitating, and cutting the tumors out by no means ensured that more wouldn't take their place, but, he said, he felt he had to continue down the route he was on - switching to a different diet and cutting back on the toxins being, in his eyes, a cuckoo way to deal with a life-threatening illness.

'I will continue fighting it,' he concluded stoically. 'And we'll see what happens.'

Oh.

Needless to say, I was sad for days afterwards.

16

The 7 Pillars of Self-Healing

Now that we're on the home stretch, I feel justified in presenting to you a round-up of what I learned in Abadiânia during the twelve days I was there and the way, I believe, based on what I've seen, the process of self-healing works.

I say *self*-healing simply because we are active participants in the process.

True healing, the kind of healing that tackles the causes of a problem rather than merely suppressing the symptoms, is not a passive endeavor. Healthcare providers must always be our first stop, that goes without saying, and they work wonders very often, but even then it's only if we're prepared to play our part too.

For simplicity, I'm lumping the principles into a single list, which I call 'the pillars of self-healing'. Seven vital components that need to be present, I would suggest, if we're to nurture harmony in our body and return it to a state of balance that is its birthright, and a precursor to good health.

These are:

1. A Willingness to Change
2. Cleansing and Purifying the Body
3. Self-Nurturing
4. Fortitude

5. Surrender
6. A Raised Level of Consciousness
7. Getting Out of Your Own Light

Pillar #1: A Willingness to Change. It stands to reason that if what you've been doing so far brought you to a place of sickness, doing more of it will likely make you even sicker.

What I've heard people say in Abadiânia, and what I'm coming to believe is probably true, is that oftentimes disease is not a random stroke of bad luck, the way we think it is; many times it's a deliberate, purposeful act of rebellion by the body, intended to shake us up and force us to reevaluate the way we're living and consider making changes. Issues vary from person to person, of course, but if your body is in crisis, then more than likely it's just letting you know that change is overdue. You're being invited to surrender up anything that no longer serves you, including habits, routines, old behaviors, stale conflicts, old fears, negativity, toxic foods, drugs, and chemicals, or whatever else has outlived its purpose in your life, and to switch instead to a more beneficial regime, one that can begin to correct longstanding damaging patterns.

Example: the average person in America drinks fifty gallons of soda each year. How can that much sugar and all those chemicals and flavorings NOT eat away at the body's tissue and nervous system? By the same token, how can a radio journalist eat cake and pastries every day of his life and drink 5000 lattes, and not eventually plug up his body with mucus, leading to some kind of disease – deafness perhaps?

To me, this is starting to make perfect sense. The Western lifestyle is killing us. Our poor, defiled organs are struggling to cope with the harm we continually inflict on them without even thinking. With stress. With discord. With struggle. With fear. With radiation from excessive exposure to technology. With poor nutrition. I see that now. I see it in my own life; I see it in the lives of others.

We each must be the custodian of our own mind and body. In the end, it's all down to us. There's no white knight coming to save us. The government can't. Big corporations won't. Doctors do their best, but there's a limit to what they can achieve. Ultimately, we are entirely responsible for doing the right thing and taking care of ourselves. Unless positive changes are made, physically, emotionally, mentally, psychologically, spiritually, wherever the problem lies, then the body has nothing new to respond to and will most likely stay in the same old low-vibration sickness state, until eventually it breaks down completely. When it does, we need to realize that it didn't happen on the spin of a roulette wheel. There was no bad luck involved. We initiated it ourselves.

Pillar #2: Cleansing and Purifying the Body. To help a new health regime kick in and begin raising the body's vibration, it seems we have to at least consider ridding ourselves of low-energy detritus from the old regime - any toxins or other demons that may have been responsible for tearing it down in the first place.

First and foremost, we have to get the right advice, and also do research, looking into possible holistic, organic ways to cleanse the body internally so that it can function at its best, ridding it of built-up toxic materials such as heavy metals, hardened mucus, stones, old rotting food, parasites, or any other malingering pathogens that may be living in our system. Apparently, fasting, done correctly and under supervision, is a time-honored way of tackling this. But there's also colonic irrigation. Many people swear by colonics, while others flinch at the very idea. Still, a colon cleanse of some kind has value, it would seem, along with liver and gallbladder flushes, a kidney cleanse, parasite cleanse, heavy metals cleanse, or whatever else the individual body may need.[29]

Of course, a process like this doesn't happen overnight. It takes time. There's sacrifice involved. But it sounds to me like a good and worthy sacrifice, one that could pay dividends over the longer term.

Who knows, with just a little extra time, effort, and discipline we may be able to establish a new ground zero for ourselves - a clean, uncompromised, toxin-free foundation from which to rebuild a healthy system that will support us for years into the future.

Pillar #3: Self-nurturing. Writing in the late 19th Century, Ralph Trine said, 'Suffering is designed to continue only so long as sin continues.' By 'sin' he was referring to the sin of abusing the body. 'The moment the violation ceases, the moment one comes into perfect harmony with the law, the cause of the suffering ceases; and though there may be residing, within, the cumulative effects of past violations, the cause is removed, and consequently...even the disease's condition that has been induced from past violations will begin to disappear...'

That's why it's important to treat yourself with respect and kindness.

The value of self-nurturing has been hammered home by countless health professionals over the years. We could pull up a thousand articles on the Internet right now that tell us everything we need to know to bring our bodies into balance and harmony. Yet do we pay any attention? I can only speak for myself here, but the answer is no. Mostly, I read the

[29] Every body is different – that's the key. No two people are physically the same, so our needs are not the same. That's why we're constantly being urged to consult with a suitably trained healthcare professional before we undertake procedures of any kind. It's an excellent idea. In all cases, get the best advice and information possible ahead of time; do only what's right for your particular body. Take no risks with your health.

articles, watch the documentaries, absorb the statistics about diabetes, stress, heart disease, cancer, and the rest, enough to be frightened out of my wits by them, then step over it all and continue on as I did before, unable to shake off old habits, even though I'm aware they're killing me.

'I'll take my chances,' is what I say. And what most people say.

Then of course we wonder why, many years later, our bodies have given up on us, we're swallowing handfuls of expensive medication, and being informed by doctors that our condition is irreversible.

Fact is, the wellness experts aren't lying to us. The health and fitness craze isn't a kooky fad that's bound to pass in time if we just give it long enough, the way some of us had hoped. The advice we've been pounded with all these years actually means something. Even the most sedentary cake-addicted journalist has to confront the facts eventually. To get healthy and stay that way is going to take consistent, positive effort in four main areas: a) exercise - including cardio, weights, and yoga or some other form of stretching; b) meditation to still the mind and de-stress the body; c) deep breathing so that the cells of the body are fed with generous amounts of oxygen every day; and d) balanced meals bursting with the right kind of nutrition for our body type, providing non-toxic food to nourish the cells, bones, blood, muscles, organs, and so on.

After hearing it repeatedly, that health requires affirmative action and that the path to healing starts on the inside and works its way out, I'm finally beginning to understand what's required of me. Not that it makes the process any more palatable, mind you, but I do, I understand.

Pillar #4: Fortitude. We are complicit in our own survival. For that reason it's vital we be explicit in our intention to rise above disease.

Healing takes a 100% commitment to getting well. Not 10%, not 40% or 50%.

Based on what I've learned, I think there are two questions a patient needs to answer right off the bat:

Do you want to live? And if so:

How much do you want to live? Enough to review your current approach to your body? Enough to overhaul your lifestyle perhaps? Enough to abandon old destructive habits and thought patterns, and treat yourself more respectfully in future?

The half-committed people are the ones who often don't make it; they're simply exhibiting the same low-vibration level of complacency that got them into trouble in the first place. High-vibration expectations of recovery, together with a steadfast attitude, are what Lukas and Dermot are using to work their way through their problems, and Amy too. In this, they are resolute.

I might add, all three of them seem incredibly cheerful. They laugh, they banter, they have fun. It's amazing how buoyant they are. A cheery disposition can make a big difference. Laughter releases endorphins in the brain; it bolsters the immune system, it relieves stress. Dwelling on illness, on the other hand, does none of these things.

In Sweden, it's said that, 'Worry gives a small thing a long shadow.' Fear tears down the spirit. Anger chews away at the body. You could eat all the organic fruits and vegetables in the world and do everything else right, but if you're anxious, angry, resentful, fearful, or bitter the whole time, you're still paving a road to disease. A sunny outlook is a key factor in raising the frequency of the body to a state of harmony and wellbeing.

Dr. Bruce Lipton writes: '...[I]f you choose to see a world full of love, your body will respond by growing in health. If you choose to believe that you live in a dark world full of fear, your body health will be compromised.'[30]

An oncologist friend of mine once confided in me: 'The moment a new cancer patient walks in through my door, I can tell right then and there if they're going to live or die.' It's in the demeanor, apparently. Those who expect to live and have the unshakable intention to overcome their illness stand a far greater chance of survival than those who are heavily invested in fear, anxiety, and the spiral of dying, and who refuse to believe there's another way out. My friend was quick to throw in a sobering caveat, however: 'It is very difficult to change thought patterns that are 'locked in' at the disease setting.'

Our urge for instant gratification is our worst enemy, because it seeks an immediate end to the problem with the minimum of effort.

Offer someone a pill that will suppress their symptoms and they'll take it, even if the side-effects of that pill are in some cases worse than the disease itself. On the other hand, tell that same person that good health is achievable, but only with faith, with sacrifice, and with a steely commitment to getting well; and that this steely commitment is likely to involve delving into any possible psychological or emotional or mental origins of the problem and adopting a new attitude, a new diet, a fresh approach to life; on top of which they may have to revolutionize their life from top to bottom, letting go of damaging anxieties, hurts, fears, and doubts – and they'll think you're out of your tiny mind. 'What? Do all of that? Oh no. You're asking too much,' they'll say. 'I'm not giving up my lifestyle. I'd rather stay as I am and wait for my physician to figure something out.'

If that were me and I were faced with the prospect of living many years in pain and dying prematurely, then nothing in the world would be too much trouble, I guarantee it. I'd begin

---

[30] *The Biology of Belief*, page 113.

immediately, 100% determined to overcome any obstacles. The changes I had to make would simply become an exciting part of the adventure. But that's me. I'm blessed with fortitude. I'm in the minority, though. When it comes down to the wire, most people, having been brainwashed into believing that illness is a normal part of life and that 'if doctors don't have the answer then there is no answer', simply won't put in the extra effort required.

When the worst happens, it's not enough to keep puttering along as you are, clinging to an outlook of resignation, doing the bare minimum to help yourself, and hoping things turn out okay. That's like running up millions of dollars on your credit card and hoping you'll pay it off by winning the lottery. I'm not saying hope isn't a good thing, because it is. But somehow the notion of hope contains within it the possibility of defeat. Sure, you *hope* things will improve, like you *hope* someday you'll hit big on the lotto. At the same time you acknowledge that the chances are slim and you probably won't win. Well, what's that if not a low vibration mindset?

A *high* vibration mindset, meanwhile, would be to live in a state of expectation. Expect a full recovery and back it up with the determination to do whatever it takes to get well.

That's what visitors to John of God are doing, I'm thinking. Everyone I've met here has arrived at a place of authentic intention - they're *determined* to do anything and everything they can to get well. Nothing is off-limits, however far from the mainstream they have to travel. Whatever it takes.

Of course, there are bound to be a few here and there who adopt the cynical view and see João himself as a miracle pill, their passport to good health without having to do very much. Most people I meet, though, are more philosophical. They regard the Big Man and his entities as a form of catalyst. A high-consciousness conduit that will carry them from where they are now to where they want to be. They believe wellness is achievable. To help it along they refuse to pollute the process with self-defeating attitudes, such as doubt, skepticism, excessive analysis, or lack of trust.

Pillar #5: Surrender. 'Remembering that there is nothing under our control but the capacity to accept or resist what is,' writes Alejandro Gomez, 'allows us to surrender and thus accept all.'

Reaching that point of surrender can take a while.

By the time Amy came to drag her M.S.-inflicted body up the hot mountainside that day in Arizona, she was crippled, her spirit all but broken. This woman was ready for rescue. Gone were any lingering fears or doubts, gone was all resistance – she was too far in the hole for that; instead there was within her a broad openness to change, a readiness to substitute one thought-form (wellness) for another (illness) and submit to whatever came.

Total surrender is about 'saying yes to healing, and doing so without judgment,' she insists. Scripture teaches, in John 5:14, that 'The prayer of faith shall save him that is sick.' Faith establishes a connection. It allows the greater power of divine consciousness, or the universal life force, or Source, whatever you want to call it, to work through us. Only when our mental defenses are down, when we quit intellectualizing and interfering, can miracles happen. Working through Amy's compliant body on the mountain, that same divine force reacted to her state of complete readiness by effecting an almost instantaneous transformation.

In fact, it's possible that this, right here, is the true essence of the process at the Casa. Healing is not something you strive for – that only creates more stress; it's something you open up to, harmonize with, and allow in. You don't go searching for it;

it finds you. By the same token, it's not what John of God *does* to you that brings relief, at least not initially, but whether you are prepared to relinquish control to something greater than yourself, raising your expectations high enough to initiate a breakthrough, and *receive* healing – that's what counts.

Carolyn Myss is one of the wisest speakers we have on this subject. '[Y]ou need to experience your own limitations,' she once wrote. 'You need to run out of air. You need to finally get yourself out of your own system so that you can surrender – not your ego, but your limitations. And finally you can get on your knees and say, 'What do you want me to do?''[31]

Bottom line: get humble!

To Dermot and Lukas, the Casa, when they arrived, felt like their Last Chance Saloon. Every other path they'd tried up to this point had culminated in failure and despair. Normally, regular guys like these, you wouldn't catch them resorting to anything as seemingly ludicrous as spiritual or psychic surgery. It's too far out on the fringes. But they were at rock-bottom. By the time they got here, their natural state of skepticism and resistance was shot. Humbled by their disease, and no longer willing to let doctors dictate their future or to accept the death sentence they'd been handed, they didn't care if what they were doing seemed outlandish, or if friends and doubters mocked them when they got home. All they wanted was to be released from the spiral of dying.

Again, the answers don't lie outside of yourself; don't sit waiting for that white knight. You have the tools you need already. They're all on the inside. In the end, this is between you and the Divine. A doctor or healer can only take it so far.

'Thoughts of strength,' Ralph Trine wrote in his book *In Tune With the Infinite*, 'engender strength within and attract it from without. Thoughts of weakness actualize weakness within

---

[31] *Spirituality and Health* magazine 2008

and attract it from without. Courage therefore begets success, as fear begets failure.'

Equally important, as Wendy pointed out, is not to make the common mistake of couching the treatment of disease in terms of combat: fighting, winning, beating the enemy. These are ego words. Words of defiance and control – the very opposite of surrender - that stress the body and add to the problem. Often, it's only when the urge to fight is waning, when the patient is at his lowest ebb, the way Lukas was when he arrived here, and his mental state is one of compliance and trust, switching from a position of fighting sickness to a position of allowing wellness, that recovery can get a foothold and true healing start to take place.

Pillar #6: A Raised Level of Consciousness. From what I've seen at the Casa, this would appear to be the most important pillar of all.

Our old friend Josie RavenWing says: 'Sometimes people arrive here with a great deal of mental negativity and they haven't really created a space in which the entities can help them. That's why their treatment may take a long time, because a lot of inner cleansing and opening needs to take place before their healing can be complete.'

As we noted earlier, the universe is energy. You, me, everything around us, vibrate at a specific frequency. A sick, troubled, depressed person's vibration is low. A healthy, happy person vibrates at a higher frequency. So it makes sense, then – or at least it does to me – that before healing can begin, the patient's consciousness somehow needs to be raised from the low-vibration state that goes with staying ill, and aligned - brought into harmony - with the higher-vibration state that accompanies being well.

As always, however, it's belief first, proof later. Believing is key.

Anyone familiar with the works of Abraham, will know that the core principle of the teachings supports this exact idea. Esther Hicks, addressing the issue of surgery at a *Law of Attraction* seminar, told her audience: 'Many will say, 'Well, it was easier to go and have that thing cut out of me than it was to clean up my thinking.' It might seem so, except that you can't cut it out. If that negative thing is still there, it will come back in another way... '

She adds that the key to healing is to seek the cause of the problem, not to suppress it. 'If you look for the vibrational root of something,' she says, '*now* you're onto something sustainable.'

I generally don't have a mind that retains quotes, but one that hangs in my head and won't leave was delivered by Dr. Wayne Dyer in his lecture series *Excuses Be Gone!*

'You don't get what you want in life,' he said, '*you get what you are.*'

That is a staggering truth, I've come to realize.

If your mind is heavily invested in the idea that you are sick, if you dwell on illness and align yourself with disease, allowing it to take control of your thoughts – 'I am a diseased person, I'm feeling terrible.' - then you are erecting a barrier to healing that could slow down recovery or even, in more extreme cases, I guess, prevent it.

Finally, motivational speaker Tony Robbins posted a tweet to his followers once that said: 'Beliefs have the power to create and the power to destroy. Human beings have the awesome ability to take any experience of their lives and create a meaning that disempowers them or one that can literally save their lives.'

It pays therefore to act like you're healthy. Speak of your health in the present tense. 'I am a healthy person.' Impress upon your mind that you are disease-free. Then behave as if that's the unequivocal truth. Do that, and apparently something shifts. Providence steps in. You start a chain reaction of untapped potential that sets you back on the road to wellness.

The best parallel I can think of is with the lottery, which is also a form of healing in its way, only in this case of a person's financial woes.

The Sobering Tale of Bud Post

On the day in 1988 that carnival truck driver Bud Post won the Pennsylvania lottery, he had just two bucks in the bank. Next thing you know, he'd bagged a whopping $16.2million jackpot. Now you'd think, wouldn't you, that this would have eased his money troubles once and for all? But you'd be so wrong. Bud described what happened next as 'a total nightmare.'

In the years that followed, he was sued, jailed for shooting at a debt collector, and swindled out of a third of his jackpot by a bullying landlady. He also bought himself a twin-engine plane, though he had no license and couldn't fly it, and invested in a couple of Florida businesses that went down the toilet. Oh, and later, the cops arrested Bud's brother for hiring a contract killer to murder him for his money. Within just a few years, everything had gone belly-up. The lucky lottery winner was a staggering $1million in debt and living on social security and food stamps. Eventually he went bankrupt, dying in 1996 a very, *very* unhappy man.

Stories like this are legend. A ridiculously high percentage of lottery winners – something like 70%, I believe - say it ruined their lives and they ended up worse off than before they started. How come?

It's actually very simple.

Poverty is a low vibrational state of being. Yet it's something that millions of us, because we believe on a subconscious level that we are not deserving of better, routinely embrace.

So, even when the floodgates open and the Bud Posts of this world acquire enough wealth to impress the large number of fake friends they're suddenly attracting to their swanky new pad in Las Vegas and who ride with them in their private plane, the one they haven't learned to pilot yet, it all seems phony. That's because they've not expanded their consciousness at all. There's no congruence between the money they have and the person they believe themselves to be on the inside, and external circumstances always readjust to match what the person really feels about himself. Poverty-conscious people never stay rich.

Remember what Wayne Dyer said: 'You don't get what you *want* in life...' - everyone talks about becoming rich someday; everyone wants more money - '... you get what you *are*.' Do you feel on the *inside* that you are deserving of riches? That's the question. No matter how much you may crave it, or how hard you work for it, you'll never attain the level of financial abundance you say you desire if, in your mind, you continue to be a penniless loser.

The same principle applies to success, finding love, making friends, and, it would seem, to healing a disease as well.

Restoring yourself to the perfect level of wellness that is your birthright is about bringing the whole body, mind, and soul into alignment and harmony. If years of low-consciousness living – the wrong foods, failing to exercise, torturing yourself with stress and lack of sleep, constant negative thinking, neglect, cynicism, smoking, and whatever else, all of which turn the body into a hostile, acidic environment – laid the foundation for sickness, then maybe replacing these with alkalizing, higher-consciousness activities – eating nutritious foods, meditation, yoga, adopting an optimistic, joyful state of mind, and so on – could someday pull you out of the pit you've dug for yourself.

According to Taoist anti-aging expert Dr. Maoshing Ni, 'Research shows that a prolonged acidic environment can give rise to inflammation and cancer and can lead to premature aging.... A diet high in acidic foods including animal products, caffeine, sugar, alcohol, and processed foods exerts pressure on your body's balancing systems as it strains to maintain pH neutrality. The process of counterbalancing the acidity can deplete the body of alkaline minerals such as potassium, magnesium, and calcium, making the person prone to chronic and degenerative disease.'[32]

The more I absorb messages like this and relate them to incidents in real life away from Abadiânia, the more I find evidence everywhere to support them.

Look what happened to Patrick Swayze.

Patrick Swayze Teaches Us a Valuable Lesson

Everyone remembers Swayze as the star of *Ghost* and *Dirty Dancing*. The guy was worshipped by his fans and adored by the creative community and of course his family. Sadly, though, in mid-life, after years as an unapologetic heavy drinker and smoker, he was diagnosed with pancreatic cancer.

In his autobiography he admitted that he felt 'anger, bitterness, and despair' at his disease.[33] Hardly surprising, and our hearts went out to him when we heard. On the other hand...

Looked at from an objective viewpoint, the man had invested so much time and effort into getting sick, hadn't he? Consistent abuse must have made his body so acidic and toxic that, I guess, in the end, it became too impaired to function properly.

At the time of his diagnosis, he told his doctor: 'Show me where the enemy is and I'll fight him.' Which, as we now know, seems to be inviting trouble. This fight exposed him to all the heavy-hitters: chemo, surgery, and drugs intended to

---

[32] *The Secrets of Self-Healing*, 2008, Penguin Books.

[33] *Time of My Life,* written with Lisa Niemi, 2009 Atria.

wipe out the symptoms without ever addressing the root cause of the cancer. In fact, during the later stages of his treatment, a member of the paparazzi snapped Swayze coming out of a hospital, lighting up a cigarette as he went.

Remember that page of false dietary wisdom I mentioned a few chapters ago? The one that said, 'Life should NOT be a journey to the grave with the intention of arriving safely in an attractive and well-preserved body, but rather to skid in sideways, Chardonnay in one hand, chocolate in the other...' and so on?

Well, I'd say Swayze was a living embodiment of that philosophy. To the very end, he willingly bought a product that is known to be responsible for the deaths of hundreds of thousands of people and ingested the carcinogenic fumes from it. That's how committed he must have been on a deep level to low-consciousness activities. He took the risk and reaped the consequences. Result: he was gone by 57.

Rene Caisse once said, 'There is no incurable disease. There are masses of incurable people.'

To me, Swayze's legacy is way more than his movies. At the very least, he leaves us with a stern lesson on the one hand in the dangers of mistreating your body, and on the other in what *not* to do if you want to recover from the serious illness you've brought on by mistreating it. It's too late for Swayze to learn this, but not too late for us.

Caisse is also noted for saying, 'You do the curing. Special remedies, regimes, or doctors don't cure...Our bodies know more about how to cure and eliminate disease than science, chemistry and healing professions will ever know.' She added: 'You earned your illness. You have to earn your health.'

True healing, according to Nurse Rene, begins when the patient decides to make positive changes in his outlook and the way he treats himself.

I imagine most doctors, hospitals, and pharmaceutical drugs companies would scoff at this. Indeed, they laughed in Rene Caisse's day too. She was vilified and ridiculed for her common sense methods, even though those same methods dated back thousands of years to the guy who launched this whole body stuff: Hippocrates. For the majority of the medical profession, there's only one way: the allopathic way. The white knight approach. Relief from the outside in. 'Here's a pill' or 'We need to operate.' But as we know, these are consciousness-*lowering* options; many times they can actually harm the body.

A Diagnosis Can Kill

Have you noticed how quick doctors are to give a name to a disease? In some ways, that's a huge problem, because the instant they do so, the patient feels tagged and classified. In his head, he takes on the burden of being one more sickness statistic and from then on sees himself in that light. This negativity stirs up stress, anxiety, worry, and fear, and inevitably lowers his or her vibration still further, working against his becoming well.

Telling someone: 'You have Parkinson's', or 'You have cancer' feeds the condition, giving it way too much power. From then on, every time you repeat that phrase and admit to being sick, you're siding with imperfection, aligning yourself with illness, promoting fear and anxiety, and by doing so, someone like Rene Caisse would suggest, actually compounding the problem, increasing the chances of it getting worse.[34]

What if a negative diagnosis is actually legitimizing what might otherwise be an innocuous complaint, giving it breadth and strength and ammunition?

---

[34] If we have to call it something, let's call it 'Perfection'. 'I am total perfection,' if held as a firm conviction, is a vibration-raising statement. Believe unfalteringly that this is true, and in many cases the body will catch up. What the mind says goes.

Deepak Chopra relates the story of a patient, an internist, who underwent a routine chest x-ray and was shocked to find he had a black spot on his lung. It's something all of us dread – a surprise diagnosis that puts a set time on how long we have left. The shock alone is enough to wreck our lives. And indeed that's what happened to the internist. Shortly after being told about the spot on his lung, he died of cancer. But then, later, something extremely sobering happened. A stack of his medical records came to light, including some decades-old x-rays, and - guess what! They showed that his lung, all those years ago, *had the same black spot on it*. That little sucker had been there the whole time and he'd not even known about it! Ultimately, it was not the spot, but the sense of doom and inevitability injected into his mind by his physician, that killed him.

When a doctor sits you down and tells you with a grave expression: 'I'm sorry, but your cancer is terminal,' your overriding inclination in that moment is to believe what he says. Why? *Because he's a doctor*. Of course you believe him. Who wouldn't? These guys hold a monopoly on our trust. We're raised to revere their brilliance and accept whatever they tell us as the truth, although, really, there is no absolute truth. Even a doctor will admit to that. Truth is a one-sided perception; it depends on who's telling it. One person's truth can often be supplanted by another, more powerful and persuasive one. It's very subjective.

In light of this, I now see that my mother may not have died of cancer all those years ago. What she died of was a condition called misplaced faith. Or 'believing everything her doctor said without questioning it.'

One day, a charming, well-educated man in a white coat told her that she had an advanced form of kidney cancer and didn't have long to live. Those words were a fast-acting poison to her spirit, lowering her consciousness and extinguishing all hope. In those days the Internet wasn't fully loaded like it is now; she couldn't do what Geena did for her husband - go online and hunt down a possible cure. My mother was old school. She trusted her doctor's prognosis: 'You're going to die.' This in turn brought on a mood of fatalistic gloom, lowering the frequency of her body's vibration and bringing it into full alignment with the disease. As a result her consciousness stayed the same until the day she fulfilled his prophecy and passed away.

Doctors have to give us the worst-case scenario, because if they don't and the worst happens, then we might sue them. I understand the thinking. All the same, the worst case is what *might* happen in certain extreme circumstances, not what *will* happen necessarily.

I sometimes find myself wondering what the effect might have been if my mother's physician had gone ahead and simply lied to her. If he'd smiled and said, 'You're going to be fine; within two months all the cancer will be gone and you'll be feeling perfectly okay' Maybe hearing those consciousness-raising words would have lifted her spirits and rekindled her expectation of survival, and she'd still be alive today. It's possible, but we'll never know.

Dr. Bruce Lipton, over decades of research into cell biology, made a very interesting discovery - that perception trumps genetics.

That is to say, *our thoughts and beliefs can override the reality of what is going on in our physical bodies,* which is a phenomenally important advance in our understanding of illness.

Recently, I was having dinner with a young woman whose brother had done just that. A few months before, he'd been told he had cancer and needed an urgent operation. Unlike most people in his position, though, he did an odd thing, one that panicked his family and friends: he refuted the diagnosis. Simple as that. The guy denied the disease its power over him.

'He drew a line,' his sister said. 'He told us, 'Don't mention this to me ever again.' At the same time he changed his diet, his attitude, he bought a dog to encourage him to exercise and have more playful fun, and generally lived life to its fullest like a man who was fully expecting it to continue.'

'And what happened?' I was intensely curious, as you can imagine.

'He's fine. I saw him again at Christmas, and he looked better than ever. He seems completely healthy.'

Wow.

Thinking this through, could it possibly be, d'you suppose, that, when a disease bombshell drops like that and we arrive at a critical crossroads where key decisions need to be made, we actually have a choice of how things will go? Of whether we stay sick or get well? Many believe so.

The prolific 19th Century English novelist Edward Bulwer-Lytton wrote: 'Refuse to be ill. Never tell people you are ill; never own up to it for yourself. Illness is one of those things which a man should resist on principle.'

'Give no oxygen to disease,' would be Mary Baker Eddy's advice to us today too, if she were alive. Brush it off. Disempower it. Refuse to give it a label. Starve it of attention. Instead, refocus. Align yourself with divine consciousness, which knows only of perfect health. Let your reaction to your condition be only high-vibration thoughts.

By raising our vibration and blocking out consciousness-lowering influences, perhaps we can cancel out all thoughts of disease and welcome in a renewed state of good health as a preferred alternative. To me, that's a really intriguing idea.

The Big Secret Behind John of God's Treatments

After everything I've witnessed at the Casa de Dom Inaçio, I'm coming around to the view that what João has done here, and brilliantly so, is build a spiritual theme park. And I say this, not to put it down, but to embrace the power of the underlying intention.

His single greatest achievement in Abadiânia is to create the infrastructure of belief. An environment conducive to recovery, using a variety of techniques and sideshows, all of them designed to break down doubt and resistance and generate an unshakable conviction in the Seeker that a return to health is not only likely, but almost certain. That degree of certitude is vital.

No-one compels you to take part in this piece of theater, or even to buy its mystical properties. But by doing so, by participating, by surrendering to the process - the workings of the current rooms, the metal instrument up the nose, the perceived power of some mystical subterranean vortex, and so on – and by spending twelve days meditating, relaxing, eating good but simple food, going from dawn to dusk in a positive, upbeat frame of mind, you quickly find your doubts and fears being replaced with love, peace, harmony, and a gentle but firm expectation of healing. These in turn bring you into alignment with the perfect frequency of divine intelligence, raising the vibration of the body more in keeping with health, after which the immune system and your other natural in-built reparative functions and instincts do the rest.

Truthfully, who cares whether there are entities or not, or if the wooden triangle is a Hotline to God, or if John of God is a hypnotist or just a clever conjurer with several dozen tricks up his sleeve that he learned at Clown College, or if the reason you have to keep your eyes closed at all material times during the procedures is because, if you opened them, you'd realize that there's absolutely nothing going on? None of that, I would suggest, matters. What *matters* is that João achieves his goal. And you can argue as much as you like about this, but all too often he does seem to. He achieves it by giving people hope and by raising their expectation of success to the point where, even in seemingly impossible circumstances, they allow their physical body to slip back into harmony and balance. In consequence, a large number of them get well again. Not all, but many.

Nurse Rene Caisse said much the same thing: **YOU CURE YOU**.

By your lifestyle, your attitudes, your hidden resentments, your unresolved conflicts from childhood, you brought yourself to this point. It's up to you now to stage your own intervention. Fact is:

- Doctors don't cure disease, we know that; they treat the symptoms, not the root cause.
- Drugs don't cure disease. Pharmaceutical drugs are chemicals. They're an invader in the body. They can help relieve a problem, but in addressing one issue they often create half a dozen more, each of which needs a new pill to deal with it.
- Radiation in itself doesn't cure disease – in actual fact, taken to excess it can be a killer in its own right.
- Herbs, health drinks, and potions don't cure disease either. They can help bring the body into balance, but they don't cure anything.

Ralph Trine wrote about healing, that it: '...almost invariably implies co-operation on the part of the one who is treated. In the cures that Christ performed, He almost always needed the co-operation of the one who appealed to him. His question almost invariably was 'Dost though believe?' He thus stimulated into activity the life-giving forces within the one cured.'[35]

He goes on to say: 'One may cure another, but to be permanently healed one must do it to himself.'

That's it. Others can help, and doctors and healers may play their part, but in the end disease is a very personal journey. Only you can heal you.

Andreas Moritz, talking specifically about how cancer is fundamentally a toxicity crisis in his book *Cancer Is Not a Disease,* may have hit on the right conclusion: 'There is no other cancer treatment that can ever closely compete with the body's own healing mechanism, which we unfortunately label as disease. Cancer is not a disease; it is a very unusual, but apparently highly efficient mechanism of survival and self-protection. We ought to give the most developed and complex system in the universe - the human body – a little more credit than it has so far received, and trust that it knows perfectly well how to conduct its own affairs, even under the grimmest of circumstances.'

Pillar #7: Getting Out of Your Own Light. A final and quite obvious, but oft-overlooked building block in the wellness wall, and one of the hardest to accomplish. Yet without it we can never claim to have surrendered completely.

Once the other six pillars are in place, then it's time to step aside and let go. Quit analyzing, quit debating, turn away from fear, turn away from the very concept of being sick. Stop cowering, and just be.

Once you've done everything you can and there's nothing left, release it. Open up to divine intelligence. Hold strong in faith. Then let whatever happens happen. Remember, there is no right or wrong outcome. Whatever's next, it's all for the

---

[35] *In Tune With the Infinite,* page 41.

good. If anything, that's the overriding message of the Casa: take your hands off the tiller and show a little faith. People have died during their stay in Abadiânia. Many others have received operations, then gone home and died anyway. It happens. And it will continue to happen. But is that any reason to doubt the process? Hardly. Sometimes it's just your time to go. In that moment, there's little to be done except comply, release, submit. Realize that the universe, Source, God – whatever you choose to call it - has your back, and trust in that. Tell yourself you'll be fine, no matter what comes.

I've alluded several times to that Buddhist retreat I attended. There were three pieces of advice I took away from it. I gave you two of them earlier; here's the third and last one. It's about death.

None of us operates alone, the monks said. We're all part of the whole. And we remain part of that whole whether we stay in our physical bodies or not.

You are eternal. Your time on earth is the briefest of rest stops on a far greater journey. If you fall ill, but you have work yet to do on this plane, then reprieve will come. If you're done here and it's time for you to return home, then embrace your grand exit with as much humility as you can muster, gather up your things, and prepare to move on to the next phase of this fantastic adventure.

Your ego, of course, always scared of giving up control, won't agree to this. It doesn't want to loosen its grip, its identity, its sense of self, its importance and invulnerability. It will doubtless try to keep a hold on what it has and resist its destiny. Your spirit, on the other hand, sees things differently. It knows not to hang on. It knows too that dying is nothing to worry about.

Author Chuck Palahniuk said: 'If death meant just leaving the stage long enough to change costume and come back as a new character...would you slow down, or speed up?"

That's all death is: a costume change. You are returning to the Source of All Things. The drop is becoming the ocean once more. But only temporarily. Then you make a fresh entrance later. Different outfit, new make-up, but it's still you. Knowing this, why fight it? When the day comes, don't cloak yourself in a shroud of fear, regret, or resistance. Go with dignity. Choose love. Choose light. Submit willingly to what lies ahead. Advance into the unknown with a mood of eager curiosity.

Above all, remind yourself of the truth of who you are. That you are not your personality. You are not your bank account. You are not your possessions. You are not your status or achievements or your trophies. And you are not – *not* - your disease. You are a spiritual being, infinite and timeless, bathed in grace. You don't die. Your body dies, but *you* – the real, eternal you - don't. You carry on from here, switching from this dimension to another, shrugging off the crude, low-vibration limitations of the earth plane and moving up to a far higher one. Maybe you even become a spirit orb, who knows? A mystical glimmer of fluorescent light, the kind that's often mistaken for dust or raindrops, something only cats see, flitting routinely through a vortex somewhere, straddling worlds, helping Seekers like us, those walking several paces behind you, to find our own greater truth.

Nobody can say for sure. That's the beautiful mystery of it all. And if somebody tries to tell you that they know, they're bluffing. Don't believe them.

As the final moment approaches, though, you could do worse than heed the words of Chief Tecumseh, head of the Shawnee Nation in the 18th Century. I thought he encapsulated the monks' teachings perfectly when he said:

'Love your life. Perfect your life. Beautify all things in your life. Seek to make your life long and its purpose in the service of your people. Prepare a noble death song for the day when you go over the great divide.... When it comes your time to die, be not like those whose hearts are filled with the fear of death, so that when their time comes they weep and pray for a little more time to live their lives over again in a different way... sing your death song and die like a hero going home.'

17

Unanswered Prayers

It's been several months since I returned from Brazil. Now and then I make a point of speaking to Angela via *Skype* to catch up on what other members of our group are up to, because you can't help but be fascinated. We may be scattered across the globe, but after the intense experience we went through together, it's hard to disentangle ourselves from one another's lives. And Angela's at the hub of that.

Today, when I call her, she is brimming with news. For starters, Amy has written a book about her miraculous breakthrough with multiple sclerosis.[36] These days she schools people with M.S., empowering them to overcome it.

Evidently Lukas is still cancer-free. 'He's busy running his foundation,' Angela reports chirpily, 'bringing sick people to Abadiânia. I see him regularly. He's doing well.' Which is an encouraging development.

So maybe he was cured after all. As always, there are no guarantees, but he's already lasted a lot longer than his doctor thought he would, and without losing any more organs.

Marty, she says, adopting a matter-of-fact tone, is back to wearing glasses again, which on the face of it is a disappointment. But apparently not. 'It turns out the entities weren't correcting his vision,' Angela says. 'They were treating something else. Whatever it was, they released it through his eyes.'

---

[36] *The Juniper Tree & Me* (2011)

Hm.

Dermot, meanwhile, remains a work in progress. But he's alive at least, which, once again, is more than his physician at home in Boston imagined would happen. Like Lukas, Dermot has traveled back to the Casa since, to continue his treatment.

There are other life-affirming stories too, not the least of which concerns the mayoral election in Abadiânia. The votes are in, and the winner was Dr. Itamar, the politician who's very João-friendly. Wilmar Arantes, the anti-Casa candidate, got trounced. And rightly so. Where's the sense in running John of God out of town? It would be entirely counter-productive in a place as poor as Abadiânia, not to mention a slap in the face to the thousands of needy people there, bringing economic catastrophe as it forced local shops and services out of business. Without a doubt the right man won. We should all give thanks for that.

In fact, everyone seems thankful for their experiences in Abadiânia, returning home either healed, or feeling enlightened, or, as in my case, equipped with answers to pressing questions. The issues that troubled me so much at the start of the book have, I feel, been laid to rest, even if the answers weren't always clear-cut or the ones I expected. In that respect, the gamble in going to Brazil paid off handsomely. The Seeker became a Finder.

'Good, I'm glad to hear it,' Angela says with a knowing smile.

Once she's done with her updates, we switch to other issues.

Despite everything I just said, there are a couple of mysteries outstanding that continue to trouble me about the Casa experience. First: the sacred waterfall! 'It's fake. I know it is. Please tell me I'm right about that. One of the Casa's gardeners pours water down a tube, right?'

On the monitor, a face half-hidden by drapes of Morticia Addams-like hair freezes with shock. 'Next!'

'No, wait - I'm serious. I saw it for myself. It's a total fake.'

'Cash,' she snorts, 'the *cachoeira* is NOT a fake waterfall, okay? Don't you *dare* write that in your book. It's completely real. You should go down there in winter, it's like Niagara.'

She's so emphatic about it that I let it go.

Second mystery: my hearing. You know how I feel about this already. Disconcertingly, my left ear is back to pre-Brazil deafness levels. Having been sprung from jail briefly, inhaling the sweet perfume of freedom for a mere two days, I've been thrown back in the auditory slammer, seemingly with no hope of parole. What on earth is going on? I'm no better off than when I started.

Once again, Angela is quick to dismiss my concerns (and my mild hysteria) as premature. 'I keep telling you, *be patient*. Have some faith. Obviously, the entities have bigger things in store for you. Your ear cleared up briefly in Abadiânia because the spirits wanted to give you a taste of what's to come if you keep pressing on. It means you have more learning to do, that's all. This is just the beginning.'

'The beginning of what, though?'

The conversation ends there. She has no idea. Can't speak for the entities, she says, and wouldn't want to second-guess their larger game plan.

Well, okay.

With effort, I *suppose* I could be talked into accepting her argument that the entities granted Wish #1 on my list by allowing my hearing to come back, even if it was only for forty-eight hours. They showed me what's possible; now the burden falls on me to bring my vibration into harmonious alignment with the idea of perfect hearing, as opposed to continually lowering it by focusing on the frustration of deafness. That would make sense.

But it's just one possibility. I have another, one that may explain many of the other 'spontaneous healings' at the Casa as well.

Way back, many chapters ago, I told you about Dr. Howard Benson. He wrote a book in 1975 called *The Relaxation Response*, which suggested that 60%, and possibly as high as 90%, of patient visits to doctors are in some way related to stress. That's an astonishing number. His antidote to those problems was quite straightforward. 'To the extent that any condition is being caused or made worse by stress,' he said during a recent interview on *Good Morning America*, 'the daily elicitation of the relaxation response will be a helpful prevention and treatment.'

Relaxation was his answer.

Now, think about that: what was our stay in Abadiânia if not twelve pleasant days of relaxation? A peaceful environment, good food, mindfulness, prayer, plenty of sleep, waves of unconditional love, and long restful conversations with wonderfully engaging people. I doubt anyone in our group encountered a single moment of stress from the moment they stepped off the bus on the first evening to the morning we left. Furthermore, any anxiety we brought with us from home began to dissipate by the third day. If 60-90% of ailments are stress-related, as Dr. Benson claims, and 100% of your time as a patient at the Casa is taken up with stress-relieving activities, including meditation, 24-hour recuperations, taking passionflower pills, and lying on crystal beds, might this not be the biggest clue yet to what John of God's secret is?

I once listened to a lecture in which the incredibly gifted medical intuitive Carolyn Myss offered her take on the recent rise in breast cancer cases. She posited the view that maybe it was a direct result of over-nurturing. The modern woman tries to be everything, she said: a great mother, a great wife, a great cook, a great provider, a great employee, a socially responsible citizen playing her part in the community, and so on. Laden with expectations and responsibilities, she is driven to trying too hard and overextends herself. This continuing strenuous effort to be all things to all people breaks down the body's natural defenses, moving it from its ideal state of ease toward one of disease. In those circumstances, is it such an unthinkable idea that a high level of emotional stress could eventually manifest itself as a physical ailment? Or that the specific ailment in question would be one that afflicts a woman's organ of nurturing – the breast?

To me, that's a breakthrough idea.

Eastern doctors plow a similar furrow. Unreleased negative emotions, they believe, can get trapped in organs of the body. So fear, for example, if indulged in excessively, resides in the kidneys, causing problems there. Anger goes to the liver; grief to the lungs; bitterness to the gall bladder, and so on.

Additionally, I've known several people who suffered with sciatica over the years, and they all had one thing in common: they were deeply frustrated with some aspect of their life and unable to see a way through. In turn, their whole body was constantly stressed out and clenched. Friends who are stubborn, willful, controlling, and whose opinions won't bend easily, have problems with arthritis, I notice, especially in the knees, and find they literally can't bend easily. What's happening in their mind is mirrored in their biology, translating into physical ailments.

Coincidence? Possibly. Nevertheless, it's intriguing, don't you think?

Superman actor Christopher Reeve slipped into a coma in 1974 after years lived as a quadriplegic following a horse-riding accident. Throughout that time, his dutiful wife Dana was on hand to take great care of him. But then something shocking happened. Soon after Christopher died, when she was suddenly free to claim her own life back, Dana went down with lung cancer. How could this be? The woman had never smoked a day in her life. Well, what if it was simply down to stress? What if the intense grief and emotional pain she endured along with her injured husband over such a long time finally got to her, corrupting her cells and giving her cancer?

Rene Caisse said this: 'Cancer patients have usually lived in relationships that have had serious negative impacts on their lives. Let go of hurts of the past. Deadly emotions can lead to cancer. Feelings used as weapons against someone, or self, can be as toxic as exposure to a lethal physical agent. Stay away from spiteful, negative, irritating, overbearing people. You don't need friends who find fault. The magic key to curing cancer, to cancer prevention, is to live, to really live...full of vigor and hope...to live with every true vital force in you.'

As with any message that resonates as strongly as this one does, her words feel like the truth. They might even offer a partial answer to other conditions as well.

Look at my ears, for instance.

It took a while, but once I'd removed all the pressures and sources of anxiety that prey on me in my everyday life in Los Angeles, and replaced them with simple harmonious things such as relaxation and happiness and restful sleep and joy – Dr. Benson called it 'an inducible, physiologic state of quietude' - then automatically my body began to unclench and unblock. It had no choice. Its response to the Casa's atmosphere of peace and wellbeing was to ease up, calm down, let go, and be tranquil. A week later I got my hearing back!

That's what your stay in Abadiânia does. It creates a forced hiatus. A twelve-day break from the insane fast-lane pace of normal life, during which your body has time to relax and reboot.

So maybe my hearing loss is not a major stepping-stone toward old-age deafness, as my doctors suggested, after all, but merely a by-product of tension. Fluid trapped in the ears by inflammation as a result of my jaw tightening up. I'm not saying that's definitely the case, but what if? And what if it's the same with cancer, only obviously on a grander scale? Or with M.S. Or migraines, and other illnesses. What if they're self-induced? Wouldn't that be something? If, in the end, we're not victims of our diseases, the way we thought. Nor are we at the butt-end of bad fortune. Nor doomed to be sick and medicated for the rest of our lives. But rather, as ordinary people we have a measure of control at our fingertips, waiting for us to use it. Sure, doctors may help, but in the end it's down to us, as ordinary, but increasingly self-aware, lay individuals, to do most of the heavy lifting, by changing our thoughts, raising our vibration, expecting positive results, and bringing ourselves into alignment with our higher good.

Find the source of the problem, remove it by adopting a different approach to living, one that's favorable to wellness rather than antagonistic to it, and the symptoms vanish too.

In other words, *you cure you.*

So that's Wish #1.

As for Wish #2, it could be argued, I guess, that the entities granted that too, since, if I'd not gone to Brazil, I doubt there'd have been any meaningful progress made toward reconciling with my father. I can't think how the opportunity would ever have arisen, quite honestly. More than likely, a long and awkward stalemate would have continued indefinitely. So in fairness, we should perhaps give her the benefit of the doubt there.

That still leaves my third wish, though, doesn't it?

'Please unblock my career and get me out of public radio.'

The work situation, I'm afraid to say, has remained stubbornly unchanged for half a year. I'm working for the same show I did before, struggling to do the same old boring reports, and back to stressing out over the myriad details that go into making radio happen. The treadmill seems never ending and I'm as unhappy as I ever was.

Of course the fault is largely my own, for hanging in there long after change was overdue. Prison inmates do the same thing. Once they get a few years' incarceration under their belt it becomes a way of life. Sometimes, when their sentence is up, they balk, terrified of venturing into the world outside. How will they fit in? Where will they go? What will they do instead of lounging around all day staring at the wall? Well, it's no different in public broadcasting. Lovely, comfortable, familiar old public broadcasting, where we, too, lounge around all day staring at the wall, only this time with headphones on.

It's a trying dilemma, one faced by millions of people who, as slaves of nine to five drudgery, toil away at jobs they don't enjoy simply to pay their bills. Meanwhile, they feel their life slips away from them. I mean, come on – we deserve better, right? That's no way to go about things.

So you know what I did earlier today?

I decided to bring it to a head.

You're going to think I'm crazy and impetuous, and I can only suppose that maybe a cloud of madness descended on me overnight, banishing any previous links I might have had to common sense, but, shortly after waking up, I was hit by an impulse. The impulse to make a dramatic change.

Not only did I feel this impulse, but I acted on it.

I went to the computer and hammered out an email to my editor, telling him I could no longer carry on. Things didn't feel right; my heart wasn't in the work, etc etc., and I therefore intended to resign. Then I hit 'send' before I could back out.

It was one of the toughest things to do. Like smoking your last cigarette before quitting for good. Or eating your last slice of chocolate cake (just kidding, that's never going to happen.)

In all honesty, it would be far-fetched to suggest that the entities provided this subconscious prompting I felt. But there's definitely something behind it. And behind all of what's happened. Of the twenty-four people in our group last fall, nobody's life has been left untouched. For some it's subtle; for others the shift has been pronounced and even dramatic. (I happen to know that there has been one marriage, and at least two sets of divorce proceedings have been commenced, since we got back). But in all cases, the regime of total relaxation at the Casa seems to have opened pathways in our minds through which subconscious promptings can flow more freely, ready to instigate change.

Whether John of God is, in the end, truly a *milagreiro*, a phenomenal spiritual entity with unrivaled cosmic powers, or just some unemployed peasant boy who had a great idea for a theme park, that's for other people to decide. In my case, I leave this experience pretty much convinced that it's the former. I've seen too much to think otherwise. Either way, what the Big Man does, at the very least, is provide Seekers like us with a rare opportunity to stand back, distance ourselves from our regular circumstances, put the past behind us, and confidently cross a threshold into a different future.

For that I will always be grateful.

'The best day of your life is the one on which you decide your life is your own,' self-help author Bob Moawad wrote. 'No apologies or excuses. No one to lean on, rely on, or blame. The gift is yours – it is an amazing journey – and you alone are responsible for the quality of it. This is the day your life really begins.'

Today, I decided, was to be that day.

Last night, when I went to bed, I was a professional broadcaster. Tonight when my head hits the pillow, I will no longer be. I won't be anything at all, actually. I'll just be some guy who left the job he's done for way too long and opted for change, without having the first clue where his new path would take him. But that's fine. Sometimes you just have to take a leap, not knowing whether the net will appear to catch you. It will, of course. It always does. But first you're required to step up and step out. Step out into the abyss, do so with unshakable faith, and the ground will rise to meet your feet. That's how it is with this stuff: belief first, proof later - always. There's no way around it.

So here I am, the scent of liberty in my nostrils, giddy with possibilities. No going back now. Things might be shaky for a while, but I now consider Wish #3 fulfilled.

'There's life before Brazil,' Susan told us on the bus that first night, 'and life after Brazil. Things will never be the same again.'

Boy, did she get that right.

Afterword

Centuries ago it was widely believed that the human body had a natural power to heal itself unaided. That view has waned slowly over the years with the rise of the modern medical profession. Nowadays, faced with serious illness, we experience a strong sense of helplessness and, feeling the need to do something, will in most cases resort to traditional medical care. At the same time, the more knowledgeable we become in this field, the more skeptical many of us are about the effectiveness of many alternative or fringe therapies, especially faith healing.

An important and probably essential aspect of a faith healer's role, therefore, is to help override that skepticism and restore belief. Belief in the *potential* for direct spiritual healing and also in the body's capacity to correct itself after an illness. For healing to occur, the patient's whole system needs to theoretically 're-boot' itself. That's quite a challenge. Yet it seems that, in certain instances, the strength of the personality of the faith healer may be enough to give the patient this kind of jolt and start paving a road back to health.

To the legendary healer John of God, for example, love, compassion, prayer, harmony, peaceful contemplation, surrender, and self-worth are the tools of cleansing and healing. The Casa de Dom Inaçio, his clinic in Brazil, offers an all-encompassing spiritual backdrop to his work dedicated to helping the thousands of pilgrims who stop by each year to reframe their concept of what it means to be sick and to replace it with a return to good health. His goal is to convince everyone who visits him that they have the 'potential for wellness.'

To cross this important threshold seems to require

a threefold strategy. The first step is for the patient to *accept* his condition. From there we move on to the greater challenge of getting him to *acknowledge* that the illness can be reversed. Lastly, the patient must be brought to a point where he *believes* that his body can be repaired and healed.

Looked at from the traditional medical standpoint, this is quite an expectation, and a real leap of faith!

As a professor of medicine with over thirty years experience in both clinical- and lab-based research, it was hard for me to make such a leap, or to review the work of John of God without any clinical data. However, experience has taught me this: that a commitment to a positive outcome is a vital element in all types of medical care. Believing you will get well is important. The motivation and the determination originate within the patient. Doctors then use their expertise to oversee and facilitate that recovery. It's probably asking too much of a patient that he should rely exclusively upon hope and expectation to heal the body, and in some cases it may even compound the problem, generating stress at the responsibility of creating his own personal healing miracle. That having been said, when it comes to healing, nothing should be off-limits, and I retain a sense of curiosity and a mind open to new possibilities, exactly as Cash Peters does in his remarkable first-hand exploration of the faith healing phenomenon.

It is interesting to note that Oprah Winfrey on her talk show devoted significant time to John of God and sent her people to investigate the Casa de Dom Inaçio. She then invited some of his patients who had recovered from serious illness to tell their stories. Based on their testimony and all the evidence, Oprah was led to the same conclusions as Cash: that something extraordinary is going on in Brazil.

The results that John of God achieves are impressive, that

much is undeniable. But what is really going on at the Casa? Is John himself channeling a divine energy, as he claims, and it's this that is responsible for the healings? Or are patients being brainwashed by virtue of their profound belief in his paranormal abilities, to the point that their body succumbs to the powerful convictions of their own mind and they believe themselves to be cured, even though they may not be?

From a medical point of view, these questions remain open to debate, but in exploring them frankly and honestly, Cash attempts to demystify the world of faith healing and show what really goes on behind the scenes.

The message we can take away from his experiences, I think, is that the power to bring about healing resides in the individual. We each have the capacity for hope and an expectation of healing, whether it be physical or emotional. As a result of this raised awareness, it's entirely possible that some people may get significantly better, while for others the experience may simply allow them to accept for the first time that there are perhaps other ways to attain wellness beyond the conventional methods that we all take for granted.

So often the overriding obstacle to recovery is fear. Fear of change, fear of anything different, fear of thinking outside the box. If we can let go of fear and be willing to allow new doors to open, new patterns of thought and pathways to healing to emerge, then from that point on, it strikes me, anything is possible.

BRIAN G.M. DURIE M.D.

BRIAN DURIE M.D. IS THE MEDICAL DIRECTOR OF APTIUM ONCOLOGY, INC. AND A SPECIALIST IN MULTIPLE MYELOMA AND RELATED DISORDERS AT THE CEDARS-SINAI OUTPATIENT CANCER CENTER IN LOS ANGELES. CALIFORNIA.

Acknowledgments

The fact that you're holding this book in your hand is a small miracle in itself.

I didn't realize when I embarked on this project how much skepticism, and in some cases outright opposition, there is these days to: a) faith-based healing; b) good nutrition, exercise, and meditation as forms of therapy for bringing the body back to wellness, rather than pharmaceutical drugs, radiation, and surgery; and c) spiritual teachings in general. It really came as a surprise.

The book, therefore, stands as testimony to the support I received from a bunch of people who felt, as I do, that this information should no longer be hidden from view. For commercial reasons that I fully understand, mainstream publishers don't allow many of the things you read here to find their way into print. That's their right. But it doesn't mean the information shouldn't be made available for discussion. How can people be expected to make wise and balanced decisions about their life and their health if all they have is one side of the story? The corporate or institutional side. Don't we ordinary guys have a say too? After all, it's our health they're playing with.

Of course, none of this would have happened without, first and foremost, Joâo Teixeira de Faria and his assistants at the Casa de Dom Inaçio, as well as the amazing people I met in Brazil - the sick, the dying, and in some cases the recovering – who opened my eyes to what's possible, and, by their courage and determination, continue to demonstrate the power of faith and how partnering up with the Divine can make a huge difference in all aspects of life, not just with our health. Out of respect to them, I changed their names, and even merged some characters together, though this was more for reasons of space. Now and then it was also necessary to bundle up several conversations into one, the better to explain the principles and concepts behind what was happening.

However, there are some people who deserve to be thanked individually.

Geena, naturally, for starting it all off.

Len Richmond, who is way ahead of his time in this field, and a neverending source of hippy wisdom and self-healing insights. Christine Sellin-Richards, a bottomless well of encouragement, whose backbone was fortunately strong enough for two. Krista Goering for reading the manuscript and describing it as 'awesome' just when I needed to hear that. And Adam Korn at DeFiore & Co. To know that this material kept him awake at night was a real shot in the arm.

Additional thanks to Ann Bradney, Stan Oléynik; to Ron and Alexandra Seigel for their advice; and to Sonia Fiore for her great talent and patience.

To Josie RavenWing (www.johnofGod-Brazil.net) for allowing me to quote from her book. To Dr. Erin Moore of the University of Southern California for her sage input. To Steve Kiesling at *Spirituality & Health* magazine for convincing me that I had what it takes to write something like this. To Sylvana Robinson for proofreading. To Jeff Rediger and Brian Durie too – thanks for pitching in and believing along with the rest of us, guys; it made a world of difference. To the nun whose name I never knew, who came to my rescue in Abadiânia, and, in so doing, taught me a lesson in compassion that I'll never forget.

And finally to Stanley Penner for pretty much everything else. I value him more than he knows. Everyone should be lucky enough to have a Stanley in their life.

C.P.

CASH PETERS is an award-winning journalist and writer. A long-time commentator on American public radio and the BBC, he also writes regularly on the subject of spirituality and health.

WWW.CASHPETERS.COM